GREAT KNITTING IN
VOGUE

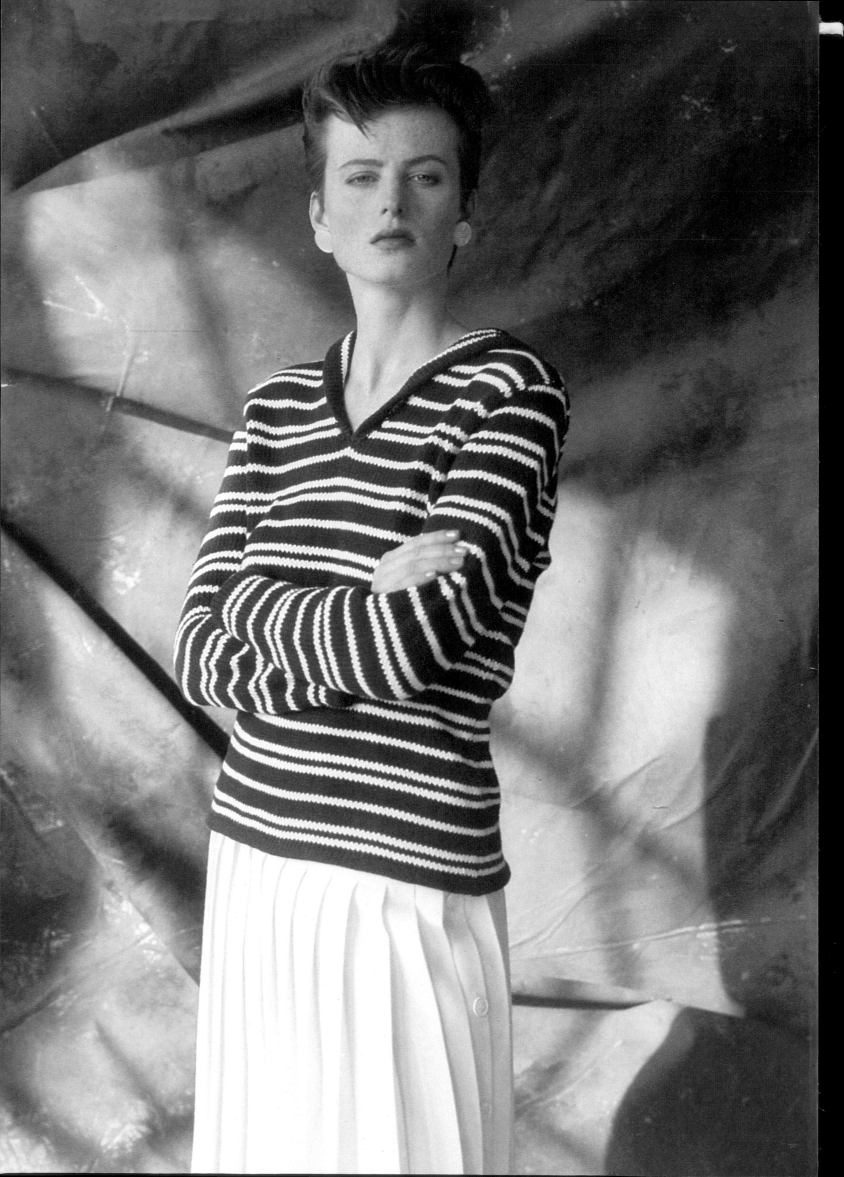

GREAT KNITTING IN VOGUE

Christina Probert

PHOTOGRAPHS BY MARIO TESTINO

St. Martin's Press   New York

To my godson Rupert

Copyright © 1985 by The Condé Nast Publications Ltd
All rights reserved
No part of this book may be used or reproduced
in any manner whatsoever without written
permission except in the case of brief
quotations embodied in critical articles or
reviews. For information, address
St Martin's Press, 175 Fifth Avenue, New York, N.Y. 10010

Library of Congress Cataloging in Publication Data
Probert, Christina
    Great Knitting in Vogue
    I. Knitting   2. Vogue (New York).   I. Title
TT820.P83 1985   746.9'2   85-10691
ISBN   0-312-34610-7

Published in Great Britain in 1985
by David & Charles (Publishers) Ltd

First U.S. Edition
10 9 8 7 6 5 4 3 2 1

Filmset in Palatino by Typesetters (Birmingham) Limited
Printed in the Netherlands by Royal Smeets Offset BV, Weert

Acknowledgements

Once again, I am indebted to all Vogue's knitting editors, past and present, who first commissioned the designs in this book, and to all the knitting yarn companies and individuals who were so co-operative in revising and reknitting the patterns, namely Art Needlework Industries, Argyll Wools Limited, Christian de Falbe, Emu Wools Ltd, Hayfield Textiles Ltd, Lister Handknitting, The Natural Dye Company, Jaeger Handknitting, Maxwell Cartlidge Ltd, Patons & Baldwins Ltd, Phildar, Laines Picaud and Browns Woolshop, Pingouin (French Wools Ltd), Richard Poppleton and Sons Ltd, Rowan Weavers Ltd, Sirdar, Sunbeam (Richard Ingham & Co Ltd), James Templeton and Son Ltd, H G Twilley Ltd, Wendy International, The Yarn Store and Yarn Works Ltd. I should like to thank Alex Kroll for his guidance throughout, Sue Horan and Essie Page for checking the patterns, Katharine Hall for the book's design, all the kind parents who entrusted their delightful children to us, and especially Lucy Page-Ratcliff for all her help and for being the perfect right-hand woman.

Colour photographs by Mario Testino.
Black and white photographs: Bailey 142; Donovan 30, 76, 78, 149; Duffy 104; Elgort 70; Honeyman 111, 132; Lousada 27, 69, 90, 123; Ogden 86, 93; Vernier 83; Zatecky 11. Charts by Andy Ingham. Drawings by Barbara Firth and Marion Appleton.

Hair by Mitch Barry on pages 14, 20, 46, 55, 59, 68, 81, 87, 91, 99, 106, 113, 114, 116, 118, 121, 122, 129, 133, 135, 143, 151; hair by Layla D'Angelo on pages 19, 23, 29, 31, 35, 40, 49, 60, 65, 73, 74, 79, 95, 96, 97, 116, 126, 131, 139, 141, 147; hair by Anthony De May for Glemby on pages 13, 17, 25, 32, 51, 62, 71, 82, 89, 92, 103; hair by Oribe on pages 10, 36, 66, 85, 100, 108, 121, 153; hair by Sacha on pages 45, 52, 56, 77, 105, 125, 136, 145, 148.

Make-up by Mark Borthwick on pages 79, 116; make-up by Jim Brussock on pages 17, 32, 51, 62, 71, 82; make-up by Leslie Chilkes on pages 13, 25, 31, 49, 89, 92, 103; make-up by Kevin on pages 10, 36, 66, 85, 100, 108, 121, 153; make-up by Jo Strettell on pages 45, 52, 56, 77, 105, 125, 136, 145, 148.

Clothes and accessories by Basile, British Shoe Corporation, Brooks Brothers, Browns, Comme des Garçons, Paul Costelloe, Dickins & Jones, Elbeo, Katharine Hamnett, Harrods, Hennes, Hobbs, Margaret Howell, Joseph, Kenzo, Libertys, Mulberry, Options at Austin Reed, Mary Quant, Scotch House, Whistles, The White House, The Yarn Store. International Textile Care Labelling Code courtesy of the Home Laundering Consultative Council.

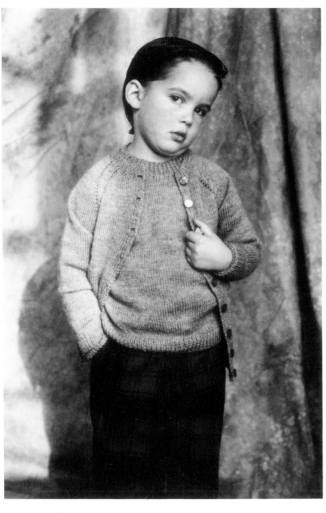

1954

Contents

KNITTING KNOW-HOW

INTERNATIONAL INFORMATION

1948

7

Introduction

Handknitting continues to go from strength to strength, more and more people are picking up needles and more and more new knitting companies are springing up, bringing exciting new ideas into the knitting world. The novelty lies both in shape and design, but above all in new yarns; mixtures of silk and linen, the latter being an important and hard-wearing new handknitting yarn, bulky wools so lightly spun that they are as weightless as the bulk nylons of the sixties, botany so heavily marled that it resembles tweed fabric when knitted up, in both heathery and bright tones.

And styles have changed quite radically. In the seventies knitting once again began to be popular after rather a lacuna in the sixties. Detailing and patterning in stitch and colour provided a new look along with raised effects which gave a 3-D appearance. By the eighties, knitting design had evolved still further. Simpler, less fussy patterns began to appear, with emphasis on yarns in natural fibres, rather than the new man-made fibres so popular in the sixties.

Here are over seventy more of the best Vogue knitting patterns published since the twenties, in Vogue and its knitting books. In this collection are designs for babies, toddlers and small children, as well as lots for men and women. The children's designs range from an enchanting baby's shawl and traditional, little-girl frocks, to scaled-down adult Arans and Fair Isles, covering a whole range of moods. For men and women there are cardigans, socks, jumpers and slipovers.

Always known for their high standard and fashionability, Vogue's knitting designs are perennial in their classic looks, whether they date from 1937 or 1957. And like all classics, they remain fashionable and wearable just as long as you want them to, according to the way in which they are accessorised, the colours in which they are knitted.

The designs themselves are unaltered, but the instructions for them have been rewritten for modern yarns, and amplified to help the modern knitter. There is a knitting know-how section at the back of the book to help beginners and to remind more experienced knitters of the various knitting processes. To assist you in your choice of patterns, each garment has been fashionably accessorised, and rephotographed in colour. The original black and white fashion shot is shown too, with a description of the design's construction.

Tension For perfect results, you must achieve the knitting tension specified in the patterns. Yarns have been chosen to correspond in character and weight to those originally used, and to produce the correct tensions. The manufacturers of the yarns chosen for the designs cannot take any responsibility for the patterns' success unless you use the correct yarn and work to the given tension. If the suggested yarn is not available, or if you are an experienced knitter and want to use a different yarn, test your tension carefully (see page 156). If the tension is wrong, the garment will be out of proportion.

Beginning The selection of Vogue originals in this book caters for knitters of every standard; and has been categorised as follows: patterns marked ★ are suitable for beginners, ★★ for knitters with some previous experience, and ★★★ for experienced knitters. Read through your pattern carefully before you begin to knit. Note that sizes are given in increasing order throughout the pattern: where only one instruction is given, this applies to all sizes. It is ofen helpful to mark each instruction for the size which you are knitting in pencil.

Alterations Garment length measurements are taken from shoulder to hem, unless otherwise specified. Alterations to body and sleeve lengths can be undertaken by experienced knitters, but be careful to mark all affected sections of the garment before you begin. On plain, unshaped designs, these alterations can usually be made after welt increases have been completed. Garments with a complicated self-pattern or Fair Isle design can be difficult to alter. Note also that lengthening increases your yarn requirement.

Abbreviations These are used to save space in knitting instructions and are explained at the beginning of each pattern. It is advisable to familiarize yourself with these before starting to knit. Asterisks (*) are used where a section of the pattern is to be repeated: the *wording will read 'repeat from *'. Where more than one section is to be repeated, two or three asterisks may be used for differentiation.

Charts These are used for multicoloured patterns. Each square of the graph paper denotes one stitch and one row. Colours are indicated by symbols. When working in stocking stitch row 1 (at the bottom of the chart) and all odd-numbered rows are knit rows, worked from right to left. Even numbered rows are purl, and worked from left to right. For further details on multicoloured knitting see page 158.

Keeping your place Mark your pattern at each stage. The easiest way to make a mistake is to lose your place. Use a ruler to underline the row which you have reached, or a card marker. Where you have to count rows, for example when increasing, use a stitch counter (available from knitting departments and shops) on your needle, or make a note of each row you knit.

Naturally Dyed Fair Isle Cardigan 1982. Instructions on page 27

Cashmere, Square-neck Twin Set 1980

Squared twin set with set-in sleeves, ribbed hem welts, cardigan with left front pocket and mitred, stocking stitch borders

★★ Suitable for knitters with some previous experience

MATERIALS

Yarn
Yarn Store Cashmere
Cardigan:
13(14:15:16:17) × 20g. hanks
Sweater:
13(14:15:16:17) × 20g. hanks

Needles
1 pair 2¾mm.
1 pair 3¼mm.
st. holder

MEASUREMENTS

Bust (both)
82(87:92:97:102) cm.
32(34:36:38:40) in.

Length (cardigan)
62 cm.
24¼ in.

Length (sweater)
60 cm.
23¾ in.

Sleeve Seam (both)
44 cm.
17¼ in.

TENSION

28 sts. and 36 rows = 10 cm. (4 in.) square over st. st. on 3¼mm. needles. If your tension square does not correspond to these measurements, see page 156 for adjustment instructions.

ABBREVIATIONS

k. = knit; p. = purl; st(s). = stitch(es); inc. = increas(ing) (see page 156); dec. = decreas(ing) (see page 157); beg. = begin(ning); rem. = remain(ing); rep. = repeat; alt. = alternate; tog. = together; sl. = slip (transfer one stitch from left needle, knitwise unless otherwise stated, to right hand needle.); cont. = continue; patt. = pattern; foll. = following; folls. = follows; mm. = millimetres; cm. = centimetres; in. = inches; st. st. = stocking st.: one row k., one row p.; g. st. = garter st.: every row k.; incs. = increases; decs. = decreases.

CARDIGAN BACK

Cast on 114(122:128:136:142) sts. with 2¾mm. needles.
Work 23 rows in k.2, p.2 rib.
Inc. row: rib 8(12:8:12:11) sts., * inc. in next st., rib 13(13:15:15:16), rep. from * to last 8(12:8:12:12) sts., inc. in next st., rib 7(11:7:11:11). [122(130:136:144:150) sts.]
Change to 3¼mm. needles.
Cont. in st. st. (k. the first row) until work measures 44(43:43:42:41) cm. (17¼(16¾:16¾:16½:16) in.). ending with a p. row.

Shape Armholes
Cast off 5 sts. at beg. of next 2 rows.
Dec. 1 st. at each end of next 5 rows, then every foll. alt. row 4(5:5:6:6) times. [94(100:106:112:118) sts.]
Cont. straight until armholes measure 18(19:19:20:21) cm. (7(7½:7½:7¾:8¼) in.), ending with a p. row.

Shape Shoulders
Cast off 5(5:5:6:6) sts. at beg. of next 6 rows and 4(6:8:7:9) sts. on foll. 2 rows.
Sl. rem. 56(58:60:62:64) sts. onto a spare needle.

CARDIGAN POCKET LINING

Cast on 24 sts. with 3¼mm. needles.
Work 22 rows in st. st.
Sl. sts. onto a spare needle.

CARDIGAN LEFT FRONT

Cast on 52(56:60:64:66) sts. with 2¾mm. needles.
Work 23 rows in k.2, p.2 rib.
Inc. row: rib 6(7:8:8:9), * inc. in next st., rib 12(13:14:15:15), rep. from * to last 7(7:7:8:9) sts., inc. in next st., rib 6(6:6:7:8). [56(60:64:68:70) sts.]
Change to 3¼mm. needles.
Cont. in st. st. (first row k.) until work measures same as back, less 2 rows, to armhole shaping.

Pocket Opening
Next row: k.19(23:28:30:33), sl. next 24 sts. onto st. holder and k. across 24 sts. from pocket lining, k. to end.
P.1 row.

Shape Armhole
Cast off 5 sts. at beg. of next row.
P.1 row.
Dec. 1 st. at armhole edge on next 5 rows, then on every foll. alt. row 4(5:5:6:6) times. [42(45:49:52:54) sts.]
Cont. straight until armhole measures 12(13:13:14:15) cm. (4¾(5:5:5½:5¾) in.), ending with a k. row.

Shape Neck
Cast off 23(24:26:27:27) sts. at beg. of next row. [19(21:23:25:27) sts.]
Cont. straight until armhole measures same as back, ending with a p. row.

Shape Shoulder
Cast off 5(5:5:6:6) sts. at beg. of next and foll. 2 alt. rows.

Work 1 row.
Cast off rem. 4(6:8:7:9) sts.

CARDIGAN RIGHT FRONT

Work as for left front, reversing shapings and omitting pocket.

CARDIGAN SLEEVES

Cast on 70(74:78:82:86) sts. with 2¾mm. needles.
Work 20 rows in st. st.
Change to 3¼mm. needles.
Cont. in st. st. for 24 rows, ending with a p. row.
To reverse work:
Next row: p.
Beg. with a k. row, work 10 rows.
Inc. 1 st. at each end of next and every foll. 12th row 12 times in all. [94(98:102:106:110) sts.]
Cont. straight until sleeve measures 44 cm. (17¼ in.) from reverse row.

Shape Top
Cast off 5 sts. at beg. of next 2 rows.
Dec. 1 st. at each end of next 7 rows, then every foll. alt. row until 46(50:54:56:60) sts. rem.
Dec. 1 st. at each end of next 10(12:14:14:16) rows.
Cast off rem. 26(26:26:28:28) sts.

CARDIGAN POCKET TOP

With 2¾mm. needles and right side of work facing, k. across 24 sts. of pocket.
Work 18 rows in st. st.
Cast off.

CARDIGAN FRONT BANDS

Cast on 16 sts. with 2¾mm. needles.
Work in st. st. until band is long enough to fit up front to neck shaping, stretched slightly.

Mitre Corner
Dec. 1 st. at each end of next 7 rows. [2 sts.]
K.2 tog., fasten off.
Work another band to match.

CARDIGAN BACK & SIDE NECK BANDS

Sew up shoulder seams.
With 2¾mm. needles and right side facing, pick up 23 sts. along straight side edge of front neck to top shoulder, 56(58:60:62:64) sts. from spare needle at back, and 23 sts. down front neck. [102(104:106:108:110) sts.]
Now work in st. st., p. first row.
Dec. 1 st. at each end of next 8 rows.
Work 1 row.
Now inc. 1 st. at each end of next 8 rows.
Cast off.

CARDIGAN FRONT NECK BANDS

With 2¾mm. needles and right side of work facing, pick up 23(24:26:27:27) sts. from front neck of left front.
Now work in st. st., p. first row.
Dec. 1 st. at inner edge and inc. 1 st. at neck edge on next 8 rows.
Work 1 row.
Dec. 1 st. at neck edge and inc. 1 st. at inner edge on next 8 rows.
Cast off.
Work other side to match.

CARDIGAN MAKING UP

Press lightly on wrong side avoiding rib.
Set in sleeves.
Sew up side and sleeve seams to beg. of cuff, reverse work and complete seam.
Sew back, side and front bands in position.
Sew up all mitred corners.
Turn bands to inside and sew to seams.
Sew pocket lining in place.
Turn pocket top in half onto inside and sew in place, then sew edges of top in position.
Press seams.
Turn cuff to outside and press lightly in place.

SWEATER BACK

Cast on 120(126:134:140:148) sts. with 2¾mm. needles.
Work 24 rows in k.2, p.2 rib.
Change to 3¼mm. needles.
Cont. in st. st. (first row k.) until work measures 42(41:41:40:40) cm. (16½(16:16: 15¾:15¾) in.), ending with a p. row.

Shape Armholes

Cast off 5 sts. at beg. of next 2 rows.
Dec. 1 st. at each end of next 5 rows, then on every foll. alt. row 3(3:4:4:5) times. [94(100:106:112:118) sts.] *.
Cont. straight until armholes measure 18(19:19:20:20) cm. (7(7½:7½:7¾:7¾) in.), ending with a p. row.

Shape Shoulders

Cast off 5(5:5:6:6) sts. at beg. of next 6 rows and 4(6:8:7:9) sts. at beg. of next 2 rows. [56(58:60:62:64) sts.]
Change to 2¾mm. needles and work 18 rows in st. st.
Cast off.

SWEATER FRONT

Work as for back to *.
Cont. straight until armholes measure 11(12:12:13:13) cm. (4¼(4¾:4¾:5:5) in.), ending with a p. row.

Divide for Neck

1st row: k.19(21:23:25:27) sts., turn, leave rem. sts. on a spare needle.
Cont. on these 19(21:23:25:27) sts. until armhole measures same as back, ending with a p. row.

Shape Shoulder

Cast off 5(5:5:6:6) sts. at beg. of next and foll. 2 alt. rows.
Work 1 row.
Cast off rem. 4(6:8:7:9) sts.
Sl. centre 56(58:60:62:64) sts. onto a spare needle.
Rejoin yarn to rem. sts. and work to match first side, reversing shapings.

SWEATER SLEEVES

Cast on 60(62:64:66:68) sts. with 2¾mm. needles.
Work 24 rows in k.2, p.2 rib.

Change to 3¼mm. needles.
Cont. in st. st. (first row k.), work 6 rows.
Inc. 1 st. at each end of next and every foll. 8th(7th:7th:6th:6th) row, 16(17:18: 19:20) times in all. [92(96:100:104:108) sts.]
Cont. straight until sleeve measures 44 cm. (17¼ in.)

Shape Top

Cast off 5 sts. at beg. of next 2 rows.
Dec. 1 st. at each end of next 7 rows, then every foll. alt. row 12(12:12:13:13) times.
Dec. 1 st. at each end of next 8(10:12: 12:14) rows.
Cast off rem. 28(28:28:30:30) sts.

SWEATER SIDE NECKBAND

With 2¾mm. needles and right side of work facing, pick up 23 sts. along straight edge of right front to top of shoulder.
Cont. in st. st., p.1 row.
Dec. 1 st. at front neck edge on next 8 rows.
Work 1 row.
Now inc. 1 st. at same edge on next 8 rows.
Cast off.
Work other side to match.

SWEATER FRONT NECKBAND

With 2¾mm. needles and right side of work facing, k.56(58:60:62:64) sts. from spare needle.
P. 1 row.
Dec. 1 st. at each end of next 8 rows.
Work 1 row.
Inc. 1 st. at each end of next 8 rows.
Cast off.

SWEATER MAKING UP

Press lightly on wrong side avoiding rib.
Sew up shoulder and neckband seams.
Set in sleeves.
Sew up side and shoulder seams.
Sew up mitred corners on front, turn neckband in half onto inside and sew to seams.
Press seams.

Fine Silk Roll-collar Sweater   1952

Plain sweater in stocking stitch with raglan sleeves, narrow roll collar and ribbed welts

★ Suitable for beginners

MATERIALS

Yarn
Maxwell Cartlidge Lotus Silk 4 ply
12(12:13:14:14) × 40g. hanks

Needles
1 pair 2¾mm.
1 pair 3¼mm.

MEASUREMENTS

Chest
97(102:107:112:117) cm.
38(40:42:44:46) in.

Length
59(61:63:65:66) cm.
23¼(24:24¾:25½:26) in.

Sleeve Seam
51(52:54:54:54) cm.
20(20½:21¼:21¼:21¼) in.

TENSION

27 sts. and 40 rows = 10 cm. (4 in.) square over st. st. on 3¼mm. needles. If your tension square does not correspond to these measurements, see page 156 for adjustment instructions.

ABBREVIATIONS

k. = knit; p. = purl; st(s). = stitch(es); inc. = increas(ing) (see page 156); dec. = decreas(ing) (see page 157); beg. = begin(ning); rem. = remain(ing); rep. = repeat; alt. = alternate; tog. = together; sl. = slip (transfer one stitch from left needle, knitwise unless otherwise stated, to right hand needle.); cont. = continue; patt. = pattern; foll. = following; folls. = follows; mm. = millimetres; cm. = centimetres; in. = inches; st. st. = stocking st.: one row k., one row p.; g. st. = garter st.: every row k.; incs. = increases; decs. = decreases; t.b.l. = through back of loops.

BACK

Cast on 126(134:142:150:158) sts. with 2¾mm. needles.
Work 13 cm. (5 in.) in k.2 t.b.l., p.2 rib patt., inc. 6 sts. evenly across last row. [132(140:148:156:164) sts.]
Change to 3¼mm. needles and st. st.
Work 18 rows.
Inc. 1 st. at each end of next and every 10th row until there are 140(148:154:162:168) sts.
Work straight until back measures 36(37:38:40:40) cm. (14(14½:15:15¾:15¾) in.), ending with a p. row.

Shape Raglans

Cast off 1(2:3:4:5) sts. at beg. of next 2 rows. *
Dec. 1 st. at each end of every k. row until 48(50:52:54:56) sts. rem.
P. 1 row.
Leave sts. on a st. holder.

FRONT

Work as for back to *.
Dec. 1 st. at each end of next 10 rows.
Now dec. 1 st. at each end of every k. row until 52(54:56:58:60) sts. rem., ending with a p. row.

Shape Neck

1st row: k.2 tog., k.5, turn.
Cont. on these sts. only for first side.
2nd row: p.2 tog., p.4.
3rd row: k.2 tog., k.1, k.2 tog.
4th row: p.2 tog., p.1.
K.2 tog. and fasten off.
Sl. centre 38(40:42:44:46) sts. onto a st. holder, rejoin yarn to inner end of rem. sts. and complete to match first side, reversing shapings.

RIGHT SLEEVE

Cast on 54(58:58:62:62) sts. with 2¾mm. needles.
Work 10 cm. (4 in.) in k.2 t.b.l., p.2 rib patt., inc. 6 sts. evenly across last row. [60(64:64:68:68) sts.]

Change to 3¼mm. needles and st. st.
Inc. 1 st. at each end of next and every foll. 6th(6th:5th:5th:5th) row until there are 110(116:122:128:134) sts.
Work straight until sleeve measures 51(52:54:54:54) cm. (20(20½:21¼:21¼:21¼) in.), ending with a p. row.

Shape Top

Cast off 1(2:3:4:5) sts. at beg. of next 2 rows.
Dec. 1 st. at each end of every k. row until 28(28:30:30:32) sts. rem., ending with a p. row.
Next row: cast off 4 sts., k. to last 2 sts., k.2 tog.
Next row: p.
Rep. last 2 rows 4 more times.
Cast off rem. 3(3:5:5:7) sts.

LEFT SLEEVE

Work as for right sleeve, reading k. for p. and p. for k. when shaping sleeve top.

COLLAR

Sew up raglan seams, leaving left back raglan sleeve open.
With right side of work facing, and 2¾mm. needles, pick up and k.16(16:16:18:18) sts. across top left sleeve shaping, 5 sts. down left front neck shaping, 38(40:42:44:46) sts. from front st. holder, 5 sts. up right front neck shaping, 16(16:16:18:18) sts. across top right sleeve shaping and 48(50:52:54:56) sts. from back st. holder. [128(132:136:144:148) sts.]
Work 12 cm. (4¾ in.) in k.2 t.b.l., p.2 rib patt.
Cast off loosely in rib with 3¼mm. needles.

MAKING UP

Sew up side, sleeve, and left back raglan seams.
Turn up cuffs and turn over collar to wrong side, sl. st. loosely in place.

Classic, warm, Fair Isle Sweater

Traditional round-neck, long-sleeved sweater with three-colour allover Fair Isle design, ribbed welts and set-in sleeves

★★ Suitable for knitters with some previous experience

MATERIALS

Yarn
ANI Scottish Homespun
3(3:4:4:5) × 28g. hanks Main Col. A
1(1:2:2:2) × 28g. hanks Col. B
1(1:1:2:2) × 28g. hanks Col. C

Needles
1 pair 3¼mm.
1 set of 4 double-pointed 3¼mm.
st. holders

MEASUREMENTS

Chest
56(61:66:71:76) cm.
22(24:26:28:30) in.
2/3(4/5:6/7:8/9:10/11) approx. age

Length
37(39:43:47:51) cm.
14½(15½:17:18½:20) in.

Sleeve Seam
24(28:34:38:40) cm.
9½(11:13½:15:15¾) in.

TENSION

28 sts. and 32 rows = 10 cm. (4 in.) square over st. st. Fair Isle patt. on 3¼mm. needles. If your tension square does not correspond to these measurements, see page 156 for adjustment instructions.

ABBREVIATIONS

k. = knit; p. = purl; st(s). = stitch(es); inc. = increas(ing) (see page 156); dec. = decreas(ing) (see page 157); beg. = begin(ning); rem. = remain(ing); rep. = repeat; alt. = alternate; tog. = together; sl. = slip (transfer one stitch from left needle, knitwise unless otherwise stated, to right hand needle.); cont. = continue; patt. = pattern; foll. = following; folls. =

follows; mm. = millimetres; cm. = centimetres; in. = inches; st. st. = stocking st.: one row k., one row p.; g. st. = garter st.: every row k.; incs. = increases; decs. = decreases.

NB See page 9 for instructions on working from patt. charts.

BACK

Cast on 70(76:82:88:94) sts. with 3¼mm. needles and A.
Work in k.1, p.1, rib for 6 cm. (2¼ in.), ending with a right side row.
Next row: p., inc. 3 sts. evenly across row. [73(79:85:91:97) sts.]
Change to st. st. and work from chart, beg. with a k. row, and stranding yarn not in use on wrong side.
Work 12 rows.
Inc. 1 st. at each end of next and every foll. 12th row until there are 81(87:95:101: 109) sts.
Cont. straight in patt. until work measures 25(27:29:32:34) cm. (10(10½: 11½:12½:13½) in.)

Shape Armholes
Cast off 3(3:4:4:5) sts. at beg. of next 2 rows.
Dec. 1 st. at each end of next 3 rows.
Now dec. 1 st. at each end of every k. row until 63(67:73:79:85) sts. rem.
Cont. straight until armholes measure 12(13:14:15:17) cm. (4¾(5:5½:5¾:6½) in.)

Shape Shoulders
Cast off 3(4:6:6:7) sts. at beg. of next 2 rows.
Cast off 6(6:6:7:8) sts. at beg. of next 4 rows.
Leave rem. 33(35:37:39:39) sts. on holder for neckband.

FRONT

Work as for back until armholes measure 7(8:9:10:12) cm. (2¾(3¼:3½:4:4¾) in.)

Shape Neck
Work 25(26:29:31:34) sts., turn and work on these sts. first.
Cast off 3 sts. at beg. of next row and foll. alt. row.
Now dec. 1 st. at neck edge on every alt. row until 15(16:18:20:23) sts. rem.
Work straight until front measures same as back to shoulder shaping, ending at armhole edge.

Shape Shoulder
Cast off 3(4:6:6:7) sts. at beg. of next row.
Work 1 row.
Cast off 6(6:6:7:8) sts. at beg. of next row.
Work 1 row.
Cast off rem. 6(6:6:7:8) sts.
Sl. centre 13(15:15:17:17) sts. onto holder for front neck.
Rejoin yarn to rem. sts. and work to match first side.

SLEEVES

Cast on 38(40:42:44:46) sts. with 3¼mm. needles and A.

Work 6 cm. (2¼ in.) in k.1, p.1 rib, ending with a right side row.
Next row: p, inc. 11(9:13:11:9) sts. evenly across row. [49(49:55:55:55) sts.]
Change to st. st. and beg. working patt. from chart, working odd rows k., and even rows p., beg. with a 5th(35th:25th: 21st:21st) row.
Work 6 rows.
Inc. 1 st. at each end of next and every foll. 6th row until there are 63(67:71:75: 79) sts.
Work straight until the same patt. row is reached as at armhole of back.

Shape Top
Cast off 3 sts. at beg. of next 2 rows.
Dec. 1 st. at each end of next 3 rows.
Work 1 row.
Dec. 1 st. at each end of next and every alt. row until 35(37:37:39:39) sts. rem.
Cast off 3 sts. at beg. of next 4 rows.
Cast off rem. sts.

NECKBAND

Sew up shoulder seams.
With right side of work facing, 3¼mm. double-pointed needles and A, k. up 33(35:37:39:39) sts. from back holder, 24(24:26:26:26) sts. down left side of neck, 13(15:15:17:17) sts. from front holder and 24(24:26:26:26) sts. up right side of neck. [94(98:104:108:108) sts.]
Arrange these sts. on 3 needles and work 12 rounds in k.1, p.1 rib.
Cast off in rib.

MAKING UP

Set in sleeves, matching patt. at armholes.
Sew up side and sleeve seams.
Fold neckband in half to wrong side and slip st. loosely in position.
Press.

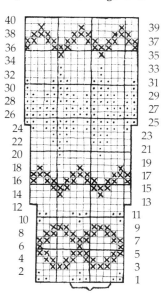

□ = Col A
▣ = Col B
▨ = Col C

Pattern
repeat
6 sts

Fine Sleeveless Pullover

Fine, textured-stitch pullover with round neck, ribbed lower welt, ribbed and shaped neck and armhole borders

★★ Suitable for knitters with some previous experience

MATERIALS

Yarn
Templeton's H & O Shetland Fleece
8(9:10:11:12) × 25g. balls

Needles
1 pair 3¼mm.
1 pair 3¾mm.
st. holder

MEASUREMENTS

Chest
87(92:97:102:107) cm.
34(36:38:40:42) in.

Length
57(59:60:62:63) cm.
22¼(23¼:23¾:24¼:24¾) in.

TENSION

32 sts. and 44 rows = 10 cm. (4 in.) square over patt. on 3¾mm. needles. If your tension square does not correspond to these measurements, see page 156 for adjustment instructions.

ABBREVIATIONS

k. = knit; p. = purl; st(s). = stitch(es); inc. = increas(ing) (see page 156); dec. = decreas(ing) (see page 157); beg. = begin(ning); rem. = remain(ing); rep. = repeat; alt. = alternate; tog. = together; sl. = slip (transfer one stitch from left needle, knitwise unless otherwise stated, to right hand needle.); cont. = continue; patt. = pattern; foll. = following; folls. = follows; mm. = millimetres; cm. = centimetres; in. = inches; st. st. = stocking st.: one row k., one row p.; g. st. = garter st.: every row k.; incs. = increases; decs. = decreases; sl. 1p. = sl. 1 st. purlwise.

FRONT

Cast on 130(138:146:154:162) sts. with 3¼mm. needles.
Work 8 cm. (3¼ in.) in k.2, p.2 rib, inc. 1 st. at beg. of last row. [131(139:147:155: 163) sts.]
Change to 3¾mm. needles and patt. as folls.:
1st row (right side): k.1, * sl.1p, k.1, rep. from * to end.
2nd row: p.
Rep. these 2 rows to form patt.
Cont. straight in patt. until front measures 15 cm. (5¾ in.), ending with a wrong side row.
Keeping patt. correct, inc. 1 st. at each

end of next and every 6th row until there are 151(159:167:175:183) sts.
Work straight on these sts. until front measures 36(37:38:39:39) cm. (14(14½:15: 15¼:15¼) in.), ending with a wrong side row.

Shape Armholes
Cast off 5(6:7:8:9) sts. at beg. of next 2 rows.
Cast off 5 sts. at beg. of next 2 rows.
Cast off 2 sts. at beg. of next 4 rows.
Cast off 1 st. at beg. of next 4(4:6:6:8) rows. [119(125:129:135:139) sts.]
Cont. straight until armholes measure (13(14:14:15:16) cm. (5(5½:5½:5¾:6¼) in.), ending with a wrong side row.

Shape Neck
1st row: patt. 51(52:53:54:55), cast off centre 17(21:23:27:29) sts., patt. 51(52:53: 54:55).
Cont. on these sts. for first side, leaving rem. sts. on holder.
Work 1 row.
** Cast off 3 sts. at neck edge on next row.
Dec. 1 st. at neck edge on next and every alt. row, AT THE SAME TIME inc. 1 st. at armhole edge on every 4th row until 35(36:37:38:39) sts. rem., ending at armhole edge.

Shape Shoulder
Cast off at beg. of next and every alt. row 5 sts. 7(6:5:4:3) times and 6 sts. 0(1:2:3:4) times.
With wrong side of rem. sts. facing, rejoin yarn to neck edge and work as for first side from ** to end.

BACK

Cast on 114(122:130:138:146) sts. with 3¼mm. needles.
Work in rib as for front, inc. 1 st. at beg. of last row. [115(123:131:139:147) sts.]
Change to 3¾mm. needles.
Work in patt. as for front until work matches front to beg. of inc., ending with a wrong side row.

Inc. 1 st. at each end of next and every 6th row until there are 135(143:151:159:167) sts.
Cont. straight until work matches front to armholes, ending with a wrong side row.

Shape Armholes
Cast off 4(5:6:7:8) sts. at beg. of next 2 rows.
Cast off 2 sts. at beg. of next 2 rows.
Cast off 1 st. at beg. of next 4(4:6:6:8) rows. [119(125:129:135:139) sts.]
Work straight until armholes measure 17(18:18:19:20) cm. (6½(7:7:7½:7¾) in.), ending with a wrong side row.

Shape Neck
1st row: patt. 34(35:36:37:38), cast off centre 51(55:57:61:63) sts., patt. 34(35:36: 37:38).
Cont. on these sts. for first side leaving rem. sts. on holder.
Dec. 1 st. at neck edge on next and foll. alt.row, AT THE SAME TIME inc. 1 st. at armhole edge on next and foll. 2 alt. rows.

Shape Shoulder
Work as for front, beg. at armhole edge.
With wrong side of rem. sts. facing, rejoin yarn at neck edge and work as for first side.

ARMBANDS

Cast on 3 sts. with 3¼mm. needles.
Work in g. st., inc. 1 st. at beg. of every 2nd row until there are 12 sts.
Work straight until band measures 36(37: 38:39:40) cm. (14(14½:15:15¼:15¾) in.) from beg. of straight section.
Dec. 1 st. at shaped edge of next and every alt. row until 3 sts. rem.
Cast off.

NECKBAND

Cast on 12 sts. with 3¼mm. needles.
Work in g. st. until neckband measures 56(58:61:63:66) cm. (22(22¾:24:24¾:26) in.)
Cast off.

MAKING UP

Sew up shoulder and side seams.
Sew armbands and neckband into circles by seaming short ends.
Sew long edges of armbands round armholes, overlapping armbands over edge st. of armholes and back-stitching neatly in place.
Sew on neckband round neck as for armbands.
Press lightly under a damp cloth with a warm iron, omitting ribbing and g. st. borders.

Chunky, Moss-stitch Jacket

1942

Thick jacket with three-quarter-length set-in sleeves, rounded collar and narrow, knitted borders around whole garment

★★ Suitable for knitters with some previous experience

NB Sleeves are three-quarter length.

MATERIALS

Yarn
Phildar Wool DK
4(5:5) × 50g. balls

Needles
1 pair 3¼mm.
1 pair 4mm.

Buttons
5

MEASUREMENTS

Chest
56(61:66) cm.
22(24:26) in.
2/3(4/5:6/7) approx. age

Length
25(28:33) cm.
9¾(11:13) in.

Sleeve Seam
10(12:14) cm.
4(4¾:5½) in.

TENSION

21 sts. and 30 rows = 10 cm. (4 in.) square over patt. on 4mm. needles. If your tension square does not correspond to these measurements, see page 156 for adjustment instructions.

ABBREVIATIONS

k. = knit; p. = purl; st(s). = stitch(es); inc. = increas(ing) (see page 156); dec. = decreas(ing) (see page 157); beg. = begin(ning); rem. = remain(ing); rep. = repeat; alt. = alternate; tog. = together; sl. = slip (transfer one stitch from left needle, knitwise unless otherwise stated, to right hand needle.); cont. = continue; patt. = pattern; foll. = following; folls. = follows; mm. = millimetres; cm. = centimetres; in. = inches; st. st. = stocking st.: one row k., one row p.; g. st. = garter st.: every row k.; incs. = increases; decs. = decreases.

RIGHT FRONT

Cast on 35(37:41) sts. with 3¼mm. needles.
K. 3 rows.

Change to 4mm. needles and work in patt. as folls.:
1st row (right side): k.1, * p.1, k.1, rep. from * to end.
2nd row: p.1,* k.1, p.1, rep. from * to end.
3rd row: p.1,* k.1, p.1, rep. from * to end.
4th row: k.1, * p.1, k.1, rep. from * to end.
These 4 rows form patt.
Work 4(0:0) more patt. rows.
1st buttonhole row: patt. 2 sts., cast off 2 sts., patt. to end.
2nd buttonhole row: patt., casting on 2 sts. over those cast off on previous row.
Patt. 8(12:14) rows.
Rep. 1st and 2nd buttonhole rows.
Cont. in this way until there are 3 buttonholes.
Work 7(9:13) rows straight after completion of 3rd buttonhole, thus ending with a right side row.

Shape Armhole

Keeping patt. correct, cont. to work buttonholes as before:
Cast off 3 sts. at beg. of next row.
Work 1 row.
Dec. 1 st. at armhole edge on next 3(5:5) rows.
Work 1 row.
Dec. 1 st. at beg. of next row. [28(28:32) sts.]
Work straight in patt. until 5 buttonholes have been worked, ending with 6(2:4) rows straight, and a wrong side row.

Shape Neck

Cast off 5 sts. at beg. of next row.
3rd size only: work 1 row, cast off 2 sts. at beg. of next and foll. alt. row.
All sizes: dec. 1 st. at neck edge on every row until 15(16:16) sts. rem.
Work straight in patt. until armhole measures 12(13:15) cm. (4¾(5:5¾) in.), ending at armhole edge.

Shape Shoulder

Cast off 5 sts. at beg. of next and foll. alt. row.
Work 1 row.
Cast off rem. 5(6:6) sts.

LEFT FRONT

Work to match right front, omitting buttonholes and reversing shapings.

BACK

Cast on 61(67:71) sts. with 3¼mm. needles.
K. 3 rows.
Change to 4mm. needles and work in patt. as for front until back matches front to beg. of armhole shaping, ending with a wrong side row.

Shape Armholes

Cast off 3 sts. at beg. of next 2 rows.
Dec. 1 st. at each end of next 3(5:5) rows.
Work 1 row.
Dec. 1 st. at each end of next row. [47(49:53) sts.]
Work straight in patt. until back matches front to beg. of shoulder shaping, ending with a wrong side row.

Shape Shoulders

Cast off 5 sts. at beg. of next 4 rows.
Cast off 5(6:6) sts. at beg. of next 2 rows.
Cast off rem. 17(17:21) sts.

SLEEVES

Cast on 35(39:43) sts. with 3¼mm. needles.
K. 3 rows.
Change to 4mm. needles and work in patt. as for front, AT THE SAME TIME inc. 1 st. at each end of every 3rd(4th:5th) row until there are 49(53:57) sts., taking inc. sts. into patt.
Work straight in patt. until sleeve measures 10(12:14) cm. (4(4¾:5½) in.), or required length, ending with a wrong side row.

Shape Top

Cast off 3 sts. at beg. of next 2 rows.
Dec. 1 st. at each end of next and every foll. alt. row until 21(25:25) sts. rem.
Dec. 1 st. at each end of every row until 11 sts. rem.
Cast off.

RIGHT FRONT BORDER

With right side facing and 3¼mm. needles, k. 48(54:60) sts. evenly up right front edge.
K. 2 rows.
Cast off.

LEFT FRONT BORDER

Work to match right front, but along left front edge.

COLLAR

Cast on 58(62:68) sts. with 3¼mm. needles.
K. 3 rows.
Change to 4mm. needles and work as folls.:
1st row (right side): k.
2nd row: k.3, p. to last 3 sts., k.3.
These 2 rows form patt.
Cont. straight in patt. as set until collar measures 4 cm. (1½ in.), ending with a 2nd row.

Shape Collar

Next row: k.7, k.2 tog., (k.12(13:15), k.2 tog.) 3 times, k.7(8:8). [54(58:64) sts.]
Work 3 rows.
Next row: k.7, k.2 tog., (k.11(12:14), k.2 tog.) 3 times, k.6(7:7). [50(54:60) sts.]
Work 1 row.
Next row: k.7, k.2 tog., (k.10(11:13), k.2 tog.) 3 times, k.5(6:6). [46(50:56) sts.]
Work 1 row.
Cast off.

MAKING UP

Sew up shoulder seams.
Sew cast-off edge of collar in position, allowing for front overlap.
Sew up side and sleeve seams.
Set in sleeves.
Sew on buttons.

Double-breasted Cotton Shirt 1938

Long-sleeved, collared shirt in stocking stitch, with ribbed yoke and double-breasted front opening

★ Suitable for beginners

MATERIALS

Yarn
Patons Cotton Top
5(5:6) × 50g. balls

Needles
1 pair 3¼mm.
1 pair 4mm.

Buttons
4

MEASUREMENTS

Chest
61(66:71) cm.
24(26:28) in.
4/5(6/7:8/9) approx. age

Length
42(46:49) cm.
16½(18:19¼) in.

Sleeve Seam
27(31:34) cm.
10½(12¼:13¼) in.

TENSION

20 sts. and 26 rows = 10 cm. (4 in.) square over st. st. on 4mm. needles. If your tension square does not correspond to these measurements, see page 156 for adjustment instructions.

ABBREVIATIONS

k. = knit; p. = purl; st(s). = stitch(es); inc. = increas(ing) (see page 156); dec. = decreas(ing) (see page 157); beg. = begin(ning); rem. = remain(ing); rep. = repeat; alt. = alternate; tog. = together; sl. = slip (transfer one stitch from left needle, knitwise unless otherwise stated, to right hand needle.); cont. = continue; patt. = pattern; foll. = following; folls. = follows; mm. = millimetres; cm. = centimetres; in. = inches; st. st. = stocking st.: one row k., one row p.; g. st. = garter st.: every row k.; incs. = increases; decs. = decreases; m.1 = make 1 st.: pick up horizontal loop lying before next st. and k. into the back of it.

BACK

** Cast on 53(57:63) sts. with 3¼mm. needles.
1st row (right side): k.1, * p.1, k.1, rep. from * to end.
2nd row: p.1, * k.1, p.1, rep. from * to end.
Rep. last 2 rows until work measures 5 cm. (2 in.), ending with a 1st row.
Next row: rib 4(1:4) sts., m.1, * rib 5, m.1, rep. from * to last 4(1:4) sts., rib 4(1:4). [63(69:75) sts.]
Change to 4mm. needles and st. st.
Beg. with a k. row, work straight until back measures 28(31:33) cm. (11(12¼:13) in.) at centre from beg., ending with a wrong side row.

Shape Armholes

Cast off 3 sts. at beg. of next 2 rows.
Dec. 1 st. at each end of every row until 47(53:55) sts. rem.
2nd size only:
Now dec. 1 st. at each end of foll. alt. row. [47(51:55) sts.] **
All sizes:
With wrong side facing, and beg. with a 1st row, work in k.1, p.1 rib over all sts. until back measures 42(46:49) cm. (16½(18:19¼) in.) at centre from beg., ending with a wrong side row.

Shape Shoulders

Cast off 4(4:5) sts. at beg. of next 2 rows, then 4(5:5) sts. at beg. of next 4 rows.
Cast off rem. 23(23:25) sts.

FRONT

Work as for back from ** to **.
All sizes:
Work yoke as folls.:
Next row: k.1, rib 11(13:14), p.23(23:25) sts., rib 12(14:15).
Next row: rib 12(14:15), turn and leave rem. 35(37:40) sts., cont. on these 12(14:15) sts. for first side as folls.:
Next row: cast on 23(23:25) sts., (k.2, p.21(21:23) on cast-on sts.), rib to end.
Keeping 2 sts. at front edge in g. st., 21(21:23) sts. in st. st. and rem. in rib, work straight until front measures 37(41:44) cm. (14½(16:17¼) in.) at centre from beg., ending at front edge.

Shape Neck

Cast off 11(11:12) sts. at beg. of next row.

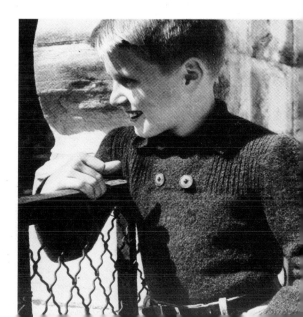

Cast off 3 sts. at beg. of foll. 3 alt. rows.
Now dec. 1 st. at neck edge on every row until 12(14:15) sts. rem.
Cont. until front matches back at armhole edge, ending with a wrong side row.

Shape Shoulder

Cast off 4(4:5) sts. at beg. of next row.
Cast off 4(5:5) sts. at beg. of foll. 2 alt. rows.
With right side facing, rejoin yarn to rem. 35(37:40) sts., k.23(23:25) sts., rib to end.
Complete to match first side, reversing all shapings and making 2 sets of buttonholes thus, 1st set to come 1 cm. (½ in.) above beg. of yoke, 2nd set to come 1 cm. (½ in.) below beg. of neck shaping:
1st buttonhole row (right side): k.2, cast off 3, k.13(13:15), cast off 3 sts., work to end.
2nd buttonhole row: work back, casting on 3 sts. over each set of those cast off.

SLEEVES

Cast on 31(33:35) sts. with 3¼mm. needles.

Work 5 cm. (2 in.) in k.1, p.1 rib as for back, ending with a 1st row.
Next row: rib 3(4:3), m.1, * rib 8(5:4), m.1, rep. from * to last 4(4:4) sts., rib 4(4:4). [35(39:43) sts.]
Change to 4mm. needles and, beg. with a k. row, work in st. st., shaping sides by inc. 1 st. at each end of 5th and every foll. 8th(10th:12th) row until there are 43(47:51) sts.
Work straight until sleeve seam measures 27(31:34) cm. (10½(12¼:13¼) in.), ending with a p. row.

Shape Top

Cast off 3 sts. at beg. of next 2 rows.
Now dec. 1 st. at each end of next and every alt. row until 19 sts. rem.
P. 1 row.
Now dec. 1 st. at each end of every row until 11 sts. rem.
Cast off.

COLLAR

Cast on 57(61:65) sts. with 3¼mm.

needles.
Work 5 rows in g. st.
Change to 4mm. needles.
Next row: k.
Next row: k.3, p. to last 3 sts., k.3.
Rep. last 2 rows 10(11:12) more times.

Shape Collar

Cast off 4 sts. at beg. of next 8 rows.
Cast off rem. 25(29:33) sts.

MAKING UP

Press lightly on wrong side, omitting ribbing on welt and cuffs, taking care not to spoil the rib yoke.
Sew up shoulder, side and sleeve seams.
Set in sleeves.
Catch down cast-on sts. of underlap on left side of yoke at back of work.
Pin cast-off edge of collar all round neck, beg. and ending at centre front, sew in position.
Press all seams.
Sew on buttons.

Cardigan with Cabled Details

1950

Stocking stitch cardigan with cable bands, garter stitch armhole and side edges, doubled button band, round neck and ribbed welts

★ Suitable for beginners

MATERIALS

Yarn
Phildar Perle 5
3 × 50g. balls

Needles
1 pair 2mm.
1 pair 2¾mm.
1 cable needle

Buttons
6

MEASUREMENTS

Chest
51 cm.
20 in.
6/12 months approx. age

Length
27 cm.
10½ in.

Sleeve Seam
17 cm.
6½ in.

TENSION

30 sts. and 40 rows = 10 cm. (4 in.) square

over st. st. on 2¾mm. needles. If your tension square does not correspond to these measurements, see page 156 for adjustment instructions.

ABBREVIATIONS

k. = knit; p. = purl; st(s). = stitch(es); inc. = increas(ing) (see page 156); dec. = decreas(ing) (see page 157); beg. = begin(ning); rem. = remain(ing); rep. = repeat; alt. = alternate; tog. = together; sl. = slip (transfer one stitch from left needle, knitwise unless otherwise stated, to right hand needle.); cont. = continue; patt. = pattern; foll. = following; folls. = follows; mm. = millimetres; cm. = centimetres; in. = inches; st. st. = stocking st.: one row k., one row p.; g. st. = garter st.: every row k.; incs. = increases; decs. = decreases; C6 = cable 6: sl. next 3 sts. onto cable needle and hold at back of work, k. next 3 sts., k. 3 sts. from cable needle; y.fwd. = yarn forward.

BACK

Cast on 87 sts. with 2¾mm. needles.
Work in rib as folls.:
1st row (right side): k.1, * p.1, k.1, rep. from * to end.
2nd row: p.1, * k.1, p.1, rep. from * to end.

Rep. last 2 rows once more.
Cont. in patt. as folls.:
1st row (right side): k.24, * p.3, k.6, rep. from * 3 more times, p.3, k.24.
2nd row: k.2, p.22, * k.3, p.6, rep. from * 3 more times, k.3, p.22, k.2.
3rd row: k.24, * p.3, C6, rep. from * 3 more times, p.3, k.24.
4th row: as 2nd.
5th row: as 1st.
6th row: as 2nd.
These 6 rows form patt.
Work straight in patt. until back measures 18 cm. (7 in.), ending with a wrong side row.

Shape Armholes

Keeping patt. correct, cast off 5 sts. at beg. of next 2 rows. [77 sts.]
Cont. straight in patt., working 2 sts. at armhole edge on every row in g.st. until armholes measure 6 cm. (2¼ in.)
Cast off.

LEFT FRONT

Cast on 49 sts. with 2¾mm. needles.
Work in rib as for back.
Cont. in patt. as folls:
1st row (right side): k.21, * p.3, k.6, rep. from * once more, p.3, k.7.
2nd row: k.10, * p.6, k.3, rep. from * once

more, p.19, k.2.
3rd row: k.21, * p.3, C6, rep. from * once more, p.3, k.7.
4th row: as 2nd.
5th row: as 1st.
6th row: as 2nd.
These 6 rows form patt.
Work straight in patt. until front matches back to armhole, ending with a wrong side row.

Shape Armhole

Cast off 5 sts. at beg. of next row. [44 sts.]
** Work straight in patt. until front matches back to shoulder, working 2 sts. at armhole edge on every row in g. st.
Cast off.

RIGHT FRONT

Cast on 55 sts. with 2¾mm. needles.
Work in rib as for back, inc. 1 st. in last rib row. [56 sts.]

Cont. in patt. as folls.:
1st row (right side): k.3, y.fwd., k.2 tog., k.5, y.fwd., k.2 tog., k.2, * p.3, k.6, rep. from * once more, p.3, k.21.
2nd row: k.2, p.19, * k.3, p.6, rep. from * once more, k.3, p.7, k.7.
3rd row: k.14, * p.3, C6, rep. from * once more, p.3, k.21.
4th row: as 2nd.
5th row: k.14, * p.3, k.6, rep. from * once more, p.3, k.21.
6th row: as 2nd.
7th row: as 5th.
8th row: as 2nd.
Rep. 3rd to 8th rows, at the same time working 4 more sets of double buttonholes as worked on 1st row, each set to be 4 cm. (1½ in.) apart.
Cont. in patt. until right front matches left front to armhole, ending with a right side row.

Shape Armhole

Cast off 5 sts. at beg. of next row. [51 sts.]
Work as for left front from **.

SLEEVES

Cast on 43 sts. with 2¾mm. needles.
Work in rib as for back, inc. 1 st. in last row. [44 sts.]
1st row (right side): k.
2nd row: k.2, p. to last 2 sts., k.2.
These 2 rows form patt.
Cont. in patt. as set, inc. 1 st. inside g. st. border at each end of every 6th row 8 times. [60 sts.]
Work straight until sleeve measures 19 cm. (7½ in.), ending with a wrong side row.

Shape Top

Cast off 18 sts. at beg. of next 2 rows. [24 sts.]

1st row (right side): k.3, * p.2, k.6, rep. from * once, p.2, k.3.
2nd row: k.5, * p.6, k.2, rep. from * once, k.3.
3rd row: k.3, * p.2, C6, rep. from * once, p.2, k.3.
4th row: as 2nd.
5th row: as 1st.
6th row: as 2nd.
These 6 rows form patt.
Work straight in patt. until strip measures 6 cm. (2¼ in.).
Cast off.

NECK BORDER

Sew back and fronts to shoulder yokes of sleeves.
(Leave 21 sts. of back free for back neck and corresponding sts. of fronts free for front neck.)
Set in sleeves, sewing to front and back at underarm.
K. up 107 sts. evenly around neck with 2mm. needles and right side facing.
1st row: p.2, * k.1, p.1, rep. from * to last st., p.1.
Double buttonhole row: k.2, p.1, y.fwd., k.2 tog., rib 5, y.fwd., k.2 tog., rib to last 2 sts., k.2.
3rd row: as 1st.
4th row: k.2, * p.1, k.1, rep. from * to last st., k.1.
5th row: as 1st.
Cast off evenly in rib.

MAKING UP

Fold right front underborder to inside and sew in position.
Buttonhole st. around buttonholes.
Sew up side and sleeve seams.
Sew on buttons.

Sleeveless Cotton Twinset 1955

Stocking stitch, sleeveless cardigan with two bands of stripes in contrast colour, bandeau top with matching stripe

★★ Suitable for knitters with some previous experience

MATERIALS

Yarn
Phildar Perle 5
8(8:9) × 40g. balls Main Col. A
1 × 40g. ball Col. B

Needles
1 pair 2mm.
1 pair 2½mm.
1 crochet hook 2½mm.

Buttons
6

Elastic (for bandeau top)
60 cm. approx.
23¾ in. approx.

MEASUREMENTS

Bust
87(92:97) cm.
34(36:38) in.

Length
Bandeau top:
34(35:36) cm.
13¼(13¾:14) in.
Cardigan:
61(62:63) cm.
24(24¼:24¾) in.

TENSION

30 sts. and 40 rows = 10 cm. (4 in.) square over st. st. on 2½mm. needles. If your tension square does not correspond to

these measurements, see page 156 for adjustment instructions.

ABBREVIATIONS

k. = knit; p. = purl; st(s). = stitch(es); inc. = increas(ing) (see page 156); dec. = decreas(ing) (see page 157); beg. = begin(ning); rem. = remain(ing); rep. = repeat; alt. = alternate; tog. = together; sl. = slip (transfer one stitch from left needle, knitwise unless otherwise stated, to right hand needle.); cont. = continue; patt. = pattern; foll. = following; folls. = follows; mm. = millimetres; cm. = centimetres; in. = inches; st. st. = stocking st.: one row k., one row p.; g. st. = garter st.: every row k.; incs. = increases; decs. = decreases; d.c. = double crochet, see page 162 for instructions; s.c. = single crochet, see page 162 for instructions.

NB When working in stripe patt. carry col. not in use loosely up side of work.

BANDEAU TOP

Cast on 114(122:130) sts. with 2mm. needles.
Work in rib as folls.:
1st row (right side): k.2, * p.2, k.2, rep. from * to end.
2nd row: p.2, * k.2, p.2, rep. from * to end.
Work 7 cm. (2¾ in.) in rib patt., ending with a 2nd row, inc. 2(2:4) sts. on last row. [116(124:134) sts.]

Shape Sides
Change to 2½mm. needles and, beg. with a k. row, work in st. st., AT THE SAME TIME inc. 1 st. at each end of every 10th(11th:13th) row 8(8:7) times. [132(140:148) sts.]
Cont. straight in st. st. until work measures 29(30:31) cm. (11¼(11¾:12¼) in.), ending with a p. row.
Now work 18 rows in st. st. stripe patt. as folls.:
4 rows B
4 rows A
2 rows B
4 rows A
4 rows B
These 18 rows form stripe patt.
Now cont. in A only:
Next row: k.
Next row: p.
Next 2 rows (fold line): k.
Change to 2mm. needles and beg. with a k. row, work 2 cm. (¾ in.) in st. st.
Cast off.

MAKING UP

Press lightly on wrong side, avoiding ribbing.
Sew up side seams.
Fold hem to wrong side at top and sew in position leaving a small gap for threading elastic.
Thread elastic through top, fasten securely, close gap.
Press all seams lightly on wrong side.

CARDIGAN
BACK

Cast on 142(148:158) sts. with 2½mm. needles and A.
Beg. with a k. row, work 11 rows in st. st.
Next row (hemline ridge): k.
Beg. with a k. row, cont. straight in st. st. until back measures 16 cm. (6¼ in.), from hemline ridge row, ending with a p. row.
Work 18 rows in stripe patt. as for bandeau top.
Now work in A only until back measures 37 cm. (14½ in.) from hemline, ending with a p. row.

Shape Armholes
Now work in stripe patt. as for bandeau top, AT THE SAME TIME when back measures 40 cm. (15¾ in.) from hemline, with right side facing, keeping stripe patt. correct, cast off 8 sts. at beg. of next 2 rows.
Dec. 1 st. at each end of next and every foll. row 5(7:9) times.
Now cast off 1 st. at each end of every alt. row until 108(110:114) sts. rem.
Work straight until armhole measures 18(19:20) cm. (7(7½:7¾) in.), ending with a p. row.

Shape Shoulders
Cast off 6 sts. at beg. of next 12(10:12) rows.
Cast off 0(5:0) sts. at beg. of next 0(2:0) rows. [36(40:42) sts.]

Shape Back Neck Facing
Cast on 2 sts. at beg. of next 8 rows. [52:56:58) sts.]
Cast off.

LEFT FRONT

Cast on 52(62:66) sts. with 2½mm. needles and A.
Beg. with a k. row, work 11 rows in st. st.
Next row: k.
Next row: cast on 48 sts., p. to end. [106(110:114) sts.]
1st row: k. to last 24 sts., sl.1, k.23.
2nd row: p.
1st and 2nd rows form patt.
Work straight in patt. as set, AT THE SAME TIME work stripes as on back until front matches back to beg. of armhole shaping, ending with a p. row.

Shape Armhole and Front Facing
Next row: cast off 8 sts., work to last st., inc. in last st.
Work 1 row.
Now dec. 1 st. at armhole edge on next and every foll. alt. row 5(7:9) times in all.

Work 1 row.
Dec. 1 st. at armhole edge on next and every foll. alt. row 4(4:5) times in all, AT THE SAME TIME inc. 1 st. at facing edge on every foll. 4th row from previous inc. until there are 93(96:98) sts.
Keeping armhole edge straight cont. to inc. 1 st. at facing edge on every foll. 4th row from previous inc. until there are 97(105:105) sts.
Work 5(3:5) rows straight.
1st and 3rd sizes only:
Inc. 1 st. at facing edge on next and every foll. 6th row until there are 100(106) sts.
Work 5 rows straight, thus ending with a wrong side row.

Shape Neck
All sizes:
Next row: k.54(53:54), turn and leave rem. sts. on a spare needle.
Dec. 1 st. at neck edge on next and every foll. row until 36(35:36) sts. rem.
Work 1 row.

Shape Shoulder
Cast off 6 sts. at beg. of next and 4 foll. alt. rows.
Work 1 row.
Cast off rem. sts.
With right side facing, rejoin yarn to rem. sts.
Cast off centre 23(29:29) sts. loosely, k. to last st., inc. in last st.
Now dec. 1 st. at neck edge on next and every foll. row 18 times in all, at the same time inc. 1 st. at facing edge on every 6th row from previous inc. until there are 9 sts. on needle.
Keeping neck edge straight, inc. 1 st. on foll. 6th row from previous inc. [10 sts.]
Work 5 rows.
Cast off.

RIGHT FRONT

Work to match left front reversing shapings, working 6 buttonholes, first to come 8 cm. (3¼ in.) from hemline, last to come 3 cm. (1¼ in.) from neck, rem. spaced evenly between.
To make double buttonhole:
1st buttonhole row (right side): k.15, cast off 5 sts., work 7 sts., cast off 5 sts., work to end.
2nd buttonhole row: work across row, casting on 5 sts. over those cast off on previous row.

MAKING UP

Press lightly on wrong side.
Sew up side seams.
Turn up hem and sew.
Sew up shoulders.
Fold front facings to right side.
Sew around neck and to back neck facing, sew tog. at lower edge.
Fold facings to wrong side and catch in position at shoulders.
Work 1 row d.c. around edge of armhole and 1 row of s.c.
Buttonhole-st. buttonholes tog.
Sew on buttons.
Press seams lightly on wrong side.

Naturally Dyed Fair Isle Cardigan 1982

Round-necked, allover-patterned cardigan with grafted shoulders, ribbed welts, and sleeves knitted downwards from shoulderline

★★★ Suitable for experienced knitters only

MATERIALS

Yarn
Natural Dye Company Wool
Naturally dyed woollen yarn in a combination of six colours, sold as a pack including six hand-made Dorset buttons, (mail order only, see page 166). Pack colours vary according to dye ingredients, shown is blue version, but a pink version is also available, see page 8, for which instructions are given.

Needles
1 pair 2¾mm.
1 pair 3¼mm.
1 circular 2¾mm. – 40 cm. (15¾ in.) long
1 circular 3¼mm. – 40 cm. (15¾ in.) long
st. holders

Buttons
included in pack: 6

MEASUREMENTS

Chest
61(66:71) cm.
24(26:28) in.
4/5(6/7:8/9) approx. age

Length
39(42:47) cm.
15¼(16½:18½) in.

Sleeve Seam
36(37:38) cm.
14(14½:15) in.

TENSION

30 sts. and 30 rows = 10 cm. (4 in.) square over Fair Isle patt. in st. st. on 3¼mm. needles. If your tension square does not correspond to these measurements, see page 156 for adjustment instructions.

ABBREVIATIONS

k. = knit; p. = purl; st(s). = stitch(es); inc. = increas(ing) (see page 156); dec. = decreas(ing) (see page 157); beg. = begin(ning); rem. = remain(ing); rep. = repeat; alt. = alternate; tog. = together; sl. = slip (transfer one stitch from left needle, knitwise unless otherwise stated, to right hand needle.); cont. = continue; patt. = pattern; foll. = following; folls. = follows; mm. = millimetres; cm. = centimetres; in. = inches; st. st. = stocking st.: one row k., one row p.; g. st. = garter st.: every row k.; incs. = increases; decs. = decreases.

PATTERN

1st pattern
Pink version	Blue version
Indigo	Natural
Natural	Privet
Pale rose	Grey
Ice blue	Sky blue
Dark rose	Dark green
Elderberry	Indigo

2nd pattern
Pink version	Blue version
Dark rose	Sky blue
Indigo	Indigo
Pale rose	Dark green
Natural	Grey
Indigo	Natural
Dark rose	Privet

BODY

Cast on 204(216:240) sts. with 2¾mm. needles and col. chosen for first stripe (base col.).
Work 30 rows (3 rows in each col.) in k.1, p.1 rib.
Next row: rib 9(4:5), * inc. in next st., rib 7(8:9), rep. from * 22 times, inc. in next st., rib 10(4:4). [228(240:264) sts.]
Change to 3¼mm. needles.
Work in patt. from chart, beg. at bottom, working k. rows from right to left and p. rows from left to right.
Work 20 rows of chart in 1st patt., then 20 rows of chart in 2nd patt., until body measures 26(28:31) cm. (10¼(11:12¼) in.) from beg., ending with a p. row.

Divide for Fronts and Back
Next row: k.57(60:65) sts., sl. last 10(11:12) of these sts. onto 1st holder, k. next 10(11:12) sts. and sl. them onto 2nd holder, now k.104(109:122) sts., sl. the last 10(11:12) of these sts. onto 3rd holder, k. next 10(11:12) sts., sl. them onto 4th holder, finally k.47(49:53) sts.

LEFT FRONT

Work on 1st group of 47(49:53) sts. as folls.:
Next row: p.
Now work in patt. on these sts., without shaping, until work measures 9(10:11) cm. (3½(4:4¼) in.) from armhole, ending

with a k. row.

Shape Neck
1st row: cast off 6(7:8) sts., p. to end.
Dec. 1 st. at neck edge on next 6(7:8) rows. [35(35:37) sts.].
Cont. without shaping until work measures 13(14:16) cm. (5(5½:6¼) in.) from beg. of armhole.
Leave sts. on holder for left shoulder.

RIGHT FRONT

Rejoin yarn at armhole edge of 47(49:53) sts. on needle for right front.
Work as for left front, reversing shapings.

BACK

Return to the 94(98:110) sts.
With wrong side facing, rejoin yarn and cont. until work measures 10(11:13) cm. (4(4¼:5) in.) from beg. of armholes, ending with a p. row.

Shape Neck
1st row: k.41(43:46), turn.
Cont. on these sts. only.
Dec. 1 st. at neck edge on next 6(8:9) rows. [35(35:37) sts.].
Cont. without shaping until work measures same as front.
Leave these sts. on holder for shoulder.
With right side facing, sl. centre 12(12:18) sts. onto holder, rejoin yarn to inner end of rem. 41(43:46) sts. and complete to match first side.

Graft Shoulder Seam

Put sts. on needles, place right sides tog. Using col. to match work, and a 3rd needle, k. first st. on front needle tog. with first st. on back needle by slipping first st. from front needle onto back needle and knitting it tog. with first st. on back needle, sl. this st. onto 3rd needle, k.

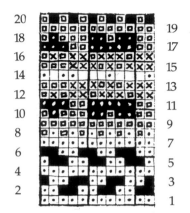

1st Pattern

□ = Natural
■ = Privet
⊠ = Grey
▣ = Sky blue
▪ = Dark green
▫ = Indigo

2nd Pattern

□ = Sky blue
■ = Indigo
⊠ = Dark green
▣ = Grey
▪ = Natural
▫ = Privet

second st. on front needle and second st. on back needle tog. onto 3rd needle as before, pull first st. knitted over second st., thus casting off first st.
Cont. in this way until all sts. are cast off. Work second seam to match.

SLEEVES

With right side of work facing, 2¾mm. circular needle and base col., k.10(11:12) sts. from 2nd holder, pick up and k.38(43:48) sts. along armhole to top of shoulder, then pick up and k.38(43:48) sts. down to 1st holder, then k.10(11:12) sts. from holder (mark last st. with coloured thread to mark end of round). [96(108:120) sts.]
Work 2 rounds in base col.
Change to 3¼mm. circular needle.
Work in patt. from chart – every row k., read chart from right to left for every row.
Next round: * k.1, k.2 tog., rep. from * to end.
Next round: * k.3, k.2 tog., rep. from * to last 4(2:0) sts., k.4(2:0). [52(58:64) sts.].

Cuff

Change to 2¾mm. circular needle.
Work 8 cm. (3¼ in.) in k.1, p.1 rib, changing col. every 3 rows to match welt.
Cast off loosely in rib.
Work 2nd sleeve as for 1st, using sts. from 4th and 3rd holders.

NECKBAND

With right side of work facing, base col. and 2¾mm. needles, pick up and k. 80(82:92) sts. round neck.
Work 9 rows in k.1, p.1 rib, 3 rows in each col.
Cast off loosely in rib.

FRONT BANDS

Buttonhole Band
With right side of work facing, 2¾mm. needles and base col., pick up and k.111(123:135) sts. along front edge.
Work 3 rows in k.1, p.1 rib.
Change col.
Next row: rib 4(5:4), * cast off 3 sts., rib 22(19:22) including st. on needle after casting off, rep. from * 3(4:4) times, cast off 3 sts., rib to end.
Next row: work in k.1, p.1 rib, casting on 3 sts. over each set of sts. cast off in previous row.
Rib 1 row.
Change col.
Rib 3 rows.
Cast off loosely in rib.

BUTTONBAND

Work buttonband to match, omitting buttonholes.
Sew on buttons.

Long Sweater with Low V-neck   1982

Long, stocking stitch sweater with low V-neck, set-in sleeves and ribbed welts, the cuffs having ribbed turnbacks

★   Suitable for beginners

MATERIALS

Yarn
Sunbeam Wool 4 ply
9(10:11:11) × 50g. balls

Needles
1 pair 2¾mm.
1 pair 3¼mm.

MEASUREMENTS

Bust
82(87:92:97) cm.
32(34:36:38) in.

Length
78(79:79:80) cm.
30½(31:31:31¼) in.

Sleeve Seam
45 cm.
17¾ in.

TENSION

28 sts. and 36 rows = 10 cm. (4 in.) square over st. st. on 3¼mm. needles. If your tension square does not correspond to these measurements, see page 156 for adjustment instructions.

ABBREVIATIONS

k. = knit; p. = purl; st(s). = stitch(es); inc. = increas(ing) (see page 156); dec. = decreas(ing) (see page 157); beg. = begin(ning); rem. = remain(ing); rep. = repeat; alt. = alternate; tog. = together; sl. = slip (transfer one stitch from left needle, knitwise unless otherwise stated, to right hand needle.); cont. = continue; patt. = pattern; foll. = following; folls. = follows; mm. = millimetres; cm. = centimetres; in. = inches; st. st. = stocking st.: one row k., one row p.; g. st. = garter st.: every row k.; incs. = increases; decs. = decreases; t.b.l. = through back of loops; p.s.s.o. = pass the sl. st. over.

FRONT

** Cast on 133(139:145:151) sts. with 2¾mm. needles.
1st row: k.2, * p.1, k.1, rep. from * to last st., k.1.
2nd row: * k.1, p.1, rep. from * to last st., k.1.
Rep. 1st and 2nd rows for 10 cm. (4 in.), ending with a 2nd row.
Change to 3¼mm. needles and st. st. **
Work until front measures 48 cm. (18¾ in.) from beg., ending with a k. row.

Divide for Neck

Next row: p.66(69:72:75) sts., cast off 1 st., p. to end.
Cont. on last set of sts.
1st row: k.
2nd row: p.
3rd row: k. to last 5 sts., k.2 tog., k.3.
4th row: p.
5th row: k.
6th row: p.3, p.2 tog., p. to end.
Rep. 1st to 6th rows 5 more times, and then 1st and 2nd rows once.

Shape Armhole

1st row: cast off 2 sts., k. to last 5 sts., k.2 tog., k.3.

2nd row: p.
3rd row: k.3, sl.1, k.1, p.s.s.o., k. to end.
4th row: p.3, p.2 tog., p. to last 5 sts., p.2 tog. t.b.l., p.3.
5th row: k.
6th row: p. to last 5 sts., p.2 tog. t.b.l., p.3.
7th row: k.3, sl.1, k.1, p.s.s.o., k. to last 5 sts., k.2 tog., k.3.
8th row: p.
Rep. 3rd to 8th rows 2(2:2:3) more times.
3rd size only: rep. 3rd to 5th rows once more.
All sizes: [33(36:36:36) sts.]
Now keeping armhole edge straight, cont. to dec. for neck on every 3rd row until 19(21:22:22) sts. rem.
Work until armhole measures 19(20:20:21) cm. (7½(7¾:7¾:8¼) in.) measured straight, ending at armhole edge.

Shape Shoulder

Cast off 4(6:6:6) sts. at beg. of next row, and 5(5:5:5) sts. at beg. of 2 foll. alt. rows.
Work 1 row.
Cast off rem. 5(5:6:6) sts.
Rejoin yarn to rem. sts. at neck edge, and cont. as folls.:
1st row: k.
2nd row: p.
3rd row: k.3, sl.1, k.1, p.s.s.o., k. to end.
4th row: p.
5th row: k.
6th row: p. to last 5 sts., p.2 tog. t.b.l., p.3.
Rep. 1st to 6th rows 5 more times, and then 1st to 3rd rows once.

Shape Armhole

Next row: cast off 2 sts., p. to end.
Now complete to match first side, reversing shapings.

BACK

Work as for front from ** to **.
Cont. until back measures same as front to armholes, ending with a p. row.

Shape Armholes

Cast off 2 sts. at beg. of next 2 rows.
3rd row: k.3, sl.1, k.1, p.s.s.o., k. to last 5 sts., k.2 tog., k.3.
4th row: p.3, p.2 tog., p. to last 5 sts., p.2 tog. t.b.l., p.3.
5th row: k.
6th row: as 4th.
7th row: as 3rd.
8th row: p.
Rep. 3rd to 8th rows 2(2:2:3) more times.
3rd size only: rep. 3rd to 5th rows once more.
All sizes: [105(111:113:115) sts.]
Work until armholes measure same as front armholes, ending with a p. row.

Shape Shoulders and Back of Neck

Next row: cast off 4(6:6:6) sts., k.20(20:21: 21) sts., including st. on needle, cast off 57(59:59:61) sts., k. to end.
Cont. on last set of sts.
1st row: cast off 4(6:6:6) sts., p. to last 2 sts., p.2 tog.
2nd row: k.2 tog., k. to end.
3rd row: cast off 5(5:5:5) sts., p. to last 2 sts., p.2 tog.
Rep. 2nd and 3rd rows once more.

Work 1 row.
Cast off rem. 5(5:6:6) sts.
Rejoin yarn to rem. sts. at neck edge.
1st row: p.2 tog., p. to end.
2nd row: cast off 5(5:5:5) sts., k. to last 2 sts., k.2 tog.
Rep. 1st and 2nd rows once more and then 1st row once.
Cast off rem. 5(5:6:6) sts.

SLEEVES

Cast on 63(65:67:69) sts. with 2¾mm. needles.
1st row: * k.1, p.1, rep. from * to last st., k.1.
2nd row: k.2, * p.1, k.1, rep. from * to last st., k.1.
Rep. 1st and 2nd rows for 10 cm. (4 in.), ending with a 2nd row.
Change to 3¼mm. needles and st. st.
Work 2 rows.
Inc. 1 st. at each end of next row, and then every 6th row until there are 103(105:109:113) sts.
Work until sleeve measures 50 cm. (19½ in.) from beg., ending with a p. row.

Shape Top

Cast off 2 sts. at beg. of next 2 rows.
3rd row: k.3, sl.1, k.1, p.s.s.o., k. to last 5 sts., k.2 tog., k.3.
4th row: p.3, p.2 tog., p. to last 5 sts., p.2 tog. t.b.l., p.3.
5th row: k.
6th row: as 4th.
7th row: as 3rd.
8th row: p.
Rep. 3rd to 8th rows 2(2:2:3) times more.
3rd size only: rep. 3rd to 5th rows once more.
All sizes: cast off rem. sts.

NECK BORDER

Press each piece lightly with warm iron and damp cloth.
Sew up right shoulder seam.
With 2¾mm. needles and right side facing, k. up 111(113:115:117) sts. down left side of front neck edge, 1 st. from the cast off st., 111(113:115:117) sts. up right side of neck, and 80(82:82:84) sts. evenly along back neck edge.
1st row: k.1, * p.1, k.1, rep. from * to within 2 sts. of the st. at point of V, p.2 tog., p.1, p.2 tog. t.b.l., rib to end.
2nd row: rib to within 2 sts. of the st. at point of V, k.2 tog. t.b.l., k.1, k.2 tog., rib to end.
Work 12 more rows in rib, at the same time dec. in this way on every row.
Cast off in rib, dec. as before.

MAKING UP

Sew up left shoulder and neck border seam.
Sew up side seams.
Sew up sleeve seams, reversing seam for 7 cm. (2¾ in.) from cast-on edge for turnback cuff.
Set in sleeves.
Press seams lightly.

Patterned Norwegian Socks

1951

Three-colour patterned socks with plain sole, heel and ribbed cuff

★★★ Suitable for experienced knitters

MATERIALS

Yarn

Pingouin Confortable Fin
2 × 50g. balls Main Col. A
1 × 50g. ball Col. B
1 × 50g. ball Col. C

Needles

1 set of 4 double-pointed 2¾mm.

MEASUREMENTS

Adult Shoe Size 10½-12

TENSION

34 sts. and 34 rows = 10 cm. (4 in.) square over patt. on 2¾mm. needles. If your tension square does not correspond to these measurements, see page 156 for adjustment instructions.

ABBREVIATIONS

k. = knit; p. = purl; st(s). = stitch(es); inc. = increas(ing) (see page 156); dec. = decreas(ing) (see page 157); beg. = begin(ning); rem. = remain(ing); rep. = repeat; alt. = alternate; tog. = together; sl. = slip (transfer one stitch from left needle, knitwise unless otherwise stated, to right hand needle.); cont. = continue; patt. = pattern; foll. = following; folls. = follows; mm. = millimetres; cm. = centimetres; in. = inches; st. st. = stocking st.: one row k., one row p.; g. st. = garter st.: every row k.; incs. = increases; decs. = decreases; p.s.s.o. = pass the sl. st. over.

CUFF

Cast on 68 sts. with 2¾mm. needles and A.
Using 2 needles only, work back and forth in k.1, p.2 rib for 8 cm. (3¼ in.), inc. in every 12th st. 5 times across last row. [73 sts.]

LEG

Using a separate small ball of B or C for each section of col., work in patt. as folls., carrying yarn not in use loosely at back of work:
1st row: p. with A.
2nd row: k. with A.
3rd row: p. with A.
4th row (right side): k. 4A, * 1B, 3A, 2C, 4A, 1C, 3A, 1C, 3A, 1C, 4A, 2C, 3A, 1B, * 7A, rep. from * to *, ending with 4A.
5th row: p. 3A, * 2B, 4A, 2C, 4A, 1C, 1A,

KEY
□ = Col A
▨ = Col B
◉ = Col C

33

1C, 1A, 1C, 1A, 1C, 4A, 2C, 4A, 2B, * 5A, rep. from * to *, ending with 3A.
Beg. with 6th row of chart, work patt. as now set in st. st., foll. chart until 55 patt. rows have been worked.
Next row: with A, k.19 sts., leave on holder for heel; work across next 35 sts. in patt.; leave rem. 19 sts. on holder for other half of heel.
Cont. to work patt. on 35 sts. for instep to end of chart.
Break off yarns.

HEEL

Place 38 sts. of heel from holders on one needle, with side edges at centre of needle.
Join in A and work as folls.:
1st row (wrong side): sl.1 purlwise, p. to end, dec. 2 sts. evenly across row. [36 sts.]
2nd row: * sl.1 purlwise, k.1, rep. from * to end.
3rd row: sl.1 purlwise, p. to end.
Rep. last 2 rows until there are 36 rows on heel, ending with a right side row.

Turn Heel

Sl.1, p.20, p.2 tog., p.1, turn; sl.1, k.7, sl.1, k.1, p.s.s.o., k.1, turn; sl.1, p.8, p.2 tog., p.1, turn; sl.1, k.9, sl.1, k.1, p.s.s.o., k.1, turn; sl.1, p.10, p.2 tog., p.1, turn.
Cont. to work towards sides of heel, having 1 st. more before dec. on each row until 22 sts. rem.
Break off yarn.

Gussets and Foot

With right side facing, a spare needle and A, pick up and k.18 sts. on side of heel, k.11 sts. of heel onto same needle, then pick up and k.18 sts. on other side of heel onto needle with rem. heel sts. [58 sts.].
Next row: turn, p. back across sts. using 2 needles.
Next row: turn, k.1, sl.1, k.1, p.s.s.o., k. to end of 1st needle, k. to within 3 sts. of end of 2nd needle, k.2 tog., k.1.
Rep. last 2 rows 10 times. [36 sts.]

SOLE

Place all sts. on one needle.
P. 1 row, dec. 1 st. at end of row. [35 sts.]

Work in st. st. until there are 76 rows from picked-up edge on side of heel.
Place 35 sole sts. and 35 instep sts. on 3 needles.
Join.
K. 1 round, k. last sole st. tog. with last instep st. on each side. [68 sts.]
K. in rounds until work measures 5 cm. (2 in.) less than desired finished length.

TOE

Beg. at centre of sole, place 17 sts. on each of 1st and 3rd needles, 34 sts. on 2nd needle.
1st round: 1st needle – k. to last 3 sts., k.2 tog., k.1; 2nd needle – k.1, sl.1, k.1, p.s.s.o., k. to last 3 sts., k.2 tog., k.1; 3rd needle – k.1, sl.1, k.1, p.s.s.o., k. to end.
2nd round: k.
Rep. last 2 rounds until 20 sts. rem.
K. 5 sts. from 1st needle and sl. them onto 3rd needle (sole sts.).
Cast off sts. from 2 needles tog.: hold 2 needles parallel and cast off 1 st. from each needle alternately to end.
Sew in seams, matching patts.

Polka-dot Jacket

Round-neck jacket with contrasting polka-dot design, set-in sleeves, moss stitch welts and buttoned front border

★★ Suitable for knitters with some previous experience

MATERIALS

Yarn
Jaeger Luxury Spun 4 ply
2 × 50g. balls Main Col. A
1 × 50g. ball Col. B

Needles
1 pair 2¾mm.
1 pair 3¼mm.
safety pins

Buttons
6

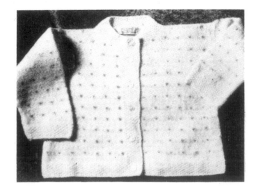

MEASUREMENTS

Chest
51 cm.
20 in. (1/2 approx. age)

Length
28 cm.
11 in.

Sleeve Seam
18 cm.
7 in.

TENSION

28 sts. and 36 rows = 10 cm. (4 in.) square over st. st. on 3¼mm. needles. If your tension square does not correspond to these measurements, see page 156 for adjustment instructions.

ABBREVIATIONS

k. = knit; p. = purl; st(s). = stitch(es); inc. = increas(ing) (see page 156); dec. = decreas(ing) (see page 157); beg. = begin(ning); rem. = remain(ing); rep. = repeat; alt. = alternate; tog. = together; sl. = slip (transfer one stitch from left needle, knitwise unless otherwise stated, to right hand needle.); cont. = continue;

patt. = pattern; foll. = following; folls. = follows; mm. = millimetres; cm. = centimetres; in. = inches; st. st. = stocking st.: one row k., one row p.; g. st. = garter st.: every row k.; incs. = increases; decs. = decreases.

N.B. When working 2 col. patt., strand yarns loosely (see page 10).

BACK

Cast on 77 sts. with 2¾mm. needles and A.
Work in border patt. as folls.:
1st row: k.1, * p.1, k.1, rep. from * to end.
Rep. this row 9 times more, inc. 1 st. at each end of last row. [79 sts.]
Change to 3¼mm. needles and work in patt. as folls.:
1st row (right side): with A, k.
2nd row: with A, p.
Join in B.
3rd row: k.4 A, 1B, * 6A, 1B, rep. from * to last 4 sts., 4A.
4th row: with A, p.
5th row: with A, k.
6th-11th rows: as 4th and 5th rows 3 times.
12th row: p. 4A, 1B, * 6A, 1B, rep. from * to last 4 sts., 4A.

13th-18th rows: as 1st and 2nd rows 3 times.

These 18 rows form patt.

N.B. Carry col. B loosely up side of work.

Cont. straight in patt. until back measures 18 cm. (7 in.) at centre from beg., ending with right side facing.

Shape Armholes

Cast off 4 sts. at beg. of next 2 rows, working in patt. throughout.

Dec. 1 st. at each end of next and every alt. row until 57 sts. rem.

Cont. straight until back measures 28 cm. (11 in.) at centre from beg., ending with right side facing.

Shape Shoulders

Cast off 5 sts. at beg. of next 6 rows.

Leave rem. 27 sts. on a spare needle.

LEFT FRONT

Cast on 41 sts. with 2¾mm. needles and A.

Work 10 rows border patt. as for back, but inc. 1 st. at end of last row. [42 sts.]

Change to 3¼mm. needles and, beg. with 1st row, work in patt. as for back, working 6 sts. at front edge in border patt. as folls.:

1st row (right side): with A, k. to last 6 sts., (p.1, k.1) 3 times.

2nd row: (k.1, p.1) 3 times, p. to end.

Join in B.

3rd row: k. 4A, 1B, * 6A, 1B, rep. from * to last 9 sts., 3A, (p.1, k.1) 3 times with A.

Cont. in patt. thus until front measures same as back at side edge, ending with right side facing.

Shape Armhole

Cast off 4 sts. at beg. of next row.

Work 1 row straight, then dec. 1 st. at beg. of next and every alt. row until 32 sts. rem.

Keeping patt. correct, work straight until front measures 24 cm. (9½ in.) at centre from beg., ending with wrong side facing.

Shape Neck

Next row: (k.1, p.1) 3 times, sl. these 6 sts. onto a safety pin for neck border, cast off 3 sts., patt. to end.

Now dec. 1 st. at neck edge on every row until 15 sts. rem.

Work straight until front matches back at armhole edge, ending with right side facing.

Shape Shoulder

Cast off 5 sts. at beg. of next and foll. 2 alt. rows.

RIGHT FRONT

Work to match left front, but make 5 buttonholes, 1st to come 2 cm. (¾ in.) above lower edge, 5th, 4 cm. (1½ in.) below beg. of neck shaping and rem. 3 spaced evenly between.

Mark position of buttons on left border with pins to ensure even spacing, then work holes to correspond.

Make buttonhole:

1st row (right side): patt. 2, cast off 2, patt. to end.

2nd row: work back, casting on 2 sts. over those cast off.

Shape Neck

Work to match left front, but 1st row will read:

Break yarn, sl. first 6 sts. on a safety pin for neck border, rejoin yarn to rem. sts., cast off 3, patt. to end.

SLEEVES

Cast on 43 sts. with 2¾mm. needles and A.

Work 10 rows in border patt. as for back, but inc. 1 st. at beg. of last row. [44 sts.]

Change to 3¼mm. needles and beg. with 1st row, work in patt. as for back, shaping sides by inc. 1 st. at each end of 5th and every foll. 6th row until there are 58 sts., taking inc. sts. into patt.

Work straight until sleeve seam measures 18 cm. (7 in.), ending with same row of patt. as on back and fronts before start of armhole shaping.

Shape Top

Cast off 4 sts. at beg. of next 2 rows, then dec. 1 st. at each end of next and every alt.

row until 32 sts. rem.

Work 1 row straight.

Dec. 1 st. at each end of every row until 16 sts. rem.

Cast off.

NECK BORDER

Sew up shoulder seams.

With right side facing, using 2¾mm. needles and A, patt. 6 sts. from safety pin on right border, pick up and k.17 sts. up right side of neck, k.27 from back, pick up and k.17 down left side, then patt. 6 sts. from safety pin on left border. [73 sts.]

Work 3 rows in border patt.

Make a buttonhole in next 2 rows, then work a further 4 rows border patt.

Cast off in patt.

MAKING UP

Press lightly on wrong side, omitting borders.

Sew up side and sleeve seams, matching patt.

Set in sleeves.

Press all seams.

Sew on buttons.

Elegant, Cotton Evening Blouse

1952

Stocking stitch blouse with deep-ribbed rounded boat neck, set-in sleeves and ribbed cuffs and hem

★★ Suitable for knitters with some previous experience

MATERIALS

Yarn
Pingouin Coton Perle 5
5(5:6:6) × 50g. balls

Needles
1 pair 2¼mm.
1 pair 3mm.
1 circular 2¼mm.–80 cm. (32 in.) long
2 st. holders

MEASUREMENTS

Bust
82(87:92:97) cm.
32(34:36:38) in.

Length
47(48:51:52) cm.
18½(18¾:20:20½) in.

Sleeve Seam
44(46:46:47) cm.
17¼(18:18:18½) in.

TENSION

32 sts. and 40 rows = 10 cm. (4 in.) square over st. st. on 3mm. needles. If your tension square does not correspond to these measurements, see page 156 for adjustment instructions.

ABBREVIATIONS

k. = knit; p. = purl; st(s). = stitch(es); inc. = increas(ing) (see page 156); dec. = decreas(ing) (see page 157); beg. = begin(ning); rem. = remain(ing); rep. = repeat; alt. = alternate; tog. = together; sl. = slip (transfer one stitch from left needle, knitwise unless otherwise stated, to right hand needle.); cont. = continue; patt. = pattern; foll. = following; folls. = follows; mm. = millimetres; cm. = centimetres; in. = inches; st. st. = stocking st.: one row k., one row p.; g. st. = garter st.: every row k.; incs. = increases; decs. = decreases.

BACK

Cast on 100(108:116:124) sts. with 2¼mm needles.
Work in k.1, p.1 rib for 9 cm. (3½ in.).
Change to 3mm. needles.
Work 4 rows in st. st.
Inc. 1 st. at each end of next and every 6th row until there are 120(128:136:144) sts.
Cont. until back measures 28(29:31:31) cm. (11(11¼:12¼:12¼) in.).

Shape Armholes
Cast off 5(7:8:9) at beg. of next 2 rows.
Dec. 1 st. at each end of every k. row until 104(108:112:116) sts. rem.
Cont. until armholes measure 9(9:10:11) cm. (3½(3½:4:4¼) in.), ending with a p. row.

Shape Neck
1st row: k.42(43:44:45) sts., turn.
Cont. shaping this side:
* Cast off at beg. of next and foll. p. rows 2(3:4:5) sts. once, 4 sts. 4 times, 3 sts. 3 times, 2 sts. twice and 1 st. 6 times.
Work 3 rows.
Next row: dec. 1 st., work to end.
Work 3 rows on rem. 4 sts.
Cast off.
Sl. centre 20(22:24:26) sts. onto holder.
Rejoin yarn to neck edge of rem. sts. and work from *, reading k. for p.

FRONT

Cast on 104(110:116:124) sts. with 2¼mm. needles.
Work 9 cm. (3½ in.) in k.1, p.1 rib.
Change to 3mm. needles.
Work in st. st. as folls.:
Inc. 1 st. at each end of next and every 6th row until there are 128(136:144:152) sts.
Cont. until front measures same as back to armholes.

Shape Armholes
Cast off 6(7:8:9) sts. at beg. of next 2 rows.
Dec. 1 st. at each end of every k. row until 106(110:114:118) sts. rem.
Cont. until armholes measure 6(7:8:8) cm. (2¼(2¾:3¼:3¼) in.), ending with a p. row.

Shape Neck
1st row: work 43(44:45:46) sts., turn, and cont. on these sts.:
** Cast off at beg. of next and foll. p. rows 4 sts. 4 times, 3 sts. twice, and 2 sts. 3 times.
Dec. 1 st. at same edge of every alt. row until 6 sts. rem.
Now dec. 1 st. at same edge on every 4th row until 4 sts. rem.
Work 5(4:3:2) rows.
Cast off.
Sl. centre 20(22:24:26) sts. onto holder.
Rejoin yarn to neck edge of rem. sts. and work from **, reading k. for p.

SLEEVES

Cast on 48(52:56:60) sts. with 2¼mm. needles.
Work 4 rows in k.1, p.1 rib.
Change to 3mm. needles.
Work 8 rows in st. st.
Inc. 1 st. at each end of next and every 8th row until there are 90(94:98:102) sts.
Cont. until sleeve measures 44(46:46:47) cm. (17¼(18:18:18½) in.).

Shape Top
Cast off 6(7:8:9) sts. at beg. of next 2 rows.
Dec. 1 st. at each end of next 5 rows.
Now dec. 1 st. at each end of every k. row until 40 sts. rem.
Cast off 3 sts. at beg. of next 8 rows.
Cast off.

NECK BORDER

Sew up shoulder seams.
With right side of work facing and circular 2¼mm. needle, k. up sts. around neck as folls.: 54(55:56:57) sts. down right back neck, 20(22:24:26) sts. from holder at centre back, 54(55:56:57) sts. up left side, 64(65:66:67) sts. down left front, 20(22:24:26) sts. from holder at centre front and 64(65:66:67) sts. up right front. [276(284:292:300) sts.]
Work in k.1, p.1 rib for 5 cm. (2 in.).
Cast off in rib.

MAKING UP

Set in sleeves.
Sew up side and sleeve seams.

Sleeveless Pullover in Cross-stitch

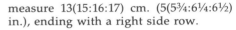

Fine, sleeveless slipover in cross-stitch rib, with round neck and ribbed welts

★★ Suitable for knitters with some previous experience

MATERIALS

Yarn
Pingouin Pingolaine 4 ply
3(3:4:4) × 50g. balls

Needles
1 pair 2¾mm.
1 pair 3¼mm.

MEASUREMENTS

Chest
56(61:66:71) cm.
22(24:26:28) in.
2/3(4/5:6/7:8/9) approx. age

Length
33(37:39:43) cm.
13(14½:15¼:16¾) in.

TENSION

35 sts. and 38 rows = 10 cm. (4 in.) square over patt. on 3¼mm. needles. If your tension square does not correspond to these measurements, see page 156 for adjustment instructions.

ABBREVIATIONS

k. = knit; p. = purl; st(s). = stitch(es); inc. = increas(ing) (see page 156); dec. = decreas(ing) (see page 157); beg. = begin(ning); rem. = remain(ing); rep. = repeat; alt. = alternate; tog. = together; sl. = slip (transfer one stitch from left needle, knitwise unless otherwise stated, to right hand needle.); cont. = continue; patt. = pattern; foll. = following; folls. = follows; mm. = millimetres; cm. = centimetres; in. = inches; st. st. = stocking st.: one row k., one row p.; g. st. = garter st.: every row k.; incs. = increases; decs. = decreases; m.1 = make 1 st.: pick up horizontal loop lying before next st. and work into back of it; cross 3 = k. into front of 3rd st. on left needle, k. into front of 1st st., then k. into front of 2nd st., sl. all 3 sts. off needle tog.

BACK

** Cast on 87(95:101:109) sts. with 2¾mm needles.
Work in rib as folls.:
1st row (right side): k.1, * p.1, k.1, rep. from * to end.
2nd row: p.1, * k.1, p.1, rep. from * to end.
Rep. these 2 rows until work measures 5 cm. (2 in.), ending with a 1st row.
Next row: rib 2(6:5:9), * m.1, rib 4, rep. from * to last 1(5:4:8) sts., m.1, rib to end. [109(117:125:133) sts.]
Change to 3¼mm. needles and work in patt. as folls.:
1st row (right side): p.1, * k.3, p.1, rep. from * to end.
2nd row: k.1, * p.3, k.1, rep. from * to end.
3rd row: k.1, * p.1, k.3, rep. from * to end.
4th row: * p.3, k.1, rep. from * to last st., p.1.
5th row: k.1, * p.1, cross 3, rep. from * to end.
6th row: as 4th.
7th row: k.2, * p.1, k.3, rep. from * to last 3 sts., p.1, k.2.
8th row: p.2, * k.1, p.3, rep. from * to last 3 sts., k.1, p.2.
9th row: * k.3, p.1, rep. from * to last st., k.1.
10th row: p.1, * k.1, p.3, rep. from * to end.
11th row: * cross 3, p.1, rep. from * to last st., k.1.
12th row: p.1, * k.1, p.3, rep. from * to end.
These 12 rows form patt.
Cont. in patt. until back measures 20(22:23:26) cm. (7¾(8½:9:10¼) in.), ending with a wrong side row.

Shape Armholes

Keeping patt. straight, cast off 5 sts. at beg. of next 2 rows.
Dec. 1 st. at each end of next 7 rows.
Work 1 row.
Dec. 1 st. at each end of next and every alt. row until 77(83:91:97) sts. rem. **
Work straight in patt. until armholes

measure 13(15:16:17) cm. (5(5¾:6¼:6½) in.), ending with a right side row.

Shape Back Neck and Shoulders

Next row: patt. 27(28:30:31), cast off 23(27:31:35) sts. (including st. on needle after casting off), patt. 27(28:30:31).
Cont. on last 27(28:30:31) sts. for first side.
*** *Next row*: cast off 7(7:8:8), patt. to end.
Next row: cast off 3, patt. to end.
Rep. last 2 rows once more.
Cast off rem. 7(8:8:9) sts. ***
With right side facing, rejoin yarn to rem. sts., patt. to end.
Now work as given for first side from *** to ***.

FRONT

Work as for back from ** to **.
Work straight in patt. until armholes measure 8(10:10:11) cm. (3¼(4:4:4¼) in.), ending with a right side row.

Shape Neck

Next row: patt. 31(32:36:37), cast off 15(19:19:23) sts. (including st. on needle after casting off), patt. 31(32:36:37).
Cont. on last 31(32:36:37) sts. for first side.
**** Work 1 row.
Cast off 3 sts. at beg. of next and foll. alt. row.
Work 1 row.
Cast off 2 sts. at beg. of next and foll. 1(1:2:2) alt. rows.
Cont. straight on rem. 21(22:24:25) sts. until front matches back to beg. of shoulder shaping, ending at armhole edge.

Shape Shoulder

Cast off 7(7:8:8) sts. at beg. of next and foll. alt. row.
Work 1 row.
Cast off rem. 7(8:8:9) sts. ****.
With right side facing, rejoin yarn to rem. sts., patt. to end.
Work as for first side from **** to ****.

MAKING UP AND BORDERS

Sew up side and shoulder seams.

Neck border
Cast on 10 sts. with 2¾mm. needles and work in g. st. until border fits around neck, starting at left shoulder: sew in position as you work.
Cast off.
Sew border ends tog. at shoulder.

Armhole Borders
Work as for neck border.
Sew border ends tog. at underarm.

Tucked Woollen Dress

Fine wool and angora dress with tucked skirt and bodice, puffed sleeves, long back button opening and doubled hems

1951

★★★ Suitable for experienced knitters only

MATERIALS

Yarn
Jaeger Luxury Spun 4 ply
5(5:6:6) × 50g. balls

Needles
1 pair 2¾mm.
1 pair 3¼mm.
2 st. holders

Buttons
7

MEASUREMENTS

Chest
46(51:56:61) cm.
18(20:22:24) in.
6 months/1(1/2:2/3:4/5) approx. age

Length
42(46:49:53) cm.
16½(18:19¼:20¾) in.

Sleeve Seam
7(7:9:9) cm.
2¾(2¾:3½:3½) in.

TENSION

28 sts. and 36 rows = 10 cm. (4 in.) square over st. st. on 3¼mm. needles. If your tension square does not correspond to these measurements, see page 156 for adjustment instructions.

ABBREVIATIONS

k. = knit; p. = purl; st(s). = stitch(es); inc. = increas(ing) (see page 156); dec. = decreas(ing) (see page 157); beg. = begin(ning); rem. = remain(ing); rep. = repeat; alt. = alternate; tog. = together; sl. = slip (transfer one stitch from left needle, knitwise unless otherwise stated, to right hand needle.); cont. = continue; patt. = pattern; foll. = following; folls. = follows; mm. = millimetres; cm. = centimetres; in. = inches; st. st. = stocking st.: one row k., one row p.; g. st. = garter st.: every row k.; incs. = increases; decs. = decreases; m.1 = make 1 st.: pick up horizontal loop lying before next st. and work into the back of it; y.fwd. = yarn forward; t.b.l. = through back of loops.

FRONT

** Cast on 105(121:137:153) sts. with 2¾mm. needles.
Work 12 rows in st. st., beg. with a k. row.
Next row: p.
The last row forms ridge for hemline.
Work a further 13 rows in st. st., beg. with a p. row.
Make hem by k. 1 st. from needle tog. with 1 st. from cast-on edge all along row.
Change to 3¼mm. needles, cont. in st. st.
Work a further 25 rows straight.
Next row: p.
Work a further 9 rows in st. st., beg. with a p. row.
To make 1st tuck: fold work on p. ridge, counting down 9 rows from ridge on wrong side of work and k. 1 st. from needle tog. with 1 st. from 10th row all along row.
Work 23 rows in st. st., beg. with a p. row.
Next row: p.
Work a further 7 rows in st. st., beg. with a p. row.
2nd tuck: fold work on p. ridge as before and k. 1 st. from needle tog. with 1 st. from 8th row all along row.
Work 21 rows in st. st., beg. with a p. row.
Next row: p.
Work 5 rows in st. st., beg. with a p. row.
3rd tuck: work as before by k. 1 st. from needle tog. with 1 st. from 6th row all along row.
Work 19 rows in st. st., beg. with a p. row.
Next row: p.
Work 3 rows in st. st., beg. with a p. row.
4th tuck: k. 1 st. from needle tog. with 1 st. from 4th row all along row.
Beg. with a p. row, cont. straight in st. st. until front measures 23(25:28:30) cm. (9(9¾:11:11¾) in.) at centre, ending with a k. row. **

Shape Skirt
Next row: p.1, * p.2 tog., rep. from * to end. [53(61:69:77) sts.]
Change to 2¾mm. needles.
Work 14 rows in st. st.
Next row: k.4(3:3:2), m.1, * k.5(6:7:8), m.1, rep. from * to last 4(4:3:3) sts., k.4(4:3:3). [63(71:79:87) sts.]

Change to 3¼mm. needles and cont. in st. st. until front measures 33(36:38:41) cm. (13(14:15:16) in.) at centre, ending with a p. row.
Work a further 6 rows straight.
Next row: p.
Work 5 rows in st. st., beg. with a p. row.
Make tuck as for 3rd tuck on skirt.
Next row: p.

Shape Armholes
Cast off 4 sts. at beg. of next 2 rows.
Now dec. 1 st. at each end of every row until 49(53:57:61) sts. rem.
Next row: p.
Work a further 4 rows straight.
Next row: p.
Work 3 rows in st. st., beg. with a p. row.
Make tuck as for 4th tuck on skirt.
Cont. in st. st. until front measures 37(41:44:48) cm. (14½(16:17¼:18¾) in.) at centre, ending with a p. row.

Divide for Neck
Next row: k.12(13:14:15), turn and leave rem. sts. on spare needle.
Cont. on these 12(13:14:15) sts. for first side.
Work 17 rows straight.
Cast off.
With right side facing, sl. centre 25(27:29:31) sts. onto a spare needle.
Rejoin yarn to rem. sts., k. to end.
Complete to correspond with first side.

BACK

Work as for front from ** to **.

Shape Skirt
Next row: p.1, (p.2 tog.) 26(30:34:38) times, turn and leave rem. sts. on a spare needle.
Change to 2¾mm. needles and cont. on these 27(31:35:39) sts. for first side as folls.:
Next row: cast on 2, k. to end. [29(33:37:41) sts.]
Now, k. 5 sts. at centre back edge on every row throughout, work a further 13 rows straight.
Next row: k.7(9:9:9), m.1, * k.5(5:6:7), m.1, rep. from * to last 2(4:4:4) sts., k.2(4:4:4). [34(38:42:46) sts.]
Change to 3¼mm. needles and cont. in st. st. until back matches front to armhole at side edge, ending with a k. row.

41

Shape Armhole

Cast off 4 sts. at beg. of next row.
Now dec. 1 st. at armhole edge on every row until 27(29:31:33) sts. rem.
Work straight until back measures 39(43:46:50) cm. (15¼(16¾:18:19½) in.) at centre, ending with a wrong side row.

Shape Neck

Next row: sl. first 15(16:17:18) sts. onto holder, rejoin yarn to rem. 12(13:14:15) sts. and work straight until back matches front at armhole edge.
Cast off.
Next row: with wrong side facing, rejoin

yarn to rem. 52(60:68:76) sts., cast on 3 sts., k.3, (k.2 tog.) twice, (p.2 tog.) 24(28:32:36) times. [29(33:37:41) sts.]
Change to 2¾mm. needles and complete to match 1st side, reversing all shapings and making 6 buttonholes, 1st to come 1 cm. (½ in.) above beg. of border, 6th 2 cm. (¾ in.) below neck shaping, and rem. spaced evenly between.
Mark position of buttons on left border with pins to ensure even spacing, then work holes to correspond.
Buttonhole row (right side): k. to last 4 sts., k.2 tog., y.fwd., k.2.

SLEEVES

Cast on 38(42:46:50) sts. with 2¾mm. needles.
Work 4 rows in st. st., beg. with a k. row.
Next row: p.
Work a further 5 rows in st. st., beg. with a p. row.
Make hem in next row as for skirt.
Next row: p.1, * m.1, p.1, rep. from * to end. [75(83:91:99) sts.]
Change to 3¼mm. needles.
Cont. in st. st. until sleeve measures 7(7:9:9) cm. (2¾(2¾:3½:3½) in.) at centre, ending with a p. row.

Shape Top

Cast off 4 sts. at beg. of next 2 rows.
Now dec. 1 st. at each end of every row until 39(39:39:39) sts. rem.
Next row: k.1, * k.2 tog., rep. from * to end. [20 sts.]
Cast off.

NECKBORDER

Sew up shoulder seams.
With right side facing and 2¾mm. needles beg. at left side of back opening and k. 15(16:17:18) sts. from holder, pick up and k.8 sts. up left side of back, 16 sts. down left side of front, k.25(27:29:31) sts. from centre, pick up and k.16 sts. up right side of front, 8 sts. down right side of back, then k.15(16:17:18) sts. from holder. [103(107:111:115) sts.]

1st, 3rd and 5th rows: k.5, p. to last 5 sts., k.5.
2nd row: k. 13(14:15:16), k.2 tog. t.b.l., k.2 tog., k.20, k.2 tog. t.b.l., k.2 tog., k.21(23:25:27), k.2 tog. t.b.l., k.2 tog., k.20, k.2 tog. t.b.l., k.2 tog., k.13(14:15:16). [95(99:103:107) sts.]
4th row: k.12(13:14:15), k.2 tog. t.b.l., k.2 tog., k.18, k.2 tog. t.b.l., k.2 tog., k.19(21:23:25), k.2 tog. t.b.l., k.2 tog., k.18, k.2 tog. t.b.l., k.2 tog., k.8(9:10:11), k.2 tog., y.fwd., k.2. [87(91:95:99) sts.]
6th row: k.11(12:13:14), k.2 tog. t.b.l., k.2 tog., k.16, k.2 tog. t.b.l., k.2 tog., k.17(19:21:23), k.2 tog. t.b.l., k.2 tog., k.16, k.2 tog. t.b.l., k.2 tog., k.11(12:13:14). [79(83:87:91) sts.]
Next row: cast off 5 sts., k. to end.
Next row: cast off 5 sts., k.6(7:8:9), inc. in each of next 2 sts., k.16, inc. in each of next 2 sts., k.17(19:21:23), inc. in each of next 2 sts., k.16, inc. in each of next 2 sts., k.6(7:8:9). [77(81:85:89) sts.]
Next row: p.
Next row: k.7(8:9:10), inc. in each of next 2 sts., k.18, inc. in each of next 2 sts., k.19(21:23:25), inc. in each of next 2 sts., k.18, inc. in each of next 2 sts., k.7(8:9:10). [85(89:93:97) sts.]
Next row: p.
Next row: k.8(9:10:11), inc. in each of next 2 sts., k.20, inc. in each of next 2 sts., k.21(23:25:27), inc. in each of next 2 sts., k.20, inc. in each of next 2 sts., k.8(9:10:11). [93(97:101:105) sts.]
Cast off purlwise.

MAKING UP

Press work lightly on wrong side.
Sew up side and sleeve seams.
Set in sleeves, gathering in excess fullness at top of sleeve head.
Fold neck border in half to wrong side at ridge and sl.-hem loosely in position all round.
Catch down cast-on sts. of borders to main work.
Press all seams.
Sew on buttons.

Silky Cotton Cardigan

1953

Casual cardigan with deep armholes and dropped shoulderline, in garter stitch rib with round neck and ribbed welts

★ Suitable for beginners

MATERIALS

Yarn
Phildar Perle 5
9(9:10:10:10) × 50g. balls

Needles
1 pair 2mm.
1 pair 2¾mm.

Buttons
7

MEASUREMENTS

Bust
82(87:92:97:102) cm.
32(34:36:38:40) in.

Length
55(56:57:58:59) cm.
21½(22:22¼:22¾:23¼) in.

Sleeve Seam
42(43:44:45:46) cm.
16½(16¾:17¼:17¾:18) in.

TENSION

28 sts. and 48 rows = 10 cm. (4 in.) square over patt. on 2¾mm. needles. If your tension square does not correspond to these measurements, see page 156 for adjustment instructions.

ABBREVIATIONS

k. = knit; p. = purl; st(s). = stitch(es); inc. = increas(ing) (see page 156); dec. = decreas(ing) (see page 157); beg. = begin(ning); rem. = remain(ing); rep. = repeat; alt. = alternate; tog. = together; sl. = slip (transfer one stitch from left needle, knitwise unless otherwise stated, to right hand needle.); cont. = continue; patt. = pattern; foll. = following; folls. = follows; mm. = millimetres; cm. = centimetres; in. = inches; st. st. = stocking st.: one row k., one row p.; g. st. = garter st.: every row k.; incs. = increases; decs. = decreases.

BACK

Cast on 121(129:137:145:153) sts. with 2mm. needles.
Work in rib as folls.:
1st rib row (right side): k.1, * p.1, k.1, rep. from * to end.
2nd rib row: p.1, * k.1, p.1, rep. from * to end.

Rep. last 2 rows for 5 cm. (2 in.), ending with a 2nd row and inc. 1 st. in last row. [122(130:138:146:154) sts.]
Change to 2¾mm. needles and work in patt. as folls.:
1st row (right side): k.2, * p.2, k.2, rep. from * to end.
2nd row: as 1st.
These 2 rows form patt.
Work straight in patt. until back measures 34 cm. (13¼ in.), ending with a wrong side row.

Shape Armholes

Cast off 5 sts. at beg. of next 2 rows. [112(120:128:136:144) sts.]
Work straight in patt. until armholes measure 21(22:23:24:25) cm. (8¼(8½: 9:9½:9¾) in.), ending with a wrong side row.

Shape Shoulders

Cast off 5(6:6:7:7) sts. at beg. of next 12(8:14:6:12) rows.
Cast off 6(5:0:6:6) sts. at beg. of next 2(6:0:8:2) rows.
Cast off rem. 40(42:44:46:48) sts.

LEFT FRONT

Cast on 70(74:78:82:86) sts. with 2mm. needles.
Work in rib as folls.:
1st row (right side): * k.1, p.1, rep. from * to last 2 sts., k.2.
2nd row: p.2, * k.1, p.1, rep. from * to end.
Rep. last 2 rows for 5 cm. (2 in.), ending with a 2nd row.
Change to 2¾mm. needles and work in patt. as for back until front matches back to armhole, ending with a wrong side row.

Shape Armhole

Cast off 5 sts. at beg. of next row. [65(69:73:77:81) sts.]
Work straight in patt. until armhole measures 15(16:17:18:19) cm. (5¾(6¼: 6½:7:7½) in.), ending with a right side row.

Shape Neck

Next row: cast off 9(10:9:10:9) sts., patt. to end.
Work 1 row.
Cast off 3 sts. at beg. of next and 4(4:5:5:6) foll. alt. rows.
Work 1 row.
Dec. 1 st. at neck edge on next and 4(4:3:3:2) foll. alt. rows. [36(39:42:45:48) sts.]

Work straight in patt. until front matches back to shoulder, ending with a wrong side row.

Shape Shoulder

Cast off 5(6:6:7:7) sts. at beg. of next and 5(3:6:2:5) foll. alt. rows.
Work 1(1:0:1:1) row.
Cast off 6(5:0:6:6) sts. at beg. of next and 0(2:0:3:0) foll. alt. rows.
Mark position of buttons on left front, first to come 2 cm. (¾ in.) from cast-on edge, then allowing for last on the 6th row of neckborder, space rem. 5 evenly between.

RIGHT FRONT

Cast on 70(74:78:82:86) sts. with 2mm. needles, and work in rib as folls.:
1st row (right side): k.2, * p.1, k.1, rep. from * to end.
2nd row: * p.1, k.1, rep. from * to last 2 sts., p.2.
Work to match left front reversing all shapings and making buttonholes as folls.:
1st buttonhole row (right side): work 6, cast off 3 sts., work to end.
2nd buttonhole row: work across, casting on 3 sts. over those cast off on previous row.

SLEEVES

Cast on 61(63:65:69:73) sts. with 2mm. needles.
Work in rib as for back, ending with a 2nd rib row, and inc. 1(3:1:1:1) sts. in last row. [62(66:66:70:74) sts.]

Change to 2¾mm. needles.
Work in patt. as for back, AT THE SAME TIME shaping sides as folls.:
1st and 2nd sizes:
Inc. 1 st. at each end of every 5th row 20(21) times, taking inc. sts. into patt.
Now inc. 1 st. at each end of every foll. 7th row until there are 116(122) sts.
3rd, 4th and 5th sizes:
Inc. 1 st. at each end of every 5th row until there are 128(134:140) sts., taking inc. sts. into patt.
All sizes:
[116(122:128:134:140) sts.]
Work straight in patt, until sleeve measures 44(45:46:47:48) cm. (17¼(17¾:
18:18½:18¾) in.).
Cast off loosely.

NECKBORDER

Sew up shoulders.
With right side facing and 2mm. needles, k. up 43(45:47:49:51) sts. up right side of neck, 51(55:57:59:61) sts. across back neck and 43(45:47:49:51) sts. down left side of neck. [137(145:151:157:163) sts.]
Work in rib as folls.:
1st row (wrong side): p.2, * k.1, p.1, rep. from * to last st., p.1.
2nd row: k.2, * p.1, k.1, rep. from * to last st., k.1.

Rep. last 2 rows once more, then 1st row again.
6th row: rib 6, cast off 3 sts., rib to end.
7th row: work back, casting on 3 sts. over those cast off on previous row.
Work 6 more rows in rib.
Cast off evenly in rib.

MAKING UP

Place centre of cast-off edge of sleeves to shoulders.
Sew in position sewing to front and back at underarm.
Sew up side and sleeve seams.
Sew on buttons.

Twin Set with Cabled Raglans 1954

Cardigan and jumper each worked in one piece from neck downwards, with cabled raglan sleeves, round necks and ribbed welts

★★★ Suitable for very experienced knitters only

MATERIALS

Yarn
Wendy Shetland 4 ply
Cardigan:
3(3:4:4) × 50g. balls
Sweater:
3(3:4:4) × 50g. balls

Needles
1 pair 3mm.
1 pair 3¼mm.
cable needle
1 circular 3¼mm., approx. 100 cm. (40 in. long)
st. holders

Buttons
Cardigan:
9(10:10:11)
Sweater:
5(5:6:7)

MEASUREMENTS

Chest
56(61:66:71) cm.
22(24:26:28) in.
2/3(4/5:6/7:8/9) approx. age.

Length
Cardigan:
39(43:43:47) cm.
15¼(16¾:16¾:18½) in.
Sweater:
38(42:42:46) cm.
15(16½:16½:18) in.

Sleeve Seam
Short Sleeve:
5(7:10:11) cm.
2(2¾:4:4½) in.

Long Sleeve:
26(29:32:36) cm.
10¼(11¼:12½:14) in.

TENSION

28 sts. and 36 rows = 10 cm. (4 in.) square over st. st. on 3¼mm. needles. If your tension square does not correspond to these measurements, see page 156 for adjustment instructions.

ABBREVIATIONS

k. = knit; p. = purl; st(s). = stitch(es); inc. = increas(ing) (see page 156); dec. = decreas(ing) (see page 157); beg. = begin(ning); rem. = remain(ing); rep. = repeat; alt. = alternate; tog. = together; sl. = slip (transfer one stitch from left needle, knitwise unless otherwise stated, to right hand needle.); cont. = continue; patt. = pattern; foll. = following; folls. = follows; mm. = millimetres; cm. = centimetres; in. = inches; st. st. = stocking st.; one row k., one row p.; g. st. = garter st.; every row k.; incs. = increases; decs. = decreases; C4B = cable 4 back: sl. next 2 sts. onto cable needle and leave at back of work, k.2, then k.2 from cable needle; y.r.n. = yarn round needle; y.o.n. = yarn over needle.

NB The cardigan is worked in one piece, as is the sweater, beg. at the neck edge and working downwards.

CARDIGAN

Cast on 86(96:106:116) sts. with 3mm. needles.

Work 5 rows in k.1, p.1 rib.
Buttonhole row: rib 2, cast off 3, rib to end.
Next row: work in rib, casting on 3 sts. over those cast off.
Rib 1 row.
Change to 3¼mm. needles.
When necessary change to circular needle and cont. working in rows:
1st row: (k.1, p.1) 4 times, k.5(7:9:11), * y.r.n., p.1, k.4, p.1, y.o.n. *, k.10(12:14: 16), rep. from * to *, k.16(18:20:22), rep. from * to *, k.10(12:14:16), rep. from * to *, k.1, turn.
2nd row: sl.1, p. to last 12(14:16:18) sts., turn.
3rd row: sl.1, k.1, * y.r.n., p.1, k.4, p.1, y.o.n. *, k.12(14:16:18), rep. from * to *, k.18(20:22:24), rep. from * to *, k.12(14: 16:18), rep. from * to *, k.3, turn.
4th row: sl.1, p. to last 11(13:15:17) sts., turn.
5th row: sl.1, k.3, * y.r.n., p.1, C4B, p.1, y.o.n., * k.14(16:18:20), rep. from * to *, k.20(22:24:26), rep. from * to *, k.14(16: 18:20), rep. from * to *, k.5, turn.
6th row: sl.1, p. to last 10(12:14:16) sts., turn.
7th row: sl.1, k.5, * y.r.n., p.1, k.4, p.1, y.o.n. *, k.16(18:20:22), rep. from * to *, k.22(24:26:28), rep. from * to *, k.16(18: 20:22), rep. from * to *, k.7, turn.
8th row: sl.1, p. to last 9(11:13:15) sts., turn.
9th row: sl.1, k.7, * y.r.n., p.1, k.4, p.1, y.o.n., * k.18(20:22:24), rep. from * to *, k.24(26:28:30), rep. from * to *, k.18(20: 22:24), rep. from * to *, k.9, turn.
10th row: sl.1, p. to last 8(10:12:14) sts., turn.
11th row: sl.1, k.9, * y.r.n., p.1, C4B, p.1,

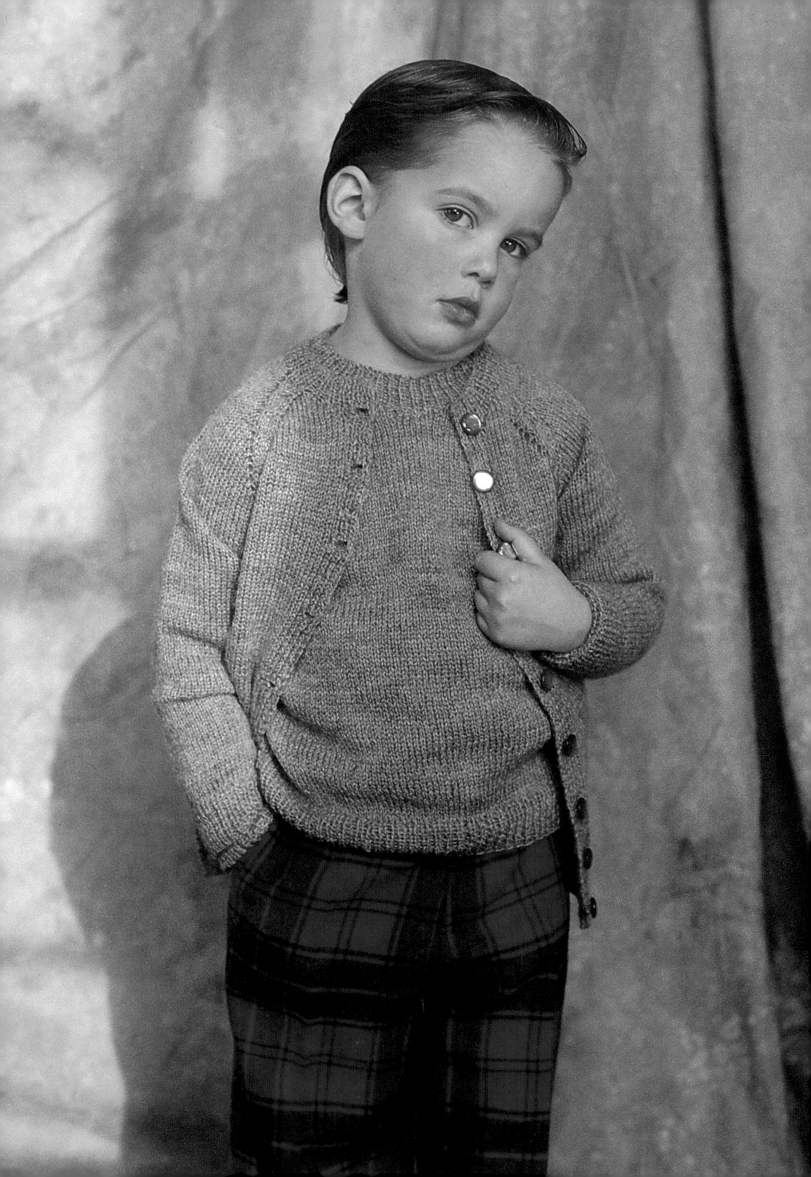

y.o.n. *, k.20(22:24:26), rep. from * to *, k.26(28:30:32), rep. from * to *, k.20(22:24:26), rep. from * to *, k.11(13:15:17), turn.

12th row: sl.1, p. to last 8 sts., k.1, turn.

13th row: sl.1, k.11(13:15:17), * y.r.n., p.1, k.4, p.1, y.o.n *, k.22(24:26:28), rep. from * to *, k.28(30:32:34), rep. from * to *, k.22(24:26:28), rep. from * to *, k. to last 7 sts., (p.1, k.1) 3 times, p.1.

14th row: (k.1, p.1) 3 times, k.1, p. to last 8 sts., (k.1, p.1) 4 times.

Keep 8 sts. in k.1, p.1 rib at each end of rows throughout.

Cont. to work in this way, making sts. on each side of cable on every right side row, having 1 more st. in each front and 2 more in the back and sleeves each time, and working C4B every 6th row.

Work 7 more rows, ending with a k. row.

22nd row: work 2, cast off 3, work to end.

23rd row: working cables, work to cast off sts., cast on 3, work to end.

Work buttonholes in this way every 15th and 16th rows to end of work.

Cont. making 8 sts. on every right side row in the same way until there are 286(312:346:372) sts., ending with a right side row.

Divide for Sleeves

Next row: (k.1, p.1) 4 times, p.99(109:122:132), cast on 2, turn.

** *Foll. row*: k.68(74:82:88), cast on 2, turn.

Work sleeve on these 70(76:84:90) sts.

Work 3 rows.

Dec. 1 st. at both ends of next and every foll. 6th row until 50(52:54:56) sts. rem.

Cont. straight until sleeve measures 24(26:27:32) cm. (9½(10¼:10½:12½) in.), ending with a p. row.

Change to 3mm. needles.

Work 3(5:5:5) cm. (1¼(2:2:2) in.) in k.1, p.1 rib.

Cast off in rib.

Rejoin yarn to sts. on left needle.

Next row: p.138(150:166:178), cast on 2 sts., turn.

Now work second sleeve from **.

Rejoin yarn to sts. on left needle and p. to last 8 sts., rib 8.

Body

1st row: work 8 sts. in rib, k. across sts. of left front, cast on 4, k. across sts. of back, cast on 4, work across sts. of right front. [162(176:194:208) sts.]

Cont. straight until work measures 34(38:38:42) cm. (13¼(15:15:16½) in.) or 5 cm. (2 in.) shorter than required length, ending with a k. row.

Change to 3mm. needles.

Work 18 rows in k.1, p.1 rib, working the last buttonhole on the 15th and 16th of these rows.

Cast off loosely in rib.

MAKING UP

Press lightly, avoiding rib.

Sew up sleeve seams and join cast-on sts. at underarms.

Sew on buttons.

Press seams.

SWEATER

Cast on 35(39:43:47) sts. with 3¼mm. needles.

1st row: (k.1, p.1) 3 times, k.8(10:12:14), * y.r.n., p.1, k.4, p.1, y.o.n., *, k.8(10:12:14), rep. from * to *, k.1.

2nd and alt. rows: p. twice into first st., p. to last 6 sts., (k.1, p.1) 3 times.

3rd row: (k.1, p.1) 3 times, k.9(11:13:15), * y.r.n., p.1, k.4, p.1, y.o.n., *, k.10(12:14:16), rep. from * to *, k.3.

5th row: (k.1, p.1) 3 times, k.10(12:14:16), * y.r.n., p.1, C4B, p.1, y.o.n *, k.12(14:16:18), rep. from * to *, k.5.

7th row: k.1, p.1, cast off 2, k.1, p.1, k.11(13:15:17), * y.r.n., p.1, k.4, p.1, y.o.n., * k.14(16:18:20), rep. from * to *, k.7.

NB On 8th row cast on 2 sts. over those cast off on 7th row.

9th row: (k.1, p.1) 3 times, k.12(14:16:18), * y.r.n., p.1, k.4, p.1, y.o.n., * k.16(18:20:22), rep. from * to *, k.9.

11th row: (k.1, p.1) 3 times, k.13(15:17:19), * y.r.n., p.1, C4B, p.1, y.o.n *, k.18(20:22:24), rep. from * to *, k.11.

12th row: cast on 2, p. to last 6 sts., (k.1, p.1) 3 times.

13th row: (k.1, p.1) 3 times, k.14(16:18:20), * y.r.n., p.1, k.4, p.1, y.o.n *, k.20(22:24:26), rep. from * to *, k.14.

14th row: as 12th.

15th row: (k.1, p.1) 3 times, k.15(17:19:21), * y.r.n., p.1, k.4, p.1, y.o.n *, k.22(24:26:28), rep. from * to *, k.17.

Break yarn, leave sts. on holder.

Work left side of neck in same way, reading each row backwards to reverse shaping, omitting buttonhole and working y.r.n. in place of y.o.n., and y.o.n. in place of y.r.n.

Now join pieces as folls.:

16th row: (p.1, k.1) 3 times, p. to end, cast on 4(6:8:10), p. across sts. of first piece to last 6 sts., (k.1, p.1) 3 times. [156(166:176:186) sts.]

When necessary change to the circular needle and cont. working in rows.

17th row: k.1, p.1, cast off 2, k.1, p.1, k.16(18:20:22), * y.r.n., p.1, C4B, p.1, y.o.n., * k.24(26:28:30), rep. from * to *, k.40(42:44:46), rep. from * to *, k.24(26:28:30), rep. from * to *, k. to last 6 sts., (p.1, k.1) 3 times.

NB On 18th row, cast on 2 sts. above cast-off sts. of 17th row.

Cont. in this way, making 8 sts. on every right side row, working cables on every 6th row and making 2(2:3:4) more buttonholes 8 rows apart until there are 284(310:344:370) sts., ending with a right side row.

Next row: cast off 6 sts. for underlap, p. until there are 97(107:120:130) sts. on needle, turn, cast on 2.

** *Foll. row*: k.64(70:78:84) sts., turn, cast on 2, sl. 35(39:44:48) sts. for back onto a holder.

Work sleeve on these 66(72:80:86) sts.

Short Sleeves

Work 4(6:8:10) rows straight.

Dec. 1 st. at both ends of next row and every 4th row until 60(64:68:72) sts. rem.

Change to 3mm. needles.

Work 6 rows in k.1, p.1 rib.

Cast off in rib.

Long Sleeves

Work 3 rows.

Dec. 1 st. at both ends of next and every foll. 6th row until 46(48:50:52) sts. rem.

Cont. straight until sleeve measures 23(26:29:33) cm. (9(10¼:11¼:13) in.), ending with a p. row.

Change to 3mm. needles.

Work 3 cm. (1¼ in.) in k.1, p.1 rib.

Cast off in rib.

Rejoin yarn to sts. on left needle, p.140(152:168:180) sts., turn and cast on 2. Work second sleeve from **, leaving 78(84:92:98) sts. for front on second st. holder.

Rejoin yarn to rem. sts. of back, p. across these 41(45:50:54) sts., break yarn.

Sl. 35(39:44:48) sts. of other half of back onto same needle. [76(84:94:102) sts.]

Rejoin yarn at beg. of k. row.

*** Cast on 2 sts. at beg. of next 2 rows.

Work 20 rows straight.

Dec. 1 st. at both ends of next and foll. 20th row.

Cont. straight in st. st. until work measures 34(37:37:41) cm. (13¼(14½:14½:16) in.) or 4(5:5:5) cm. (1½(2:2:2) in.) shorter than required length, ending with a p. row.

Change to 3mm. needles.

Work 12(18:18:18) rows in k.1, p.1 rib.

Cast off loosely in rib.

Rejoin yarn to sts. for front at beg. of a k. row.

Complete as for back from ***.

NECKBAND

With right side of work facing and 3mm. needles, pick up and k.76(86:96:106) sts. around neck edge.

Work 8 rows in k.1, p.1 rib, working the last buttonhole on the 3rd and 5th rows.

Cast off loosely in rib.

MAKING UP

Press work lightly avoiding rib.

Sew up side and sleeve seams.

Catch down base of underlap.

Sew on buttons.

Press seams.

Rib-and-twist stitch Sweater

1948

Crew-neck sweater in stocking stitch with twisted rib panels, set-in sleeves and ribbed welts

★★ Suitable for knitters with some previous experience

MATERIALS

Yarn
Patons Clansman 4 ply
8(8:9:9:10) × 50g. balls

Needles
1 pair 2¾mm.
1 pair 3¼mm.

MEASUREMENTS

Chest
92(97:102:107:112) cm.
36(38:40:42:44) in.

Length
65(66:66:67:67) cm.
25½(26:26:26¼:26¼) in.

Sleeve Seam
46(46:47:47:47) cm.
18(18:18½:18½:18½) in.

TENSION

28 sts. and 36 rows = 10 cm. (4 in.) square over st. st. on 3¼mm. needles. If your tension square does not correspond to these measurements, see page 156 for adjustment instructions.

ABBREVIATIONS

k. = knit; p. = purl; st(s). = stitch(es); inc. = increas(ing) (see page 156); dec. = decreas(ing) (see page 157); beg. = begin(ning); rem. = remain(ing); rep. = repeat; alt. = alternate; tog. = together; sl. = slip (transfer one stitch from left needle, knitwise unless otherwise stated, to right hand needle.); cont. = continue; patt. = pattern; foll. = following; folls. = follows; mm. = millimetres; cm. = centimetres; in. = inches; st. st. = stocking st.: one row k., one row p.; g. st. = garter st.: every row k.; incs. = increases; decs. = decreases; m.1 = make 1 st.: pick up horizontal loop lying before next st. and work into back of it; Tw.2R = k. into front of 2nd st. on left needle, then k. into front of first st. on left needle and sl. both sts. off needle tog.; Tw.2L = k. into back of 2nd st. on left needle, then k. into front of first st. on left needle and sl. both sts. off needle tog.

BACK

** Cast on 119(127:135:143:151) sts. with 2¾mm. needles.
1st row (right side): k.1, * p.1, k.1, rep. from * to end.
2nd row: p.1, * k.1, p.1, rep. from * to end.
Rep. last 2 rows until work measures 7 cm. (2¾ in.), ending with a 1st row.
Next row: p.3(7:3:7:4), m.1, (p.3(6:4:8:5), m.1) 3(1:3:1:3) times, p.3(6:4:8:4), * k.1, (p.1, k.1) 4 times, p.3(2:5:4:5), m.1,

(p.4(3:4:3:5), m.1) 1(2:1:2:1) times, p.4(3:4:3:5), rep. from * 3 times, k.1, (p.1, k.1) 4 times, p.3(7:3:7:4), m.1, (p.3(6:4: 8:5), m.1) 3(1:3:1:3) times, p.3(6:4:8:4). [135(143:151:159:167) sts.]
Change to 3¼mm. needles and work in patt. as folls.:
1st row (right side): k.19(21:23:25:27), * p.1, (k.1, p.1) 4 times, k.13(14:15:16:17), rep. from * 3 times, p.1, (k.1, p.1) 4 times, k.19(21:23:25:27).
2nd row: p.19(21:23:25:27), * k.1, (p.1, k.1) 4 times, p.13(14:15:16:17), rep. from * 3 times, k.1, (p.1, k.1) 4 times, p.19(21:23: 25:27).
3rd-8th rows: as 1st and 2nd 3 times.
9th row: k.17(19:21:23:25), Tw.2R, * p.1, (k.1, p.1) 4 times, Tw.2L, k.9(10:11:12:13), Tw.2R, rep. from * 3 times, p.1, (k.1, p.1) 4 times, Tw.2L, k.17(19:21:23:25).
10th row: as 2nd.
11th row: k.21(23:25:27:29), * p.1, (k.1, p.1) twice, k.17(18:19:20:21), rep. from * 3 times, p.1, (k.1, p.1) twice, k.21(23:25: 27:29).
12th row: p.21(23:25:27:29), * k.1, (p.1, k.1) twice, p.17(18:19:20:21), rep. from * 3 times, k.1, (p.1, k.1) twice, p.21(23:25: 27:29).
13th-20th rows: as 11th and 12th 4 times.
21st row: k.19(21:23:25:27), Tw.2R, * p.1, (k.1, p.1) twice, Tw.2L, k.13(14:15:16:17), Tw.2R, rep. from * 3 times, p.1, (k.1, p.1) twice, Tw.2L, k.19(21:23:25:27).
22nd row: as 12th.
These 22 rows form patt.
Work straight in patt. until back measures 43 cm. (16¾ in.) from beg., ending with a wrong side row.

Shape Armholes

Keeping patt. straight, cast off 4 sts. at beg. of next 2 rows, then dec. 1 st. at each end of next and every foll. alt. row until 103(107:111:115:119) sts. rem. **
Work straight until back measures 65(66:66:67:67) cm. (25½(26:26:26¼:26¼ in.) from beg., ending with a wrong side row.

Shape Shoulders

Cast off 11(10:11:12:11) sts. at beg. of next 2 rows.
Cast off 10(11:11:11:12) sts. at beg. of next 4 rows.
Leave rem. 41(43:45:47:49) sts. on a spare needle.

FRONT

Work as for back from ** to **.
Work straight until front measures 57(58:58:59:59) cm. (22¼(22¾:22¾:23¼:23¼) in.) from beg., ending with a wrong side row.

Divide for Neck

Next row: patt. 39(40:41:42:43), turn and leave rem. sts. on a spare needle.
Cont. on these 39(40:41:42:43) sts. for first side.
Dec. 1 st. at neck edge on next and every alt. row until 31(32:33:34:35) sts. rem.
Work straight until front matches back to shoulder, ending with a wrong side row.

Shape Shoulder

Cast off 11(10:11:12:11) sts. at beg. of next row.
Cast off 10(11:11:11:12) sts. at beg. of foll. 2 alt. rows.
With right side facing, sl. centre 25(27:29:31:33) sts. on a spare needle.
Rejoin yarn to rem. sts., patt. to end.
Complete to match first side.

SLEEVES

Cast on 63(67:67:71:71) sts. with 2¾mm. needles.

Work 7 cm. (2¾ in.) in k.1, p.1 rib as for back, ending with a 1st row.
Next row: p.3(4:4:3:3), (m.1, p.2(5:5:3:3)) 2(1:1:2:2) times, * k.1, (p.1, k.1) 4 times, p.3(2:2:5:5), (m.1, p.4(3:3:4:4)) 2(3:3:2:2) times, rep. from * once, k.1, (p.1, k.1) 4 times, p.3(4:4:3:3), (m.1, p.2(5:5:3:3)) 2(1:1:2:2) times. [71(75:75:79:79) sts.].
Change to 3¼mm. needles and patt.
1st row (right side): k.9(10:10:11:11), * p.1, (k.1, p.1) 4 times, k.13(14:14:15:15), rep. from * once, p.1, (k.1, p.1) 4 times, k.9(10:10:11:11).
2nd row: p.9(10:10:11:11), * k.1, (p.1, k.1) 4 times, p.13(14:14:15:15), rep. from * once, k.1, (p.1, k.1) 4 times, p.9(10:10:11:11).
These 2 rows set patt.
Cont. in patt. to match back, shaping sides by inc. 1 st. at each end of 11th and every foll. 8th row until there are 99(103:103:107:107) sts., taking inc. sts. into st. st.
Cont. straight until sleeve seam measures 46(46:47:47:47) cm. (18(18:18½:18½:18½) in.), ending with a wrong side row.

Shape Top

Working in patt., cast off 4 sts. at beg. of next 2 rows.

Now dec. 1 st. at each end of next and every alt. row until 51 sts. rem.
Work 1 row straight, then dec. 1 st. at each end of every row until 27 sts. rem.
Cast off.

Neck Border

Sew up right shoulder seam.
With right side facing and 2¾mm. needles, beg. on left front shoulder, pick up and k.31 sts. down left side of neck, k.25(27:29:31:33) from centre, pick up and k.31 sts. up right side, then k.41 (43:45:47:49) from back. [128(132:136:140:144) sts.]
Work 7 rows in k.1, p.1 rib.
Cast off evenly in rib.

MAKING UP

Press work lightly on wrong side, omitting welt, cuff and neck ribbing, taking care not to spoil patt.
Sew up left shoulder seam, then sew up neck border with a flat seam.
Sew up side and sleeve seams.
Set in sleeves.
Press all seams.

Cosy Plaid Socks

1952

Four-colour plaid socks in fine wool, in adjustable size with plain foot and ribbed top

★★ Suitable for knitters with some previous experience

MATERIALS

Yarn
Rowan Botany 3 ply
3 × 25g. hanks Main Col. A
1 × 25g. hank Col. B
1 × 25g. hank Col. C
1 × 25g. hank Col. D

Needles
1 set of 4 double-pointed 2¾mm.
3 st. holders

MEASUREMENTS

Length (adjustable)
24-30 cm.
9½-11¾ in.

Length from Top to Heel Base
30 cm.
11¾ in.

TENSION

18 sts. and 22 rows to 5 cm. (2 in.) square over st. st. on 2¾mm. needles. If your tension square does not correspond to these measurements, see page 156 for adjustment instructions.

ABBREVIATIONS

k. = knit; p. = purl; st(s). = stitch(es); inc. = increas(ing) (see page 156); dec. = decreas(ing) (see page 157); beg. = begin(ning); rem. = remain(ing); rep. = repeat; alt. = alternate; tog. = together; sl. = slip (transfer one stitch from left needle, knitwise unless otherwise stated, to right hand needle.); cont. = continue; patt. = pattern; foll. = following; folls. = follows; mm. = millimetres; cm. = centimetres; in. = inches; st. st. = stocking st.: one row k., one row p.; g. st. = garter st.: every row k.; incs. = increases; decs. = decreases; p.s.s.o. = pass the sl. st. over.

NB Twist yarns on wrong side of work when changing col. to avoid a hole.

Cast on 64 sts. with A: 22 sts. on first and third needles, 20 sts. on second needle. Take care not to twist sts.

Work 9 cm. (3½ in.) in rounds of k.2, p.2 rib.

Inc. round: k.3, * k. twice into next st., k.6, rep. from * to last 5 sts., k. twice into next st., k.4. [73 sts.]

Place a coloured marker at end of last round to mark centre back.

Work in patt. as folls.:

1st round: k.6A, * join in C, k.1C, k.11A, join in D, k.1D, k.11A, rep. from * to end, joining in a new small ball of C and D each time and ending last rep. with k.6A.

2nd round: k.6A, * 1C, 11A, 1D, 11A, rep. from *, ending last rep. k.6A.

Rep. last round 6 times more.

Join in 4th ball of C.

9th round: k.18C, * 1D, 23C, rep. from * to last 7 sts., k.1D, 6C.

10th round: as 9th.

Break 4th ball of C, use A.

Rep. 2nd round 8 times.

Break A, join in B.

Rep. 2nd round 8 times, using B instead of A.

Join in 4th ball of D.

27th round: k.6D, * 1C, 23D, rep. from * to last 19 sts., k.1C, 18D.

28th round: as 27th.

Break 4th ball of D, use B.

Rep. 2nd round 8 times, using B instead of A.

Rep. last 36 rounds once more.

Break B, first ball of C and 3rd ball of D.

Divide for Heel and Instep

Sl. first and last 16 sts. of round onto 2 separate holders.

Join A to rem. 41 sts. at beg. of k. row.

Work 36 rows in patt., working to and fro and p. every alt. row.

Now break all coloured wools and leave these sts. on holder.

Sl. 32 sts. from first two holders onto one needle for heel.

Join A to beg. of k. row.

1st row: k.3, * k. twice into next st., k.7, rep. from * to last 5 sts., k. twice into next st., k.4. [36 sts.]

2nd row: sl. 1 purlwise, p. to end.

3rd row: * keeping yarn at back, sl.1 purlwise, k.1, rep. from * to end.

Rep. last 2 rows 17 times.

Turn Heel

Next row: sl.1, p.20, p.2 tog., p.1, turn.

Next row: sl.1, k.7, sl.1, k.1, p.s.s.o., k.1, turn.

Next row: sl.1, p.8, p.2 tog., p.1, turn.

Next row: sl.1, k.9, sl.1, k.1, p.s.s.o., k.1, turn.

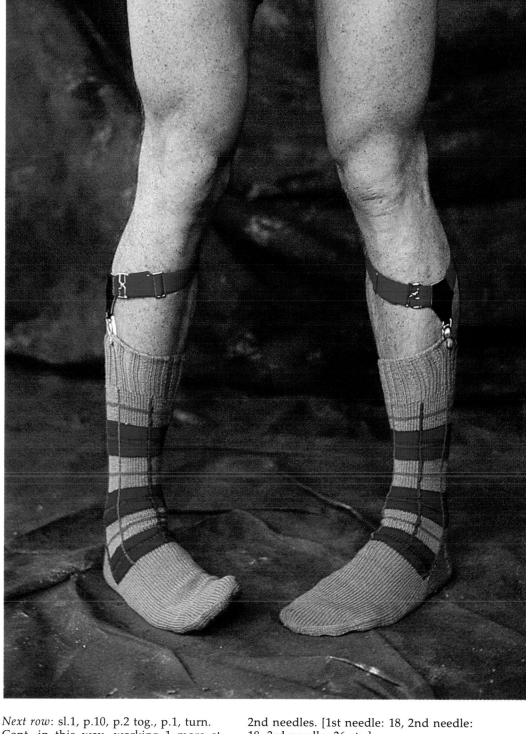

Next row: sl.1, p.10, p.2 tog., p.1, turn.

Cont. in this way, working 1 more st. before the dec. on every row until 22 sts. rem.

Now with same needle, k. up 18 sts. up left side of heel.

With another needle pick up 18 sts. up right side of heel and sl. first 11 sts. of heel onto same needle. [29 sts. on each needle.]

Return to sts. at end of 1st needle and work to and fro on these 2 needles.

1st row: p.

2nd row: k.1, sl.1, k.1, p.s.s.o., k. to last 3 sts., k.2 tog., k.1.

Rep. last 2 rows until 34 sts. rem.

Now with 3rd needle, k. across instep sts. on holder as folls.:

k.5, * k.2 tog., k.12, rep. from * to last 8 sts., k.2 tog., k.6. [36 sts.]

Sl. first and last sts. of instep onto 1st and 2nd needles. [1st needle: 18, 2nd needle: 18, 3rd needle: 36 sts.]

Work in rounds without further shaping until foot measures 5 cm. (2 in.) less than desired length.

Shape Toe

1st round: 1st needle – k.1, sl.1, k.1, p.s.s.o., k. to end; 2nd needle – k. to last 3 sts., k.2 tog., k.1; 3rd needle – k.1, sl.1, k.1, p.s.s.o., k. to last 3 sts., k.2 tog., k.1.

2nd round: k.

Rep. last 2 rounds until 20 sts. rem.

Put the 2 sets of 5 sts. onto one needle.

Cast off both sets of sts. tog.: hold 2 needles parallel and cast off 1 st. from each needle alternately, to end.

Press work on wrong side with a damp cloth omitting ribbing.

Sew up seams.

Self-welt, V-neck Sweater   1955

V-neck sweater in broken rib with single rib welts and neck edging knitted all-in-one with sweater front

★★ Suitable for knitters with some previous experience.

MATERIALS

Yarn
Poppleton Lana DK
11(12:13:14:15) × 50g. balls

Needles
1 pair 3mm.
1 pair 4mm.
1 3½mm. crochet hook

MEASUREMENTS

Chest
92(97:102:107:112) cm.
36(38:40:42:44) in.

Length
68(71:73:74:76) cm.
26¾(27¾:28½:29:29¾) in.

Sleeve Seam
46(47:49:50:51) cm.
18(18½:19¼:19½:20) in.

TENSION

22 sts. and 28 rows = 10 cm. (4 in.) square over patt. on 4mm. needles. If your tension square does not correspond to these measurements, see page 156 for adjustment instructions.

ABBREVIATIONS

k. = knit; p. = purl; st(s). = stitch(es); inc. = increas(ing) (see page 156); dec. = decreas(ing) (see page 157); beg. = begin(ning); rem. = remain(ing); rep. = repeat; alt. = alternate; tog. = together; sl. = slip (transfer one stitch from left needle, knitwise unless otherwise stated, to right hand needle.); cont. = continue; patt. = pattern; foll. = following; folls. = follows; mm. = millimetres; cm. = centimetres; in. = inches; st. st. = stocking st.: one row k., one row p.; g. st. = garter st.: every row k.; incs. = increases; decs. = decreases; d.c. = double crochet.

BACK

** Cast on 99(105:111:117:123) sts. with 3mm. needles.
Work in rib as folls.:
1st row (right side): * k.1, p.1, rep. from * to last st., k.1.
2nd row: * p.1, k.1, rep. from * to last st., p.1.
These 2 rows form rib.
Cont. until work measures 8 cm. (3¼ in.) from beg., ending with a wrong side row.

Change to 4mm. needles.
Work in patt. as folls.:
1st row (right side): k.
2nd row: p.1, * k.1, p.1, rep. from * to end.
These 2 rows form patt. **
Cont. straight until work measures 47(49:50:50:51) cm. (18½(19¼:19½:19½:20) in.) from beg., ending with a wrong side row.

Shape Armholes

Keeping patt. correct, cast off 4(5:6:7:8) sts. at beg. of next 2 rows, then dec. 1 st. at each end of next and every foll. alt. row 5 times in all.
Work straight in patt. on these rem. 81(85:89:93:97) sts. until work measures 21(22:23:24:25) cm. (8¼(8½:9:9½:9¾) in.) from beg. of armhole shaping, ending with a wrong side row.

Shape Neck and Shoulders

Next row: patt. 22(24:26:28:30) sts., then cast off next 37 sts. and patt. to end.
Now cont. in patt. on these rem. sts., casting off 11(12:13:14:15) sts. at beg. of next and foll. alt. row.
Rejoin yarn to neck edge of rem. sts.
Work 1 row.
Complete to match first side.

FRONT

Work as for back from ** to **.
Cont. straight in patt. until work measures 44(46:47:47:48) cm. (17¼(18: 18½:18½:18¾) in.) from beg., ending with a wrong side row.

Shape Neck

Next row: k.55(58:61:64:67) sts., then turn and leave rem. 44(47:50:53:56) sts. on spare needle.

Patt. 5 rows.
Next row: k. to last 14 sts., k.2 tog., k. to end.
Patt. 1 row.

Shape Armhole

Cast off 4(5:6:7:8) sts. at beg. of next row.
Dec. 1 st. at neck edge, as before, on every 4th(4th:4th:6th:6th) row from previous dec., and AT THE SAME TIME dec. 1 st. at armhole edge on the next 5 right-side rows.
Cont. to dec. at neck edge only until 34(36:38:40:42) sts. rem.
Patt. straight until front matches back to shoulder, ending at armhole edge.

Shape Shoulder

Cast off 11(12:13:14:15) sts. at beg. of next row and on the foll. alt. row.
Work straight in patt. on rem. 12 sts. for a further 9 cm. (3½ in.)
Cast off.
Return to rem. sts. and cast on 11 sts. at centre edge for underlap.
Complete to match first side, reversing all shapings.

SLEEVES

Cast on 51(55:59:63:67) sts. with 3mm. needles and work in rib as on back welt for 8 cm. (3¼ in.), ending with a wrong side row.
Change to 4mm. needles.
Work in patt., inc. 1 st. at each end of every 6th(6th:6th:8th:8th) row until there are 79(83:87:91:95) sts., working inc. sts. into patt.
Work straight in patt. until sleeve measures 46(47:49:50:51) cm. (18(18½: 19¼:19½:20) in.) from beg., ending with a wrong side row.

Shape Top

Cast off 6 sts. at beg. of next 2 rows, then dec. 1 st. at each end of next and every foll. alt. row until 41 sts. rem., ending with a wrong side row.
Cast off 3 sts. at beg. of next 8 rows.
Cast off rem. 17 sts.

MAKING UP

Sew up shoulder seams.
Sew ends of neckband tog., then sew to back neck.
Sew underlap to wrong side at centre front.
Set in sleeves, sew up side and sleeve seams.
Do not press.
With right side facing and crochet hook, work 1 row d.c. all round neck edge.

Rabbit-design Sweater

1954

Long sweater in stocking stitch with contrasting, knitted-in rabbits on front, set-in sleeves and ribbed welts

★ Suitable for adventurous beginners

MATERIALS

Yarn
Emu Superwash 4 ply
3(4:4:4) × 50g. balls Main Col. A
1(1:1:1) × 50g. ball Col. B

Needles
1 pair 3mm.
1 pair 3¼mm.
2 st. holders

MEASUREMENTS

Chest
56(61:66:71) cm.
22(24:26:28) in.
2/3(4/5:6/7:8/9) approx. age

Length
34(36:38:41) cm.
13¼(14:15:16) in.

Sleeve Seam
25(29:32:35) cm.
9¾(11¼:12½:13¾) in.

TENSION

14 sts. and 18 rows = 5 cm. (2 in.) square over st. st. on 3¼mm. needles. If your tension square does not correspond to these measurements, see page 156 for adjustment instructions.

ABBREVIATIONS

k. = knit; p. = purl; st(s). = stitch(es); inc. = increas(ing) (see page 156); dec. = decreas(ing) (see page 157); beg. = begin(ning); rem. = remain(ing); rep. = repeat; alt. = alternate; tog. = together; sl. = slip (transfer one stitch from left needle, knitwise unless otherwise stated, to right hand needle.); cont. = continue; patt. = pattern; foll. = following; folls. = follows; mm. = millimetres; cm. = centimetres; in. = inches; st. st. = stocking st.: one row k., one row p.; g. st. = garter st.: every row k.; incs. = increases; decs. = decreases; p.s.s.o. = pass slipped st. over.

BACK

Cast on 80(88:96:104) sts. with 3mm. needles and A.
Work 18 rows in k.1, p.1 rib.
Change to 3¼mm. needles.
Beg. with a k. row, work straight in st. st. until work measures 23(24:25:27) cm. (9(9½:9¾:10½) in.) from cast-on edge, ending with a p. row.

Shape Armholes

Cast off 3(4:5:6) sts. at beg. of next 2 rows and 2 sts. at beg. of foll. 2 rows.
5th row: k.1, sl.1, k.1, p.s.s.o., k. until 3 sts. rem., k.2 tog., k.1.
6th row: p.
Rep. 5th and 6th rows until 64(68:74:80) sts. rem.
Cont. straight until armholes measure 11(12:13:14) cm. (4¼(4¾:5:5½) in.), ending with a p. row.

Shape Shoulders

Cast off 8(9:10:11) sts. at beg. of next 2 rows and 9(9:10:11) sts. at beg. of foll. 2 rows.
Leave rem. 30(32:34:36) sts. on holder until required for neckband.

FRONT

Work as for back until 20 rows have been worked in st. st.
Now work the rabbit patt. from chart as folls.:
Odd-numbered k. rows, are read from right to left, and even-numbered p. rows, are read from left to right.
Carry yarn not in use loosely across back of work, catching it in every 5 sts. if necessary.
1st row: k.4(8:12:16) with A, join in B, and work 72 sts. from 1st row of chart, k.4(8:12:16) with A.
Work from 2nd to 15th row of chart, working the end 4(8:12:16) sts. on each row with A.
Break off B, and cont. entirely with A.
Beg. with a p. row, work as for back until armholes measure 6(7:8:9) cm. (2¼(2¾:

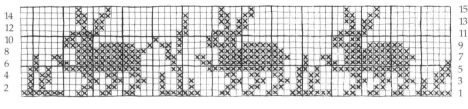

☐ = Col A
☒ = Col B

3¼:3¾) in.), ending with a p. row. [64(68:74:80) sts.]

Shape Neck
Next row: k.23(24:26:28), turn and work on these sts. leaving rem. sts. on a spare needle.
1st row: p.
2nd row: k. until 3 sts. rem., k.2 tog., k.1.
Rep. these 2 rows until 17(18:20:22) sts. rem.
** Cont. straight until armhole measures same as back armhole, ending at armhole edge.

Shape Shoulder
Cast off 8(9:10:11) sts. at beg. of next row, work 1 row straight then cast off rem. 9(9:10:11) sts.
With right side of work facing sl. next 18(20:22:24) sts. onto a holder until required for neckband, then rejoin A to first of rem. 23(24:26:28) sts.
1st row: k.
2nd row: p.
3rd row: k.1, sl.1, k.1, p.s.s.o., k. to end.
Rep. 2nd and 3rd rows until 17(18:20:22) sts. rem.
Now work from ** to end as for 1st shoulder.

SLEEVES

Cast on 44(46:48:50) sts. with 3mm. needles and A.
Work 18 rows in k.1, p.1 rib.
Change to 3¼mm. needles.
Beg. with a k. row, work 4 rows in st. st.
Next row: k.1, k. twice into next st., k. until 2 sts. rem., k. twice into next st., k.1.
Work 5 rows straight.
Rep. the last 6 rows until there are 62(66:70:74) sts.
Cont. straight until sleeve seam measures 25(29:32:35) cm. (9¾(11¼:12½:13¾) in.), ending with a p. row.

Shape Top
Cast off 3(4:5:6) sts. at beg. of next 2 rows and 2 sts. at beg. of foll. 2 rows.
5th row: k.1, sl.1, k.1, p.s.s.o., k. until 3 sts. rem., k.2 tog., k.1.
6th row: p.
Rep. 5th and 6th rows until 38 sts. rem.
Cast off 6 sts. at beg. of next 4 rows then cast off rem. 14 sts.

NECKBAND

Sew up right shoulder seam.
With right side of work facing, using A and 3mm. needles, pick up and k. 24 sts. down left front neck edge, k. across 18(20:22:24) sts. at centre front, pick up and k.24 sts. up right front neck edge and finally k. across 30(32:34:36) sts. at back neck edge. [96(100:104:108) sts.].
Work 6 rows in k.1, p.1 rib.
Cast off loosely in rib.

MAKING UP

Sew up remaining shoulder seam, carrying seams across neckband.
Set in sleeves.
Sew up side and sleeve seams.

Twist-rib and Cable Sweater

Round-neck, cable and twist-rib-pattern sweater with set-in sleeves, twist-rib welts and neckband

★★ Suitable for knitters with some previous experience

MATERIALS

Yarn
ANI Shetland 2 ply
14(14:15:16) × 28g. hanks

Needles
1 pair 2¾mm.
1 pair 3¾mm.
1 cable needle
st. holder

MEASUREMENTS

Chest
92(97:102:107) cm.
36(38:40:42) in.

Length
60(61:62:64) cm.
23½(24:24½:25) in.

Sleeve Seam
48(50:51:51) cm.
19(19½:20:20) in.

TENSION

30 sts. and 36 rows = 10 cm. (4 in.) square over slightly stretched patt. on 3¾mm. needles. If your tension square does not correspond to these measurements, see page 156 for adjustment instructions.

ABBREVIATIONS

k. = knit; p. = purl; st(s). = stitch(es); inc. = increas(ing) (see page 156); dec. = decreas(ing) (see page 157); beg. = begin(ning); rem. = remain(ing); rep. = repeat; alt. = alternate; tog. = together; sl. = slip (transfer one stitch from left needle, knitwise unless otherwise stated, to right hand needle.); cont. = continue; patt. = pattern; foll. = following; folls. = follows; mm. = millimetres; cm. = centimetres; in. = inches; st. st. = stocking st.: one row k., one row p.; g. st. = garter st.: every row k.; incs. = increases; decs. = decreases; t.b.l. = through back of loop.

FRONT

Cast on 144(150:158:164) sts. with 2¾mm. needles.
Work 26 rows in k.1 t.b.l., p.1, twist rib.
Next row: work in twist rib to last 2 sts., k.2 tog. [143(149:157:163) sts.]
Next row: beg. with a p. st., twist rib 15(11:15:11) sts., * inc. in next st., twist rib 13 sts. *, rep. from * to * to last 15(11:15:11) sts., inc. in next st., twist rib to end. [152(159:167:174) sts.]
Change to 3¾mm. needles.
Work in rib and cable patt. as folls.:
1st row: beg. with k.1 t.b.l., work 12(8:12: 8) sts. in twist rib, * k.8, beg. with p.1, twist rib next 7 sts., * rep. from * to * to last 20(16:20:16) sts., k.8, beg. with p.1, twist rib to end.
2nd row: beg. with p.1, twist rib first 12(8: 12:8) sts., * p.8, beg. with k.1 t.b.l., twist rib next 7 sts., * rep. from * to *, to last 20(16:20:16) sts., p.8, beg. with k.1 t.b.l., twist rib to end.

3rd to 6th rows: rep. 1st and 2nd rows twice more each.
7th row: beg. with k.1 t.b.l., work 12(8:12: 8) sts. in twist rib, * sl. next 4 sts. onto cable needle and leave at front of work, k.4, k.4 from cable needle, beg. with p.1, twist rib next 7 sts., * rep. from * to * to last 5(1:5:1) sts., twist rib to end.
8th row: as 2nd.
These 8 rows form patt.
Rep. these 8 patt. rows 13(14:14:15) times more, then work rows 1 to 4 inclusive 1(0:1:0) times more.

Shape Armholes
Keeping patt. correct, cast off 6 sts. at beg. of next 2 rows.
Cast off 2 sts. at beg. of next 4 rows.
Now dec. 1 st. at beg. of every row until 118(127:131:142) sts. rem. **
Cont. straight in patt., working beg. and end 10(7:9:7) sts. of each row in twist rib until a total of 21½(22:22½:23) patts. have been worked.

Shape Neck
Work 52(56:58:63) sts., turn.
Work on these sts. first.
Cast off 4(5:5:6) sts. at beg. of next row.
Cast off 4(4:4:5) sts. at beg. of next 2 alt. rows.
Cast off 2 sts. at beg. of foll. 2 alt. rows, ending at armhole edge. [36(39:41:43) sts.]

Shape Shoulder
Cast off 12(13:13:14) sts. at beg. of next row and on the foll. alt. row.
Work 1 row, thus ending at armhole edge.
Cast off rem. 12(13:15:15) sts.
Sl. centre 14(15:15:16) sts. onto holder for neck.
Rejoin wool to rem. 52(56:58:63) sts., and work to match left side.

BACK

Work as for front to **.
Cont. straight in patt. until 22½(23:23½: 24) patts. have been worked.
Work 2 more rows.

Shape Shoulders
Cast off 12(13:13:14) sts. at beg. of next 4 rows.
Cast off 12(13:15:15) sts. at beg. of next 2 rows.
Leave rem. 46(49:49:56) sts. on holder for back of neck.

SLEEVES

Cast on 64(68:68:72) sts. with 2¾mm. needles.
Work 31 rows in twist rib.
Next row: working in twist rib, inc. 8 sts. evenly across row. [72(76:76:80) sts.]
Change to 3¾mm. needles and work in patt. as folls:
1st row: beg. with k.1 t.b.l., twist rib 2(4: 4:6) sts., k.8, * beg. p.1, twist rib 7, k.8, *, rep from * to * to last 2(4:4:6) sts., beg. with p.1, twist rib to end.
This row sets patt.
With sts. as set, patt. 7 rows as for front.

Inc. 1 st. at each end of next and every foll. 6th row until there are 114(118:118: 122) sts.
N.B. Incorporate extra sts. into patt., after one extra cable appears at each side, work rem. inc. sts. in twist rib only.
Cont. straight in patt. until work measures 48(50:51:51) cm. 19(19½:20:20) in. or required length.

Shape Top
Cast off 6 sts. at beg. of next 2 rows.
Cast off 2 sts. at beg. of every row until 42(46:46:50) sts. rem.
Cast off.

NECKBAND

Sew up left shoulder seam.
With 2¾mm. needles pick up and k.46 (49:49:56) sts. from back of neck, 32 sts. from shaped left front neck edge, 14(15: 15:16) sts. from centre front and 32 sts. from shaped right front neck edge. [124 (128:128:136) sts.]
Work 13 rows in twist rib.
Cast off in twist rib.

MAKING UP

Sew up right shoulder seam, including neckband.
Sew up side and sleeve seams.
Set in sleeves.
Turn neckband in half onto wrong side and stitch.
Press lightly.

Sweater with Cabled Cross-stitch

Round-neck sweater in stocking stitch with cable crosses on yoke and cuff, with set-in sleeves and shoulder buttoning

★★ Suitable for knitters with some previous experience

MATERIALS

Yarn
Wendy Ascot 4 ply
3(4:4) × 50g. balls

Needles
1 pair 3mm.
1 pair 3¼mm.
1 cable needle
1 crochet hook
st. holder

Buttons
3

MEASUREMENTS

Chest
56(61:66) cm.
22(24:26) in.
2/3(4/5:6/7) approx. age

Length
36(39:42) cm.
14(15¼:16½) in.

Sleeve Seam
23(26:29) cm.
9(10¼:11¼) in.

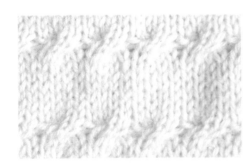

TENSION

28 sts. and 36 rows = 10 cm. (4 in.) square over st. st. on 3¼mm. needles. If your tension square does not correspond to these measurements, see page 156 for adjustment instructions.

ABBREVIATIONS

k. = knit; p. = purl; st(s). = stitch(es); inc. = increas(ing) (see page 156); dec. = decreas(ing) (see page 157); beg. = begin(ning); rem. = remain(ing); rep. = repeat; alt. = alternate; tog. = together; sl. = slip (transfer one stitch from left needle, knitwise unless otherwise stated, to right hand needle.); cont. = continue; patt. = pattern; foll. = following; folls. = follows; mm. = millimetres; cm. = centimetres; in. = inches; st. st. = stocking st.: one row k., one row p.; g. st. = garter st.: every row k.; incs. = increases; decs. = decreases; C4 = cable 4: sl. the next 2 sts. onto cable needle and hold at back of work, k.2 sts., k. sts. from cable needle.

BACK

Cast on 77(82:87) sts. with 3mm. needles.
1st row (right side): p.2, * k.3, p.2, rep. from * to end.
2nd row: k.2, * p.3, k.2, rep. from * to end.
Rep. these 2 rows for 4 cm. (1½ in.), ending with a right side row.
Inc. 7(10:13) sts. evenly across next row. [84(92:100) sts.]
Change to 3¼mm. needles.
Beg. with a k. row, work 10 rows in st. st.
Cable row: k.18(20:22), * C4, k.18(20:22), rep. from * twice.
St. st. 11(13:15) rows.
Cable row: k.7(8:9), * C4, k.18(20:22), rep. from * twice, C4, k.7(8:9).
St. st. 11(13:15) rows.
Rep. the last 24(28:32) rows once.
Cable row: k.18(22:26), (C4) 12 times, k.18(22:26).
St. st. 7 rows.

Shape Armholes

Cast off 4(5:6) sts. at beg. of next 2 rows. [76(82:88) sts.]
Dec. 1 st. at both ends of next 4 right side rows working (C4) 12 times across centre 48 sts. on the first of these rows. [68(74:80) sts.]
Work 3 rows straight.

Next row: k.10(13:16), (C4) 12 times, k.10(13:16).
Work 9 rows straight.
Cable row: k.2(1:4), (C4) 16(18:18) times, k.2(1:4).
St. st. 9 rows.
Cont. in patt. as set on the last 10 rows until armholes measure 13(14:14) cm. (5(5½:5½) in.), ending with a wrong side row.

Shape Shoulders

Cast off 6(7:8) sts. at beg. of each of next 4 rows and 7 sts. at beg. of foll. 2 rows.
Leave rem. 30(32:34) sts. on a spare needle, until needed for neckband.

FRONT

Work as for back until front measures 6 rows less than back to beg. of shoulder shaping, ending with a wrong side row. [68(74:80) sts.]

Shape Neck

Next row: patt. 24(26:28), turn and work on these sts. leaving rem. 44(48:52) sts. on a spare needle.
Dec. 1 st. at neck edge on next 5 rows. [19(21:23) sts.]

Shape Shoulder

Cast off 6(7:8) sts. at beg. of next row and foll. alt. row.
Work 1 row straight.
Cast off rem. 7 sts.
Next row: with right side of work facing sl. centre 20(22:24) sts. onto holder and rejoin yarn to first of rem. 24(26:28) sts., patt. to end.
Complete to match first side.

SLEEVES

Cast on 52(56:60) sts. with 3mm. needles.
1st row: k.
2nd row: p.
Cable row: k.2, (C4) 12(13:14) times, k.2.
St. st. 9 rows then rep. cable row.
P. 1 row.
Change to 3¼mm. needles.
Inc. row: k.1(3:5), * inc., k.6, rep. from * 6 times, inc., k.1(3:5). [60(64:68) sts.]
Beg. with a p. row, work straight in st. st. until sleeve measures 23(26:29) cm. (9(10¼:11¼) in.), ending with a p. row.

Shape Top

Cast off 4(5:6) sts. at beg. of next 2 rows.

Now dec. 1 st. at both ends of every right side row until 32 sts. rem. on all sizes.
P. 1 row.
Dec. 1 st. at both ends of next 8 rows.
Cast off rem. 16 sts.

NECKBAND

Sew up right shoulder seam.
With right side of work facing and 3mm. needles, pick up and k. 17 sts. down left front neck, k. across 20(22:24) sts. at centre front, pick up and k. 17 sts. up right front neck then k. across 30(32:34) sts. of back neck. [84(88:92) sts.]
P. 1 row.
Cable row: (C4) 21(22:23) times.
Work 5 rows in p.2, k.2 rib then rep. cable row.
P. 1 row.
Cast off.

MAKING UP

Sew up left shoulder seam for 3 cm. (1¼ in.) from armhole edge.
Set in sleeves.
Sew up side and sleeve seams.
Work 1 row of double crochet (see page 162) across left back shoulder.
Work 1 row of double crochet across left front shoulder making 3 button loops.
Sew 3 buttons to back shoulder to correspond with button loops.

Raised Pattern Sweater

1960

Short- or long-sleeved sweater with raised pattern bands, raglan sleeves and ribbed welts

★ Suitable for beginners

MATERIALS

Yarn
Yarnworks Cotton
Short Sleeved Version:
3(4:4:5) × 50g. balls
Long Sleeved Version:
4(5:5:6) × 50g. balls

Needles
1 pair 3¼mm.
1 pair 4mm.

MEASUREMENTS

Chest
46(51:56:61) cm.
18(20:22:24) in.
6 months/1(1/2:2/3:4/5) approx. age

Length
27(30:34:38) cm.
10½(11¾:13¼:15) in.

Sleeve Seam
Short version:
5(5:5:5) cm.
2(2:2:2) in.

Long version:
19(22:24:27) cm.
7½(8½:9½:10½) in.

TENSION

20 sts. and 30 rows = 10 cm. (4 in.) square over patt. on 4mm. needles. If your tension square does not correspond to these measurements, see page 156 for adjustment instructions.

ABBREVIATIONS

k. = knit; p. = purl; st(s). = stitch(es); inc. = increas(ing) (see page 156); dec. = decreas(ing) (see page 157); beg. = begin(ning); rem. = remain(ing); rep. = repeat; alt. = alternate; tog. = together; sl. = slip (transfer one stitch from left needle, knitwise unless otherwise stated, to right hand needle.); cont. = continue; patt. = pattern; foll. = following; folls. = follows; mm. = millimetres; cm. = centimetres; in. = inches; st. st. = stocking st.: one row k., one row p.; g. st. = garter st.: every row k.; incs. = increases; decs. = decreases; t.b.l. = through back of loops.

BACK

Cast on 49(55:59:65) sts. with 3¼mm. needles.
1st row (right side): k.1 t.b.l., * p.1 t.b.l., k.1 t.b.l., rep. from * to end.
2nd row: p.1 t.b.l., * k.1 t.b.l., p.1 t.b.l., rep. from * to end.
These 2 rows form rib, rep. for 4 cm. (1½ in.), ending with a wrong side row.
Change to 4mm. needles, beg. patt. as folls.:
1st row (right side): k.
2nd row: p.
3rd row: k.
4th row: k. t.b.l.
5th row: k.
6th row: p.1, * k.1, p.1, rep. from * to end.
7th row: k.
8th row: k.1, * p.1, k.1, rep. from * to end.
9th row: k.
10th row: k. t.b.l.
These 10 rows form patt.
Work in patt. until back measures 16(19: 22:24) cm. (6¼(7½:8½:9½) in.) from beg., ending with a wrong side row.

Shape Raglan
Cast off 3 sts. at beg. of next 2 rows.
Dec. 1 st. at each end of next row then every foll. 4th row 5(2:2:2) times more. [31(43:47:53) sts.]
Dec. 1 st. at each end of every foll. alt. row 5(11:12:15) times. [21(21:23:23) sts.]
Work 1 row.
Break yarn, leave these sts. on holder.

FRONT

Work as for back.

SLEEVES

Short version only:
Cast on 41(43:43:45) sts. with 3¼mm. needles.
Work 4 rows in rib as for back.
Change to 4mm. needles.

Work in patt. as for back until sleeve measures 5 cm. (2 in.) from beg., ending with same patt. row as back to armhole.

Shape Raglan
Cast off 3 sts. at beg. of next 2 rows.
Dec. 1 st. at each end of next and every foll. 4th row 4(3:4:6) more times. [25(29:27:25) sts.]
Dec. 1 st. at each end of every foll. alt. row 5(7:6:5) times. [15 sts.]

Shape Neck
Next row: patt. 7, cast off 1 st., patt. to end.
Next row: patt. 7, join in a 2nd ball of yarn, and patt. rem. 7 sts.
Working both sides at same time with separate balls of yarn, and, keeping raglan edge straight, dec. 1 st. at neck edge on next 4 rows [3 sts. at each side of neck].
Cast off.

Long version only:
Cast on 29(31:33:35) sts. with 3¼mm. needles.
Work 4 cm. (1½ in.) in rib as for back, ending with a wrong side row.
Change to 4mm. needles and work in patt as for back AT THE SAME TIME inc. 1 st. at each end of 3rd and every foll. 6th(6th:10th:10th) row 5(5:4:4) more times. [41(43:43:45) sts.]
Cont. straight in patt. until sleeve measures 19(22:24:27) cm. (7½(8½:9½: 10½) in.) from beg., ending with same patt. row as back to armhole.

Shape Raglan and Neck
Work as for short version of sleeve.

NECKBANDS

Back Neckband
With 3¼mm. needles, pick up and k. 11 sts. from half of sleeve top, k.21(21:23:23) sts. from back neck, pick up and k. 11 sts. from half of other sleeve top. [43(43:45: 45) sts.]
Beg. with a 2nd rib row, work 5 rows in rib.
Cast off in rib.

Front Neckband
Work as for back neckband.

MAKING UP

Sew up side and sleeve seams.
Sew up raglans.
Overlap neckbands at shoulders and sew straight edges along shaped edges of shoulders.

Rugged, Two-colour Ski Sweater 1958

Thick, stocking stitch sweater with horizontally-knitted stripes on body and sleeves, circular-knitted yoke and ribbed welts and collar

★ Suitable for adventurous beginners

MATERIALS

Yarn
Yarn Store Natural British Wool
3(4:4) × 100g. hanks Main Col. A
3(4:4) × 100g. hanks Col. B

Needles
1 pair 4mm.
1 pair 5½mm.
1 circular 5½mm.
1 set of 4 double-pointed 4mm.
1 set of 4 double-pointed 5½mm.

MEASUREMENTS

Bust
87(92:97) cm.
34(36:38) in.

Length
60(60:62) cm.
23¾(23¾:24¼) in.

Sleeve Seam
44(45:46) cm.
17¼(17¾:18) in.

TENSION

17 sts. and 21 rows = 10 cm. (4 in.) square over st. st. on 5½mm. needles. If your tension square does not correspond to these measurements, see page 156 for adjustment instructions.

ABBREVIATIONS

k. = knit; p. = purl; st(s). = stitch(es); inc. = increas(ing) (see page 156); dec. = decreas(ing) (see page 157); beg. = begin(ning); rem. = remain(ing); rep. = repeat; alt. = alternate; tog. = together; sl. = slip (transfer one stitch from left needle, knitwise unless otherwise stated, to right hand needle.); cont. = continue; patt. = pattern; foll. = following; folls. = follows; mm. = millimetres; cm. = centi- metres; in. = inches; st. st. = stocking st.: one row k., one row p.; g. st. = garter st.: every row k.; incs. = increases; decs. = decreases.

NB Body and sleeves are worked vertically.

BACK

Cast on 60(60:63) sts. with 5½mm. needles and A to form underarm edge.
Work in stripe patt. as folls.:
1st row: k. in A.
2nd row: p. in A.
3rd row: k. in B.
4th row: p. in B.
These 4 rows form stripe patt.
Work straight in stripe patt. for 48(51:53) cm. (18¾(20:20¾) in.)
Cast off.

Waist Rib
With 4mm. needles and B, and right side facing, pick up and k.88(92:98) sts. along one long edge.
Work in k.1, p.1 rib for 6 cm. (2¼ in.)
Cast off in rib.

TOP

With 5½mm. needles and A and right side facing, pick up and k. 87(92:97) sts. along upper edge.

Chart 1

Chart 2

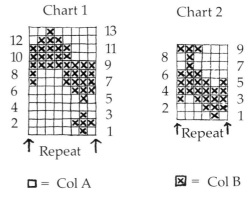

□ = Col A   ☒ = Col B

P. 1 row.
Break off A. Join in B and work in st. st. Cast off 5 sts. at beg. of next 2 rows. Sl. rem. 77(82:87) sts. onto a spare needle to be worked later for yoke.

FRONT

Work as for back.

SLEEVES

Cast on 8(10:12) sts. with 5½mm. needles and A for underarm section of sleeve seam.
Working in stripe patt. as on back, cast on 7 sts. at beg. of every p. row 8 times. [64(66:68) sts.]
Cont. straight until work measures 24(25:26) cm. (9½(9¾:10¼) in.) from last cast-on sts., ending with a k. row.
Cast off 7 sts. at beg. of every p. row 8 times.
K. 1 row.
Cast off rem. 8(10:12) sts.

CUFFS

With 4mm. needles and B and right side facing, pick up and k.46(46:48) sts. from cuff edge.
Work in k.1, p.1 rib for 6 cm. (2¼ in.)

Cast off in rib.

TOP

With 5½mm. needles and A and right side facing, pick up and k.69(72:75) sts. across top edge.
P. 1 row.
Break off A.
Join in B and work in st. st., casting off 5 sts. at beg. of next 2 rows.
Leave rem. 59(62:65) sts. on spare needle.

YOKE

With right side facing, sl. 77(82:87) sts. of back, 59(62:65) sts. of one sleeve, 77(82:87) sts. of front and 59(62:65) sts. of other sleeve onto circular needle. [272(288:304) sts.]
With A, work as folls.:
1st round: k.
2nd round: ** k.6(3:9), * k.2 tog., k.9(7:5), rep. from * 10(14:18) more times, k.2 tog., k.7(4:8), rep. from ** once more. [248(256:264) sts.]
3rd round: k.
4th round: k.
5th round: ** k.3(6:7), * k.2 tog., k.3, rep. from * 22 more times, k.2 tog., k.4(5:8), rep. from ** once more. [200(208:216) sts.]
6th round: k.

7th to 19th rounds: work from chart 1, reading chart from right to left each time.
20th round: with A only, k.
21st round: * k.2 tog., k.2, rep. from * to end of round. [150(156:162) sts.]
22nd to 30th rounds: work from chart 2. Cont. with A.
31st round: k.
32nd round: k., dec. 20 sts. evenly spaced across round. [130(136:142) sts.]
33rd round: k.
34th round: with 5½mm. double-pointed needles, work as 32nd round. [110(116: 122) sts.]
35th round: with 4mm. double-pointed needles, k.
36th round: as 32nd. [90(96:102) sts.]
37th round: k.
Break off A.

Turtle Neck

Join in B and k.1 round, dec. 6(6:6) sts. evenly. [84(90:96) sts.]
Work 5 cm. (2 in.) in k.1, p.1 rib.
Change to 5½mm. needles and cont. in rib for 7 cm. (2¾ in.).
Cast off in rib.

MAKING UP

Sew up side and sleeve seams. Press lightly.

Duck-pattern Shirt

Long- or short-sleeved fitting shirt in stocking stitch with contrasting, embroidered duck design, ribbed collar and welts

★★ Suitable for knitters with some previous experience

MATERIALS

Yarn
Patons Clansman 4 ply
2(3:3) × 50g. balls Main Col. A
1(1:1) × 50g. ball Col. B
Oddments of yarn Col. C

Needles
1 pair 2¾mm.
1 pair 3¼mm.

Buttons
6 small

MEASUREMENTS

Chest
46(51:56) cm.
18(20:22) in.
6 months/1(1/2:2/3) approx. age

Length
30(33:38) cm.
11¾(13:15) in.

Short Sleeve Seam
7(9:10) cm.
2¾(3½:4) in.

Long Sleeve Seam
19(21:24) cm.
7½(8¼:9½) in.

TENSION

28 sts. and 36 rows = 10 cm. (4 in.) square over st. st. on 3¼mm. needles. If your tension square does not correspond to these measurements, see page 156 for adjustment instructions.

ABBREVIATIONS

k. = knit; p. = purl; st(s). = stitch(es); inc. = increas(ing) (see page 156); dec. = decreas(ing) (see page 157); beg. = begin(ning); rem. = remain(ing); rep. = repeat; alt. = alternate; tog. = together; sl. = slip (transfer one stitch from left needle, knitwise unless otherwise stated, to right hand needle.); cont. = continue; patt. = pattern; foll. = following; folls. =

follows; mm. = millimetres; cm. = centimetres; in. = inches; st. st. = stocking st.: one row k., one row p.; g. st. = garter st.: every row k.; incs. = increases; decs. = decreases; m.1 = make 1 st.: pick up horizontal loop lying before next st. and work into the back of it; y.fwd. = yarn forward; y.b. = yarn back.

NB Twist yarns on wrong side of work when changing col. to avoid a hole.

BACK

** Cast on 65(73:79) sts. with 2¾mm. needles and B.
K. 1 row.
Join in A, and work in border patt. as folls.:
1st row (right side): k.2B, * with A y.fwd., p.1, y.b., k.1B, rep. from * to last st., k.1B.
2nd row: k.1B, * p.1B, with A y.b., k.1, y.fwd., rep. from * to last 2 sts., p.1B, k.1B.
These 2 rows form patt.

Cont. in patt. until work measures 4(4:5) cm. (1½(1½:2) in.), ending with a 2nd row.
Break B.
Next row: with A, k.
Next row: p.5(6:7), m.1, * p.9(10:8), m.1, rep. from * to last 6(7:8) sts., p.6(7:8). [72(80:88) sts.]
Change to 3¼mm. needles and st. st.
Beg. with a k. row, work straight until back measures 20(23:25) cm. (7¾(9:9¾) in.) from beg., ending with a p. row.

Shape Armholes
Cast off 4 sts. at beg. of next 2 rows.
Now dec. 1 st. at each end of next and every alt. row until 52(56:60) sts. rem.
Work 1 row straight. **

Divide for Opening
Next row: k.24(26:28) sts., turn, leave rem. sts. on a spare needle.
Next row: cast on 4 sts., k.4, p. to end. [28(30:32) sts.]
Now, cont. in st. st., k.4 sts. at inside edge on every row, until back measures 30(33:38) cm. (11¾(13:15) in.) from beg., ending with a wrong side row.

Shape Shoulder
Cast off 4(5:4) sts. at beg. of next row.
Cast off 4(4:5) sts. at beg. of foll. 2 alt. rows.
Cast off rem. 16(17:18) sts.
With right side facing, rejoin yarn to rem. 28(30:32) sts., k. to end.
Next row: p. to last 4 sts., k.4.
Make 1st buttonhole in next row as folls.: k.2, y.fwd., k.2 tog., k. to end.
Complete to match 1st side with the addition of 5 more buttonholes, worked on every foll. 4th row.

FRONT
Work as for back from ** to **.
Cont. straight until front measures 27(30:34) cm. (10½(11¾:13¼) in.) from

beg., ending with a wrong side row.

Divide for Neck
Next row: k.20(21:22) sts., turn, and leave rem. sts. on a spare needle.
Cont. on these 20(21:22) sts. for 1st side, dec. 1 st. at neck edge on every row until 12(13:14) sts. rem.
Work straight until front matches back armhole edge, ending with a wrong side row.
Now shape shoulder as for back.
With right side facing, rejoin yarn to rem. sts., cast off centre 12(14:16) sts., k. to end.
Complete to match first side.

SHORT SLEEVES
Cast on 45(49:53) sts. with 2¾mm. needles and B.
K. 1 row.
Beg. with a 1st row, work 4(4:5) cm. (1½(1½:2) in.) in border patt. as for back, ending with a 2nd row.
Break B.
Next row: with A, k.
Next row: with A, p.4, m.1, * p.9(10:11), m.1, rep. from * to last 5 sts., p.5. [50(54:58) sts.]
Change to 3¼mm. needles and, beg. with a k. row, work straight in st. st. until sleeve seam measures 7(9:10) cm. (2¾(3½:4) in.), ending with a p. row.

Shape Top
*** Cast off 4 sts. at beg. of next 2 rows.
Now dec. 1 st. at each end of next and every alt. row until 38 sts. rem.
Work 1 row straight.
Now dec. 1 st. at each end of every row until 14 sts. rem.
Cast off. ***

LONG SLEEVES
Cast on 39(43:47) sts. with 2¾mm. needles and B.
K. 1 row.

Beg. with a 1st row, work 4(4:5) cm. (1½(1½:2) in.) in border patt, as for back, ending with a 2nd row.
Break B.
Next row: with A, k.
Next row: with A, p., inc. 1 st. at end of row. [40(44:48) sts.]
Change to 3¼mm. needles and, beg. with a k. row, work in st. st., shaping sides by inc. 1 st. at each end of 5th(1st:5th) and every foll. 10th(12th: 12th) row until there are 50(54:58) sts.
Cont. straight until sleeve seam measures 19(21:24) cm. (7½(8¼:9½) in.), ending with a p. row.

Shape Top
Work as for short sleeves from *** to ***.

COLLAR
Cast on 55(59:63) sts. with 2¾mm. needles and B.
K. 1 row.
Now, beg. with a 1st row, work 5(6:7) cm. (2(2¼:2¾) in.) in border patt. as for back.
Cast off.
Make another piece in the same way.

MAKING UP
Press work lightly on wrong side, taking care not to spoil patt.
Using chart, embroider 1 large and 4 small ducks across front of sweater, feet of ducks to come 2(3:4) cm. (¾(1¼:1½) in.) above end of border patt.
Work bodies in B.
Work eyes, legs and beaks in C.
Sew up shoulder, side and sleeve seams.
Set in sleeves.
Sew cast-off edge of each collar piece round neck, beg. at centre front and ending in centre of back opening border.
Sew cast-on edge of button border neatly behind buttonhole border.
Press all seams.
Sew on buttons.

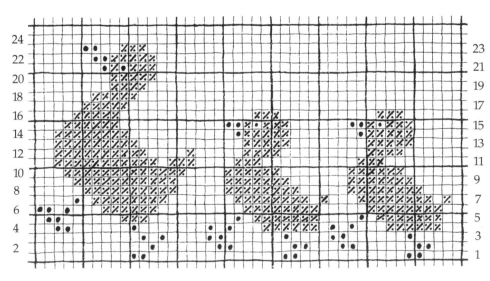

□ = Col A
🖾 = Col B
▣ = Col C

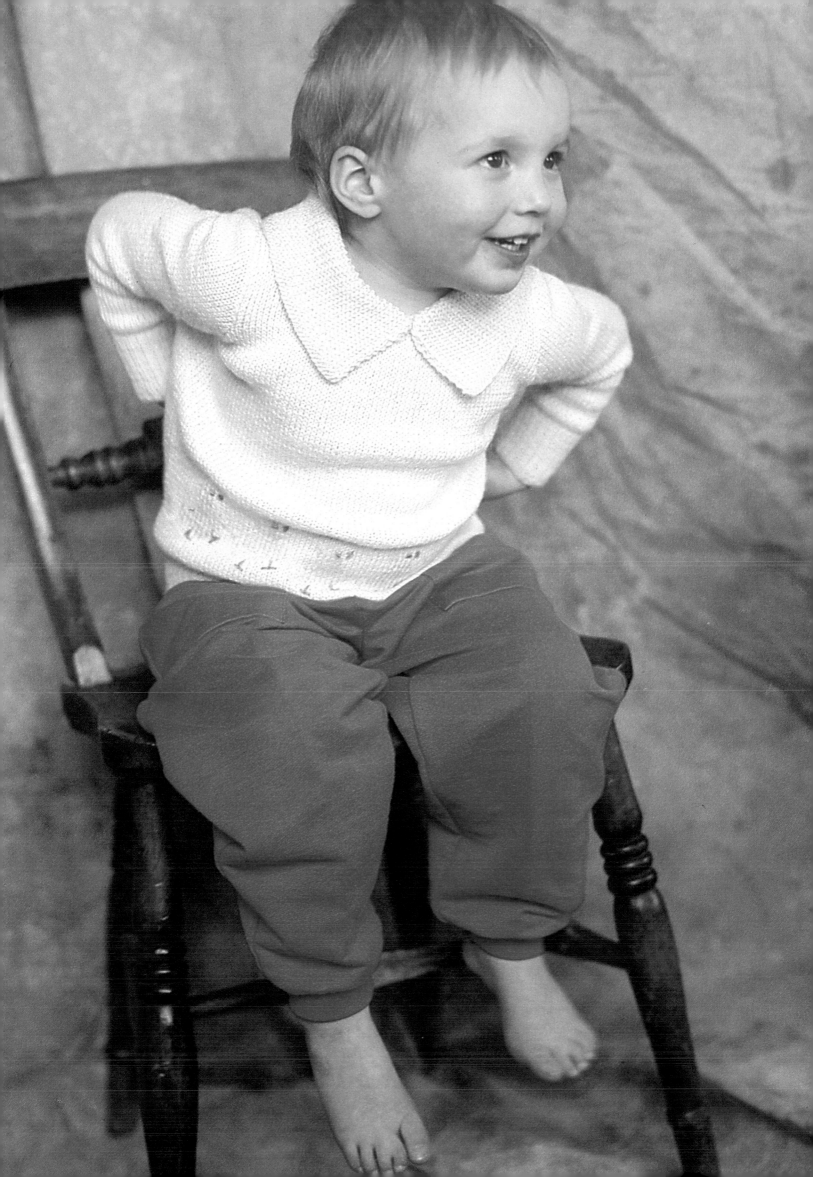

Broken Cable Heavyweight Sweater 1949

Hip-length sweater in broken cable pattern with ribbed welts

★★ Suitable for knitters with some previous experience

MATERIALS

Yarn
Sirdar Talisman DK
14(14:15) × 50g. balls

Needles
1 pair 3¼mm.
1 pair 4mm.
1 cable needle
st. holders

MEASUREMENTS

Chest
97(102:107) cm.
38(40:42) in.

Length
66(68:70) cm.
26(26¾:27½) in.

Sleeve Seam
46(49:50) cm.
18(19¼:19½) in.

TENSION

30 sts. and 30 rows = 10 cm. (4 in.) square over patt. on 4mm. needles. If your tension square does not correspond to these measurements, see page 156 for adjustment instructions.

ABBREVIATIONS

k. = knit; p. = purl; st(s). = stitch(es); inc. = increas(ing) (see page 156); dec. = decreas(ing) (see page 157); beg. = begin(ning); rem. = remain(ing); rep. = repeat; alt. = alternate; tog. = together; sl. = slip (transfer one stitch from left needle, knitwise unless otherwise stated, to right hand needle.); cont. = continue; patt. = pattern; foll. = following; folls. = follows; mm. = millimetres; cm. = centimetres; in. = inches; st. st. = stocking st.: one row k., one row p.; g. st. = garter st.: every row k.; incs. = increases; decs. = decreases; CR2R = sl. next 2 sts. on cable needle and leave at back, k.2, then p.2 from cable needle; CR2L = sl. next 2 sts. on cable needle and leave at front, p.2, then k.2 from cable needle; m.1 = make 1 st.: pick up horizontal loop lying before next st. and k. into the back of it.

BACK

Cast on 120(124:128) sts. with 3¼mm. needles.
Work in k.2, p.2 rib for 8(10:12) cm. (3¼(4:4¾) in.), ending with a wrong side row.
Next row: rib 2(2:1) m.1, (rib 3, m.1) 39(40:42) times, rib to end. [160(165:161) sts.]

1st size: p. next row. [160 sts.]
2nd size: p. next row, inc. 3 sts. evenly across row. [168 sts.]
3rd size: p. next row, inc. 3 sts. evenly across row. [174 sts.]
All sizes:
Change to 4mm. needles.
Work in patt. as folls.:
1st row (right side): p.7(4:7), k.6, (p.8, k.6) 10(11:11) times, p.7(4:7).
2nd row: k.7(4:7), p.6, (k.8, p.6) 10(11:11) times, k.7(4:7).
3rd row: as 1st.
4th row: as 2nd.
5th row: p.5(2:5), * CR2R, k.2, CR2L, p.4, rep. from * to end, ending last rep. p.5(2:5).
6th row: k.5(2:5), * (p.2, k.2) twice, p.2, k.4, rep. from * to end, ending last rep. k.5(2:5).
7th row: p.5(2:5), * (k.2, p.2) twice, k.2, p.4, rep. from * to end, ending last rep. p.(5:2:5).
8th, 10th, 12th, 14th, 16th, 18th rows: as 6th.
9th, 11th, 13th, 15th, 17th rows: as 7th.
19th row: p.5(2:5), * CR2L., k.2, CR2R, p.4, rep. from * to end, ending last rep. p.5(2:5).
20th row: as 2nd.
21st row: as 1st.
22nd row: as 2nd.
These 22 rows form patt.
Cont. straight in patt. until back measures 43(44:45) cm. (16¾(17¼:17¾) in.), ending with a wrong side row.

Shape Armholes

Cast off 13(10:13) sts. at beg. of next 2 rows. [134(148:148) sts.] **
Cont. on rem. sts., in patt. as set, until armholes measure 23(24:25) cm. (9(9½:9¾) in.) from cast-off edge of arm-shaping, ending with a wrong side row.

Shape Shoulders

Cast off 44(51:51) sts. at beg. of next 2 rows.
Leave rem. sts. on a holder.

FRONT

Work as for back to **
Cont. on rem. sts. in patt. until armholes measure 17(18:19) cm. (6½(7:7½) in.), ending with a wrong side row.

Shape Neck

Next row: patt. 54(61:61) sts., turn, work on these sts. only.
Sl. rem. sts. onto spare needle.
Dec. 1 st. at neck edge on next 6 rows, then on every foll. alt. row until 44(51:51) sts. rem.
Work a few rows straight on rem. sts. until same number of rows have been worked as for back to shoulder line,

ending with a wrong side row.

Shape Shoulder

Cast off all sts. in patt.
Sl. centre 26 sts. onto holder.
Rejoin yarn to inner end of rem. 54(61:61) sts. and complete to match first side.

SLEEVES

Cast on 60(64:68) sts. with 3¼mm. needles.
Work in k.2, p.2, rib for 8(10:12) cm. (3¼(4:4¾) in.), ending with a wrong side row.
Next row (right side): rib 4(6:8), m.1, (rib 1, m.1) 51(51:53) times, rib to end. [112(116:122) sts.]
1st and 2nd sizes: p. next row.
3rd size: p. next row, inc. 1 st. at each end of this row. [112(116:124) sts.]
Change to 4mm. needles and cont. in patt. as folls.:
1st row (right side): p.4(6:3), k.6 (p.8, k.6) 7(7:8) times, p.4(6:3).
2nd row (wrong side): k.4(6:3), p.6, (k.8, p.6) 7(7:8) times, k.4(6:3).
Cont. on sts. as set, working in patt. as for back.
Inc. 1 st. at each end of every 8th row until there are 140(144:150) sts., working extra sts. into patt.
Work on all sts. in patt. until sleeve measures 50(52:54) cm. (19½(20½:21¼) in.) from cast-on edge, ending with a wrong side row.
Next row: cast off all sts. in patt.

NECKBAND

Sew up right shoulder seam.
With 3¼mm. needles and right side facing, pick up and k. foll. sts., 20 sts. from left side front, 26 sts. from centre front, 20 sts. from right side front and 46 sts. from centre back. [112 sts.]
Work 3 cm. (1¼ in.) in k.2, p.2 rib.
Cast off ribwise.

MAKING UP

Sew up rem. shoulder seam and neck-band seam.
Set in sleeves, sewing last 13(10:13) row-ends of sleeves to cast-off sts. of back and front armhole shaping.
Sew up side and sleeve seams.

Two-colour, Criss-cross Sweater

1982

Raglan-sleeved, allover patterned sweater in two colours with round neck and ribbed welts

★★ Suitable for knitters with some previous experience

MATERIALS

Yarn

Christian de Falbe Pure Wool
11(12:14) × 25g. balls Main Col. A
2 × 25g. balls Col. B

Needles

1 pair 3¼mm.
1 pair 4mm.

MEASUREMENTS

Chest

61(66:71) cm.
24(26:28) in.
4/5(6/7:8/9) approx. age.

Length

38(42:46) cm.
15(16½:18) in.

Sleeve Seam

30(33:35) cm.
11¾(13:13¾) in.

TENSION

13 sts. = 5 cm. (2 in.) and 20 rows = 7 cm. (2¾ in.) over patt. on 4mm. needles. If your tension does not correspond to these measurements, see page 156 for adjustment instructions.

ABBREVIATIONS

k. = knit; p. = purl; st(s). = stitch(es); inc. = increas(ing) (see page 156); dec. = decreas(ing) (see page 157); beg. = begin(ning); rem. = remain(ing); rep. = repeat; alt. = alternate; tog. = together; sl. = slip (transfer one stitch from left needle, knitwise unless otherwise stated, to right hand needle.); cont. = continue; patt. = pattern; foll. = following; folls. = follows; mm. = millimetres; cm. = centimetres; in. = inches; st. st. = stocking st.: one row k., one row p.; g. st. = garter st.: every row k.; incs. = increases; decs. = decreases; T2L = twist 2 sts. left: p. into back of 2nd st. and k. into front of first st., taking both off needle tog.; T2R = twist 2 sts. right: k. into front of 2nd st. and p. into back of first st., taking both off needle tog.; Tw.2 = twist 2 sts.: k. into front of 2nd st., then into front of 1st st., taking both off needle tog.

BACK

Cast on 72(78:84) sts. with 3¼mm. needles and A.
Work 13 rows in k.1, p.1 rib.
1st size only:
Next row: rib 2, (inc. in next st., rib 5) 11 times, inc. in next st., rib 3. [84 sts.]
2nd and 3rd sizes only:
Next row: rib (6:9), (inc. in next st., rib 5) (12:12) times, rib (0:3). [(90:96) sts.]
All sizes:
Change to 4mm. needles and patt., working in A unless given otherwise:
1st row: (k.1, p.4, k.1) 14(15:16) times.
2nd row: (p.1, k.4, p.1) 14(15:16) times.
3rd row: k.1, (p.4, Tw.2) 13(14:15) times, p.4, k.1.
4th row: as 2nd.
5th row: (T2L, p.2, T2R) 14(15:16) times.
6th row: (k.1, p.1, k.1) 28(30:32) times.
7th row: (p.1, T2L, T2R, p.1) 14(15:16) times.
8th row: (k.2, p.2, k.2) 14(15:16) times.
9th row: (p.2, Tw.2, p.2) 14(15:16) times.
10th row: as 8th.
11th row: (p.1, T2R, T2L, p.1) 14(15:16) times.
12th row: as 6th.
13th row: (T2R, p.2, T2L) 14(15:16) times.
14th row: as 2nd.
15th row: as 3rd.
16th row: p. (1B, 4A, 1B) 14(15:16) times.
17th row: k. (1A, 1B, 1A) 28(30:32) times.
18th row: p. (2A, 2B, 2A) 14(15:16) times.
19th row: as 17th.
20th row: as 16th.
These 20 rows form patt.
Cont. in patt. until work measures 23(26:28) cm. (9(10¼:11) in.).

Shape Raglan

Keeping patt. correct, cast off 1 st. at beg. of next 2 rows.
3rd row: work in patt., dec. 1 st. at each end of row.
4th row: as 3rd.
5th row: work straight in patt.
Rep. these 3 rows until 26(28:28) sts. rem.
Leave sts. on holder.

FRONT

Work as for back until 44(46:46) sts. rem.

Shape Neck

Next row: patt. 15 sts., turn and work on

these sts. as folls.:
Cont. to dec. at raglan edge as before, but AT THE SAME TIME dec. 1 st. at neck edge on next 5 alt. rows.
Now dec. at raglan edge only until 2 sts. rem.
Fasten off.
Place centre 14(16:16) sts. on holder.
Rejoin yarn to rem. sts. and work to match first side.

SLEEVES

Cast on 38 sts. with 3¼mm. needles and A.
Work 13 rows in k.1, p.1 rib.
Next row: (inc. in next st., rib 3) 9 times, inc. in next st., rib 1. [48 sts.]
Change to 4mm. needles.
Work in patt., inc. 1 st. at each end of 3rd and every foll. 5th row until there are 66(70:76) sts., working the extra sts. into patt.
Cont. straight until work measures 30(33:35) cm. (11¾(13:13¾) in.), ending on same patt. row as on back at beg. of armhole.

Shape Raglan

Work as for back until 8 sts. rem.
Leave sts. on holder.

NECKBAND

Sew sleeve raglans to front raglan seams using backstitch.

Sew right sleeve raglan to back raglan seam using backstitch.

With 3¼mm. needles and A, k. across 8 sts. of left sleeve, pick up and k. 12 sts. from left front neck, k. across 14(16:16) sts. of front neck, pick up and k.12 sts. from right front neck, k. across 8 sts. of right sleeve and 26(28:28) sts. of back neck. [80(84:84) sts.]

Work 5 cm. (2 in.) in k.1, p.1 rib.

Cast off loosely with a 4mm. needle.

MAKING UP

Sew up rem. raglan seam using backstitch.

Sew up neckband seam using a flat seam.

Sew up side and sleeve seams.

Fold neckband in half to wrong side and slipstitch into place.

Press lightly with damp cloth.

Roll-collar Cotton Sweater 1981

Short cotton sweater in stocking stitch with elbow-length raglan sleeves and narrow rollover collar

★ Suitable for beginners

MATERIALS

Yarn
Twilleys Pegasus Cotton
4(4:5) × 100g. balls

Needles
1 pair 5mm.
1 pair 6½mm.
1 circular 6½mm.

MEASUREMENTS

Bust
87(92:97) cm.
34(36:38) in.

Length
54(57:60) cm.
21¼(22¼:23¾) in.

Sleeve Seam
18 cm.
7 in.

TENSION

8 sts. and 10 rows = 6 cm. (2¼ in.) square over st. st. on 6½mm. needles. If your tension square does not correspond to these measurements, see page 156 for adjustment instructions.

ABBREVIATIONS

k. = knit; p. = purl; st(s). = stitch(es); inc. = increas(ing) (see page 156); dec. = decreas(ing) (see page 157); beg. = begin(ning); rem. = remain(ing); rep. = repeat; alt. = alternate; tog. = together; sl. = slip (transfer one stitch from left needle, knitwise unless otherwise stated,

to right hand needle.); cont. = continue; patt. = pattern; foll. = following; folls. = follows; mm. = millimetres; cm. = centimetres; in. = inches; st. st. = stocking st.: one row k., one row p.; g. st. = garter st.: every row k.; incs. = increases; decs. = decreases.

BACK

Cast on 58(58:62) sts. with 5mm. needles and work 9 rows in k.2, p.2 rib, inc. 0(1:1) st. at each end of last rib row and inc. 0(1:0) st. at centre of last rib row. [58(61:64) sts.]

Change to 6½mm. needles and cont. in st. st. until work measures 36(37:38) cm. (14(14½:15) in.) from beg., ending with a p. row.

Shape Raglans
Cast off 4 sts. at beg. of next 2 rows. [50(53:56) sts.]

Next row: k.2, k.2 tog., k. to last 4 sts., k.2 tog., k.2.

Next row: p. **

Rep. these 2 rows until 22(21:22) sts. rem. Leave sts. on a spare needle.

FRONT

Work as for back to **

Rep. these 2 rows until 30(29:30) sts. rem., ending with a right side row.

Shape Neck
1st row: p. 9 sts., turn.

Cont. to shape raglan as set on back and dec. 1 st. at neck edge on every right side row until 1 st. rem.

Fasten off.

Sl. centre 12(11:12) sts. onto a spare needle to be worked later as collar.

Rejoin yarn to rem. sts. and complete as for 1st side, reversing all shapings.

SLEEVES

Cast on 38(42:46) sts. with 5mm. needles and work 9 rows in k.2, p.2 rib, (for first and second sizes only, inc. 1 st. at each

end of last rib row). [40(44:46) sts.]
Change to 6½mm. needles and work in st. st., but inc. 1 st. at each end of 12th row. [42(46:48) sts.]
Cont. until work measures 18 cm. (7 in.) from beg., ending with a p. row.

Shape Raglans
Cast off 2 sts. at beg. of next 2 rows.
Next row: k.2, k.2 tog., k. to last 4 sts., k.2 tog., k.2.
Next row: p.
Rep. these 2 rows until 10 sts. rem.

Leave sts. on a spare needle.

ROLL COLLAR
Press all pieces, avoiding rib, with a warm iron and damp cloth.
Sew up raglan edges of sleeves to those of front and back.
With right side facing, beg. at right back neck, using 6½mm. circular needle, k. across the 22(21:22) sts. of back neck, 10 sts. of left sleeve, pick up and k.6 sts. along left neck edge, k. across the

12(11:12) sts. of front neck, pick up and k.6 sts. along right neck and then k. across the 10 sts. of right sleeve. [66(64:66) sts.]
K. 16 rounds.
Cast off loosely: collar rolls over to show p. side.
Press all seams and collar on reverse side with warm iron and damp cloth.

MAKING UP
Sew up sleeve and side seams.

Round-neck, Buttoned Playshirt 1948

Stocking stitch shirt with horizontal dash stitch panels, three-buttoned front placket and ribbed welts

★ Suitable for beginners

MATERIALS

Yarn
Phildar Perle 5
3(3:4:4) × 50g. balls

Needles
1 pair 2mm.
1 pair 2¾mm.
1 set of four double-pointed 2mm.

Buttons
4 small

MEASUREMENTS

Chest
51(56:61:66) cm.
20(22:24:26) in.
1/2(2/3:4/5:6/7) approx. age

Length
31(34:37:40) cm.
12¼(13¼:14½:15¾) in.

Sleeve Seam
23(25:29:31) cm.
9(9¾:11¼:12¼) in.

TENSION

30 sts. and 40 rows = 10 cm. (4 in.) square over st. st. with 2¾mm. needles. If your tension square does not correspond to these measurements, see page 156 for adjustment instructions.

ABBREVIATIONS

k. = knit; p. = purl; st(s). = stitch(es); inc. = increas(ing) (see page 156); dec. = decreas(ing) (see page 157); beg. = begin(ning); rem. = remain(ing); rep. = repeat; alt. = alternate; tog. = together;

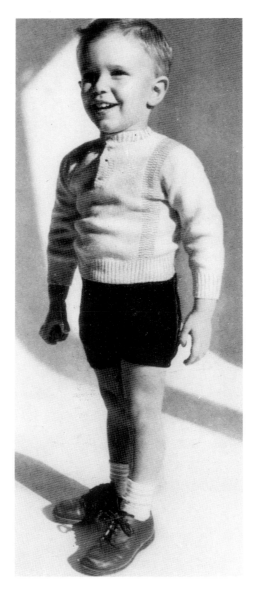

sl. = slip (transfer one stitch from left needle, knitwise unless otherwise stated, to right hand needle.); cont. = continue; patt. = pattern; foll. = following; folls. = follows; mm. = millimetres; cm. = centimetres; in. = inches; st. st. = stocking st.: one row k., one row p.; g. st. = garter st.: every row k.; incs. = increases; decs. = decreases; m.1 = make 1 st.: pick up horizontal loop lying before next st. and work into back of it.

BACK
** Cast on 73(81:89:97) sts. with 2mm. needles and work in rib as folls.:
1st row (right side): k.1, * p.1, k.1, rep. from * to end.
2nd row: p.1, * k.1, p.1, rep. from * to end.
Rep. last two rows for 5 cm. (2 in.), ending with a 1st row.
Inc. row: rib 6(6:4:4), (m.1, rib 6(7:8:9)) 10 times, m.1, rib to end. [84(92:100:108) sts.]
Change to 2¾mm. needles and work in patt. as folls.:
1st row (right side): k.18(21:24:27), p.2, k.44(46:48:50), p.2, k.18(21:24:27).
2nd row: p.15(18:21:24), k.3, p.2, k.3, p.38(40:42:44), k.3, p.2, k.3, p.15(18: 21:24).
These 2 rows form patt.
Work straight in patt. until back measures 20(22:24:26) cm. (7¾(8½:9½: 10¼) in.), ending with a wrong side row.
Shape Armholes
Keeping patt. correct, cast off 4 sts. at beg. of next 2 rows.
Dec. 1 st. at each end of next 3(5:7:9) rows.
Work 1 row.
Dec. 1 st. at each end of next and 0(0:1:1) foll. alt. row. [68(72:74:78) sts.] **

Work straight in patt. until armholes measure 11(12:13:14) cm. (4¼(4¾:5:5½) in.), ending with a wrong side row.

Shape Shoulders

Cast off 5 sts. at beg. of next 6 rows.
Cast off 4 sts. at beg. of next 2 rows.
Cast off rem. 30(34:36:40) sts.

FRONT

Work as for back from ** to **.
Work 1 row, thus ending with a wrong side row.

Divide for Opening

Next row: k.10(11:11:12), p.2, k.26(27: 28:29), leave these sts. on a spare needle. With right side facing, cast on a further 8 sts. for button border and work as folls.:
Next row: k.3, p.2, k.21(22:23:24), p.2, k.10(11:11:12). [38(40:41:43) sts.]
Next row: p.7(8:8:9), k.3, p.2, k.3, p.15(16: 17:18), k.3, p.2, k.3.
Cont. working in patt. as set until front measures 4(4:5:5) cm. (1½(1½:2:2) in.) less than back to beg. of shoulder shaping, ending with a wrong side row.

Shape Neck

Next row: cast off 11 sts., patt. to end.
Dec. 1 st. at neck edge on next 6(8:8:11) rows.
Now dec. 1 st. on every foll. alt. row 2(2:3:2) times. [19 sts.]
Cont. straight in patt. until front matches back to shoulder shaping, ending with a right side row.

Shape Shoulder

Cast off 5 sts. at beg. of next and 2 foll. alt. rows.
Work 1 row.
Cast off rem. sts.
With wrong side facing, rejoin yarn to rem. sts., and work as folls.:
Next row: k.3, p.2, k.3, patt. to end. [38(40:41:43) sts.]
Cont. in patt. as set, working 3 button-holes, 1st to come 1 cm. (½ in.) from beg. of opening, last to come 2 rows from neck, rem. buttonhole midway between, making each buttonhole as folls.:
1st row (right side): patt. to last 6 sts., cast off 3 sts., patt. to end.
2nd row: patt. 3 sts., cast on 3 sts., patt. to end.
Complete to match first side, reversing shapings.

SLEEVES

Cast on 47(51:53:61) sts. with 2mm. needles and work in rib as for back, for 5 cm. (2 in.), ending with a 1st rib row.
Inc. row: rib 3(1:1:3), (m.1, rib 4(6:5:7)) 10(8:10:8) times, m.1, rib to end. [58(60: 64:70) sts.]
Change to 2¾mm. needles and, beg. with a k. row, work in st. st., shaping sides by inc. 1 st. at each end of every 18th(16th:20th:22nd) row 3(4:4:4) times, 3 sts. in from edge. [64(68:72:78) sts.]
Work straight until sleeve measures 23(25:29:31) cm. (9(9¾:11¼:12¼) in.), ending with a p. row.

Shape Top

Cast off 4 sts. at beg. of next 2 rows.
Dec. 1 st. at each end of next and every foll. alt. row until 34(34:34:42) sts. rem.
Dec. 1 st. at each end of every row until 20 sts. rem.
Cast off.

NECK BORDER

Sew up shoulder seams.
With right side facing and set of 2mm. needles, k. up 8 sts. from button border, 22(24:26:28) sts. up right side of neck to shoulder, 35:(39:43:47) sts. across back neck, 22(24:26:28) sts. down left side of neck, and 8 sts. from buttonhole border. [95(103:111:119) sts.]
Work forward and back in rows.

1st row (wrong side): p.2, * k.1, p.1, rep. from * to last st., p.1.
2nd row: k.2, * p.1, k.1, rep. from * to last st., k.1.
Rep. 1st row once more.
1st buttonhole row: rib to last 7 sts., cast off 3 sts., rib to end.
2nd buttonhole row: rib, casting on 3 sts. over those cast off on previous row.
Rib 3 rows.
Cast off evenly in rib.

MAKING UP

Sew up side and sleeve seams.
Set in sleeves.
Sew cast-on edge of button border neatly behind buttonhole border.
Sew on buttons.

Satin-edged Lacy Shawl

Large, fine shawl with satin ribbon edging

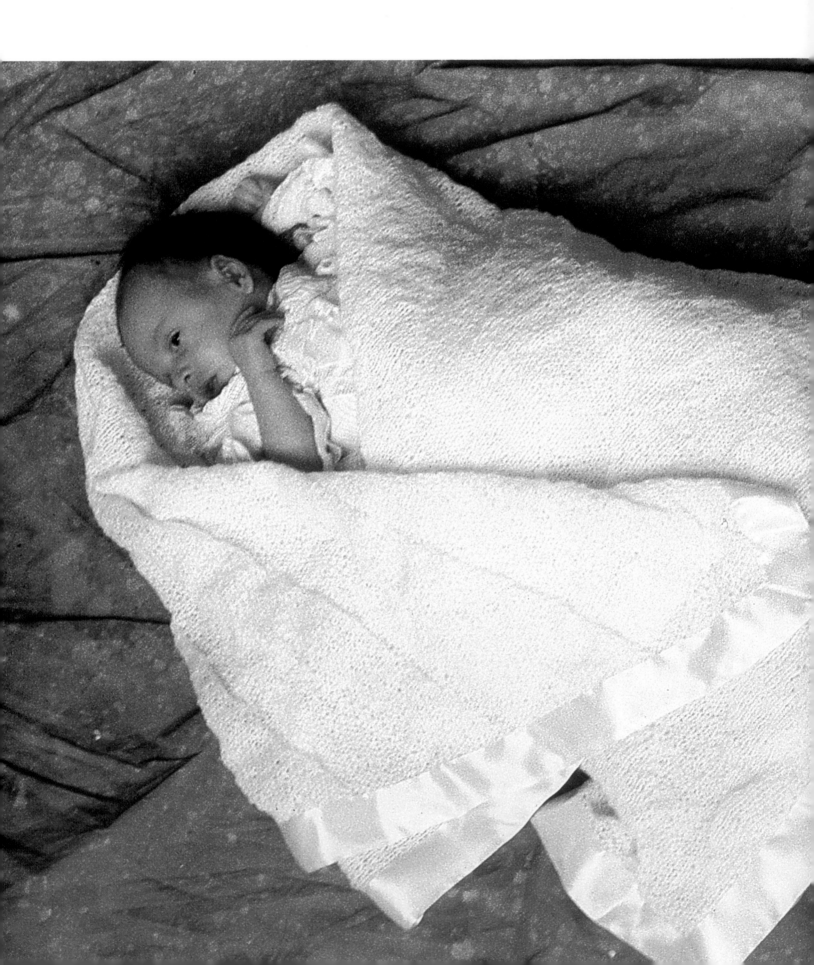

MATERIALS

Yarn
Sunbeam Pure New Wool 3 ply
17 × 25g. balls

Needles
1 pair 5mm. – extra long

Ribbon or blanket binding
5 metres

MEASUREMENTS

123 × 120 cm. approx.
48 × 47 in. approx.

TENSION

24 sts. and 28 rows = 10 cm. (4 in.) square over patt. on 5mm. needles. If your tension square does not correspond to these measurements, see page 156 for adjustment instructions.

ABBREVIATIONS

k. = knit; p. = purl; st(s). = stitch(es); inc. = increas(ing) (see page 156); dec. = decreas(ing) (see page 157); beg. = begin(ning); rem. = remain(ing); rep. = repeat; alt. = alternate; tog. = together; sl. = slip (transfer one stitch from left needle, knitwise unless otherwise stated, to right hand needle.); cont. = continue; patt. = pattern; foll. = following; folls. = follows; mm. = millimetres; cm. = centimetres; in. = inches; st. st. = stocking st.: one row k., one row p.; g. st. = garter st.: every row k.; incs. = increases; decs. = decreases.

TO MAKE

Cast on 288 sts.
1st row (right side): * k.12, p.12, rep. from * to end.
2nd row: as 1st.
3rd row: p.1, * k.12, p.12, rep. from * to last 23 sts., k.12, p.11.
4th and every alt. row: work across sts. as set.
5th row: p.2, * k.12, p.12, rep. from * to last 22 sts., k.12, p.10.
7th row: p.3, * k.12, p.12, rep. from * to last 21 sts., k.12, p.9.
9th row: p.4, * k.12, p.12, rep. from * to last 20 sts., k.12, p.8.
Cont. in this way, moving sts. over by one st. on every alt. row until work measures 120 cm. (47 in.) from beg., ending with a wrong side row.
Cast off loosely.

MAKING UP

Press.
Stitch on the binding all round edge of shawl, forming mitred corners.
Press edges.

Thick Cotton Grandpa Vest

Long, loose, cotton sweater-vest with three-button placket opening from wide, round neck, long sleeves and ribbed welts

★★ Suitable for knitters with some previous experience

MATERIALS

Yarn
Twilleys 100% Cotton Stalite
11(12) × 50g. balls

Needles
1 pair 3mm.
1 pair 3¾mm.
st. holders

Buttons
3×15mm.

MEASUREMENTS

Bust
92(97) cm.
36(38) in.

Length
69(71) cm.
27(27¾) in.

Sleeve Seam
54(55) cm.
21¼(21½) in.

TENSION

24 sts. and 34 rows = 10 cm. (4 in.) square over st. st. on 3¾mm. needles. If your tension square does not correspond to these measurements, see page 156 for adjustment instructions.

ABBREVIATIONS

k. = knit; p. = purl; st(s). = stitch(es); inc. = increas(ing) (see page 156); dec. = decreas(ing) (see page 157); beg. = begin(ning); rem. = remain(ing); rep. = repeat; alt. = alternate; tog. = together; sl. = slip (transfer one stitch from left needle, knitwise unless otherwise stated, to right hand needle.); cont. = continue; patt. = pattern; foll. = following; folls. = follows; mm. = millimetres; cm. = centimetres; in. = inches; st. st. = stocking st.: one row k., one row p.; g. st. = garter st.: every row k.; incs. = increases; decs. = decreases; p.s.s.o. = pass the sl. st. over; t.b.l. = through back of loops; y.fwd. = yarn forward.

BACK

* Cast on 108(114) sts. with 3mm. needles. Work 9 cm. (3½ in.) in k.2, p.2 rib.
Inc. row: K.0(3) sts., * k.6, inc. in next st., rep. from * to last 3(6) sts., k. to end. [123(129) sts.]
Change to 3¾mm. needles.
Beg. p., cont. straight in st. st. until work measures 45 cm. (17¾ in.) from cast-on edge, ending with a p. row.
Fasten off. *

Shape Armholes
Next row: sl. the first 9 sts. onto a st. holder, rejoin yarn, k. to last 9 sts., put these on a st. holder, turn and cont. on rem. 105(111) sts.
Work a further 69(77) rows, thus ending with a p. row.

Shape Neck
Next row: k.45(47) sts., turn.
Cont. on these sts., dec. 1 st. at neck edge on every row as folls.:
1st row: p.2, p.2 tog., p. to end.
2nd row: k. to last 4 sts., k.2 tog., k.2.

Rep. these 2 rows until 34(36) sts. rem. Leave these sts. on st. holder for shoulder seam.
Leave centre 15(17) sts. (for back neck edge) on st. holder.
Rejoin yarn to neck edge of rem. 45(47) sts.
1st row: k.2, sl.1, k.1, p.s.s.o., k. to end.
2nd row: p. to last 4 sts., p.2 tog. t.b.l., p.2.
Complete to match first side.

POCKET LINING

Cast on 21 sts. with 3¾mm. needles.
Work 10 cm. (4 in.) in st. st., ending with a p. row.
Leave sts. on st. holder.

FRONT

Work as for back from * to *.

Shape Armhole
Next row: sl. the first 9 sts. onto a st. holder, k.13. sts., sl. next 21 sts. onto a st. holder, and in place of these k. across 21 sts. of pocket lining, k.15(18) sts., turn.
Working on these 49(52) sts., cont. straight for 33(41) rows.

Shape Neck
Next row: k.43(45) sts., leave rem. 6(7) sts. on a st. holder for neck edge, turn.
1st row: p.
2nd row: k. to last 4 sts., k.2 tog., k.2.
Rep. these 2 rows until 34(36) sts. rem.
Work straight for 28 rows.
Leave sts. on a st. holder for shoulder seam.
Leave centre 7 sts. on a holder for front opening and cont. on rem. 58(61) sts.
Work to match other side of front omitting pocket and working 2nd row as folls. to reverse shapings: k.2, sl.1, k.1, p.s.s.o., k. to end.

BORDERS AND SHOULDER SEAMS

Buttonhole Border
With 3mm. needles and right side facing, rib 7 sts. on holder as folls.:
1st row: k.2 t.b.l., * p.1, k.1 t.b.l., rep. from * once, k.1 t.b.l.

2nd row: k.1 t.b.l., * p.1, k.1 t.b.l., rep. from * to end.
These 2 rows form rib.
Work 6 rows.
Make buttonhole: work 2 sts., y.fwd., k.2 tog., rib to end.
Work 13(17) rows.
Make buttonhole as before.
Work 9(13) rows.
Leave sts. on a st. holder.

Button Border
Cast on 7 sts. with 3mm. needles.
Work 32(40) rows in rib as for buttonhole border, leave on st. holder.

Graft Shoulder Seams
Work each seam as folls.:
Put 34(36) sts. from the back and those from the front onto spare needles.
Place front and back with right sides tog.
Put first st. from front needle onto back needle, k. this and first st. on back needle tog., and leave on right needle.
Rep. once more.
Now cast off first st. put on right needle over second st. put on right needle.
Cont. in this way to end.

Neck Border
With 3mm. needles and right side facing, rib across 7 sts. of button border, k. across 6(7) sts. on front neck st. holder, pick up and k.41 sts. up side front, 1 st. at shoulder seam, 11 sts. down side back, 15(17) sts. on back st. holder, 11 sts. up side back, 1 st. from shoulder seam, 41 sts. down side front, 6(7) sts. on front st. holder and rib across 7 sts. of buttonhole border. [147(151) sts.]
Work 7 rows in k.1, p.1 twisted rib, making a buttonhole on the 4th row.
Cast off in rib.

POCKET TOP

With 3mm. needles, pick up and k.21 sts. on st. holder.
Work 7 rows in k.1, p.1 twisted rib.
Cast off in rib.

SLEEVES

With 3¾mm. needles and right side facing, k.9 sts. from st. holder, 111(115) sts. evenly along armhole edge (centre st. from shoulder seam) and 9 sts. on st. holder. [129(133) sts.]
Now work in st. st., dec. 1 st. at each end of the 2nd and every foll. 4th row.
Dec. row: k.2, sl.1, k.1, p.s.s.o., k. to last 4 sts., k.2 tog., k.2.
Cont. dec. as set until 53(55) sts. rem.
Work 2 rows, dec. 1 st. at end of last row. [52(54) sts.]
Change to 3mm. needles and work 9 cm. (3½ in.) in k.2, p.2, rib.
Cast off loosely in rib.

MAKING UP

With wrong side facing, block and press (see page 160) each piece, omitting ribbing, with a steam iron.
Sew up side and sleeve seams, borders, pocket lining and sides of pocket top.
Sew on buttons.

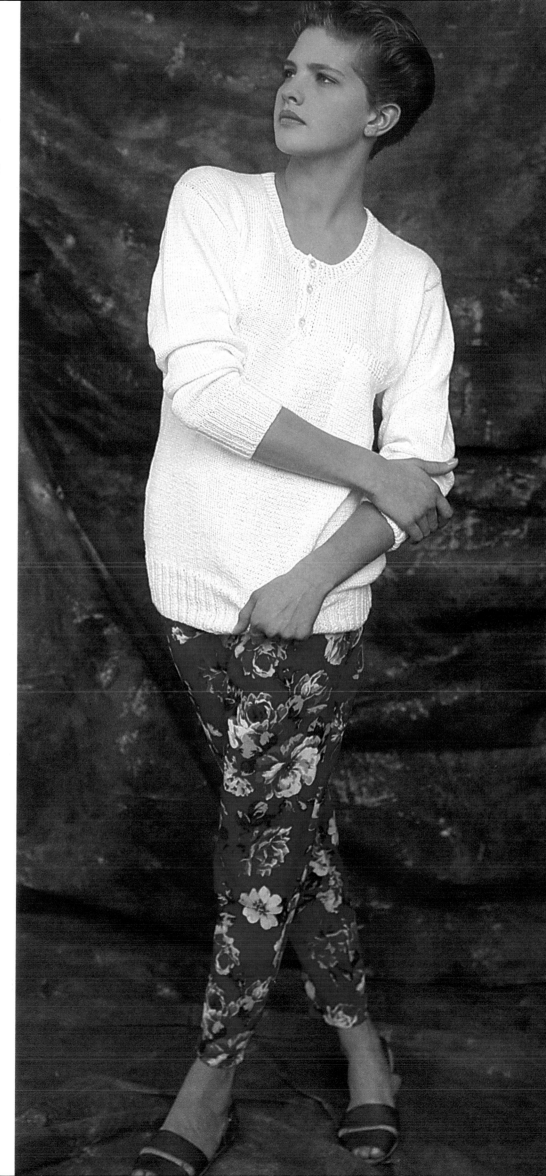

Fisherman's Rib Sloppy Joe

Long, loose fisherman's rib sweater with V-neck, raglan sleeves, ribbed, doubled-over neck border and ribbed welts

★★ Suitable for adventurous beginners

MATERIALS

Yarn
Sirdar Majestic DK
14(15:16) × 50g. balls

Needles
1 pair 3¾mm.
1 pair 4½mm.

MEASUREMENTS

Bust
87(92:97) cm.
34(36:38) in.

Length
71(72:73) cm.
27¾(28¼:28½) in.

Sleeve Seam
43(44:46) cm.
16¾(17¼:18) in.

TENSION

21 sts. and 42 rows = 10 cm. (4 in.) square over patt. on 4½mm. needles. If your tension square does not correspond to these measurements, see page 156 for adjustment instructions.

ABBREVIATIONS

k. = knit; p. = purl; st(s). = stitch(es); inc. = increas(ing) (see page 156); dec. = decreas(ing) (see page 157); beg. = begin(ning); rem. = remain(ing); rep. = repeat; alt. = alternate; tog. = together; sl. = slip (transfer one stitch from left needle, knitwise unless otherwise stated, to right hand needle.); cont. = continue; patt. = pattern; foll. = following; folls. = follows; mm. = millimetres; cm. = centimetres; in. = inches; st. st. = stocking st.: one row k., one row p.; g. st. = garter st.: every row k.; incs. = increases; decs. = decreases; p.s.s.o. = pass the sl. st. over; t.b.l. = through back of loops; k.1blw. = k. 1 st. below: k. next st. lying 1 row below next st. on left needle, slipping st. off needle in usual way after working.

BACK

Cast on 101(107:113) sts. with 3¾mm. needles.
Work in rib as folls.:
1st row: * k.1, p.1, rep. from * to last st., k.1.
2nd row: k.2, * p.1, k.1, rep. from * to last st., k.1.
Work 17 more rows in rib.
Change to 4½mm. needles and work in fisherman's rib as folls.:
1st row (right side): k.
2nd row: k.1, * p.1, k.1blw., rep. from * to last 2 sts., p.1, k.1.
These 2 rows form fisherman's rib patt.
Cont. in patt. until work measures 46 cm. (18 in.), ending with a 2nd row. **

Shape Raglan
Dec. 1 st. at each end of next and every foll. 4th row until 67(71:75) sts. rem.
Now dec. 1 st. at each end of every foll. alt. row until 29(31:33) sts. rem.
Work 1 row.
Leave sts. on a spare needle.

FRONT

Work as for back to **.

Shape Raglan and Divide for Neck
Next row: k.2 tog., k. until there are 49(52:55) sts. on right needle, turn.
Leave rem. sts. on a spare needle.
* Work 3 rows straight.
Dec. 1 st. at raglan edge on next row.
Work 3 rows straight.

Shape Neck
Cont. dec. 1 st. at raglan edge on next and every foll. 4th row, AT THE SAME TIME dec. 1 st. at neck edge on next and every foll. 8th row until 25(27:28) sts. rem.
Cont. to dec. at neck edge on every 8th row from previous dec. and, AT THE SAME TIME, dec. 1 st. at raglan edge on every alt. row until 2 sts. rem.
Work 1 row.
K.2 tog. and fasten off.
Return to rem. sts., leave centre st. on a thread.
Rejoin yarn, k. to last 2 sts., k.2 tog.
Now work to match other side from *.

SLEEVES

Cast on 45(45:49) sts. with 3¾mm. needles.
Work 19 rows in rib as for back.
Change to 4½mm. needles.
Work in patt. as for back, inc. 1 st. at each end of 9th and every foll. 10th row until there are 71(73:75) sts.
Cont. without shaping until sleeve measures 43(44:46) cm. (16¾(17¼:18) in.) ending with a 2nd row.

Shape Raglan
Dec. 1 st. at each end of next and every foll. 4th row until 25(23:21) sts. rem.
Now dec. 1 st. at each end of every foll. alt. row until 11 sts. rem.
Work 1 row.
Leave sts. on safety pin.

NECKBAND

Sew up raglans, leaving back left raglan seam open.
With right side of work facing and 3¾mm. needles, rib across 11 sts. from left sleeve: k.1, (p.1, k.1) 5 times, pick up and k. 58(62:66) sts. down left side of neck, work centre st. on thread, pick up and k.58(62:66) sts. up right side of neck, work across 11 sts. from sleeve as folls.: (k.1, p.1) 5 times, k.1, then work across sts. from back of neck as folls.: * p.1, k.1, rep. from * to last st., p.1.
Next row: rib as set to within 2 sts. of centre st., p.2 tog., p. centre st., p.2 tog. t.b.l., rib to end.
Next row: rib to within 2 sts. of centre st., sl.1, k.1, p.s.s.o., k. centre st., k.2 tog., rib to end.
Rep. last 2 rows 3 more times.
Now work 8 rows, inc. 1 st. at each side of centre st. on every alt. row.
Cast off.

MAKING UP

Sew up raglan and neckband seam.
Fold neckband in half onto inside and catch st. in place.
Sew up side and sleeve seams.

Square-necked, T-shirt Sweater

Stocking stitch sweater with all-in-one cap sleeves, square neck with rib border, and ribbed welts

★ Suitable for adventurous beginners

MATERIALS

Yarn
Wendy Ascot 4 ply
3(3:4:4:4) × 50g. balls

Needles
1 pair 3mm.
1 pair 3¼mm.
1 set of 5 double-pointed 3mm.
2 st. holders

MEASUREMENTS

Chest
61(66:71:76:82) cm.
24(26:28:30:32) in.
4/5(6/7:8/9:10/11:11/12) approx. age

Length
37(40:45:49:52) cm.
14½(15¾:17¾:19¼:20½) in.

TENSION

28 sts. and 36 rows = 10 cm. (4 in.) square over st. st. on 3¼mm. needles. If your tension square does not correspond to these measurements, see page 156 for adjustment instructions.

ABBREVIATIONS

k. = knit; p. = purl; st(s). = stitch(es); inc. = increas(ing) (see page 156); dec. = decreas(ing) (see page 157); beg. = begin(ning); rem. = remain(ing); rep. =

repeat; alt. = alternate; tog. = together; sl. = slip (transfer one stitch from left needle, knitwise unless otherwise stated, to right hand needle.); cont. = continue; patt. = pattern; foll. = following; folls. = follows; mm. = millimetres; cm. = centimetres; in. = inches; st. st. = stocking st.: one row k., one row p.; g. st. = garter st.: every row k.; incs. = increases; decs. = decreases; p.s.s.o. = pass the sl. st. over.

BACK

Cast on 82(90:98:106:114) sts. with 3mm. needles.
Work 8 cm. (3¼ in.) in k.1, p.1 rib, ending with a right side row.
Inc. row: p.2(2:3:3:4), * p. twice into next st., p.10(11:12:13:14), rep. from * 6 times, p. twice into next st., p. to end. [90(98:106:114:122) sts.]
Change to 3¼mm. needles.
Beg. with a k. row, work straight in st. st. until work measures 21(23:27:30:32) cm. (8¼(9:10½:11¾:12½) in.) from cast-on edge, ending with a p. row.

Shape Sleeves
Cast on 2 sts. at beg. of each of the next 10 rows. [110(118:126:134:142) sts.]
Cont. straight in st. st. until straight sleeve edge measures 11(12:13:14:15) cm. (4¼(4¾:5:5½:5¾) in.), ending with a p. row.

Shape Shoulders and Neck
Next row: cast off 7(8:9:10:11) sts., k. until there are 30(32:34:36:38) sts. on needle, turn, leaving rem. sts. on a spare needle.
Work 1 row straight.
** Cast off 6(7:8:9:10) sts. at beg. of next and foll. alt. row.
Work 1 row straight.
Cast off 6 sts. at beg. of next and foll. 2 alt. rows.
With right side facing sl. centre 36(38:40:42:44) sts. onto a holder.
Rejoin yarn to first of the rem. 37(40:43:46:49) sts.
Work 1 row straight.
Next row: cast off 7(8:9:10:11) sts. at beg. of next row.
Work 1 row straight.
Now work as for first side from ** to end.

FRONT

Work as for back until straight sleeve edge measures 8(9:10:11:12) cm. (3¼(3½:

4:4¼:4¾) in.), ending with a p. row. [110(118:126:134:142) sts.]

Shape Neck
Next row: k.37(40:43:46:49) sts., turn, leaving rem. sts. on a spare needle.
Cont. straight in st. st. until sleeve edge measures same as back sleeve, ending at side edge.

Shape Shoulder
Cast off 7(8:9:10:11) sts. at beg. of next row.
Work 1 row straight.
Cast off 6(7:8:9:10) sts. at beg. of next and foll. alt. row.
Work 1 row straight.
Cast off 6 sts. at beg. of next and foll. 2 alt. rows.
With right side facing, sl. centre 36(38:40:42:44) sts. onto a holder.
Rejoin yarn to first of the rem. 37(40:43:46:49) sts.
Work as for first side to end.

NECKBAND

Sew up shoulder seams.
With double-pointed needles, k. up sts. around neck edge as folls.:
1st needle – k.36(38:40:42:44) sts. from holder at back neck edge; 2nd needle – k. up 36 sts. along neck edge of left shoulder; 3rd needle – k. across 36(38:40:42:44) sts. at front neck edge; 4th needle – k. up 36 sts. along neck edge of right shoulder. [144(148:152:156:160) sts.]
Work in rounds of k.1, p.1 rib as folls.:
1st round: 1st needle – sl. 1, k.1, p.s.s.o., * k.1, p1, rep. from * to last 2 sts., k.2 tog.; work across rem. 3 needles in same way.
2nd round: work straight in rib as set on needles.
3rd round: 1st needle – sl.1, k.1, p.s.s.o., rib to last 2 sts., k.2 tog.; work across rem. 3 needles in same way.
Rep. 2nd and 3rd rounds 3 times.
Cast off loosely in rib.

SLEEVE BANDS

With 3mm. needles and right side facing, pick up and k.78(82:84:90:96) sts. along sleeve edge.
Work 9 rows in k.1, p.1 rib.
Cast off loosely in rib.

MAKING UP

Sew up side and sleeve seams.
Press.

Finely Patterned Polo-neck Sweater 1956

Long, loose sweater with generous raglan sleeves, ribbed welts and polo collar, in stocking stitch with patterned stripes

★★ Suitable for knitters with some previous experience

MATERIALS

Yarn
Lister-Lee Motoravia 4 ply
11(12:12:13:14) × 50g. balls

Needles
1 pair of 2¼mm.
1 pair of 3mm.
1 set of double-pointed 2¼mm.
4 st. holders

MEASUREMENTS

Chest
92(97:102:107:112) cm.
36(38:40:42:44) in.

Length
60(63:66:69:72) cm.
23¾(24¾:26:27:28¼) in.

Sleeve Seam
46 cm.
18 in.

TENSION

30 sts. and 40 rows = 10 cm. (4 in.) square over patt. on 3mm. needles. If your tension square does not correspond to these measurements, see page 156 for adjustment instructions.

ABBREVIATIONS

k. = knit; p. = purl; st(s). = stitch(es); inc. = increas(ing) (see page 156); dec. = decreas(ing) (see page 157); beg. = begin(ning); rem. = remain(ing); rep. = repeat; alt. = alternate; tog. = together; sl. = slip (transfer one stitch from left needle, knitwise unless otherwise stated, to right hand needle.); cont. = continue; patt. = pattern; foll. = following; folls. = follows; mm. = millimetres; cm. = centimetres; in. = inches; st. st. = stocking st.: one row k., one row p.; g. st. = garter st.: every row k.; incs. = increases; decs. = decreases; p.s.s.o. = pass the sl. st. over.

BACK

Cast on 160(168:176:184:192) sts. with 2¼mm. needles.
Work 8 cm. (3¼ in.) in k.1, p.1 rib.
Change to 3mm. needles and patt.
1st row (right side): k.3, * k. into front and back of each of next 2 sts., k.6, rep. from * to last 5 sts., k. into front and back of each of next 2 sts., k.3.
2nd row: p.3, * p.2 tog. twice, p.6, rep. from * to last 7 sts., p.2 tog. twice, p.3.

These 2 rows form. patt.
NB When counting sts., disregard the extra sts. inc. in 1st patt. row.
Work in patt. until back measures 35(37:38:39:41) cm. (13¾(14½:15:15¼:16) in.), ending with a 2nd patt. row.

Shape Raglans
Cast off 5 sts. at beg. of next 2 rows.
Dec. 1 st. at each end of next 5 rows.
Work 1 row.
* *9th row*: k.1, k. twice into each of next 2 sts., k.2 tog., work to last 5 sts., sl.1, k.1, p.s.s.o., k. twice into each of next 2 sts., k.1.
10th row: work to end, keeping patt. correct.
Rep. last 2 rows until 48(50:52:54:56) sts. rem.
Leave sts. on holder.

FRONT

Work as for back until 78(80:82:84:86) sts. rem., ending with a p. row.

Shape Neck
1st row: k.1, k. twice into each of next 2 sts., k.2 tog., work until there are 28 sts. on needle (not counting inc. sts.), turn. Finish this side first.
Work 1 row.
3rd row: k.1, k. twice into each of next 2 sts., k.2 tog., work to last 2 sts., k.2 tog.
Rep. last 2 rows until 6 sts. rem., ending with a p. row.
Next row: k.1, k. twice into each of next 2 sts., k.3 tog.
Next row: p.1, p.2 tog. twice, p.1.
Next row: k.1, k. twice into next st., k.2.
Next row: p.2 tog. twice, p.1.

Next row: k.1, k.2 tog.
Cast off.
Sl. centre 20(22:24:26:28) sts. onto holder. Rejoin wool to rem. sts. and work to correspond with first side.

SLEEVES

Cast on 80(80:88:88:96) sts. with 2¼mm. needles.
Work 8 cm. (3¼ in.) in k.1, p.1 rib.
Change to 3mm. needles and patt. as for back.
Work 4 rows.
Inc. 1 st. at each end of next and every 4th row until there are 132(138:144:150:156) sts., taking inc. sts. into patt.
Work straight until sleeve measures 46 cm. (18 in.), ending with a 2nd patt. row.

Shape Raglan Top
Cast off 5 sts. at beg. of next 2 rows.
Dec. 1 st. at each end of next 7(2:9:4:3) rows.
Work 1(0:1:0:1) row, ending with 2nd patt. row.
Now work as for back from * until 18(22:16:20:22) sts. rem.
Leave sts. on holder.

COLLAR

Sew up raglan seams.
With right side of work facing and double-pointed needles, k. up sts. round neck as folls.: (k.1, p.1) across 18(22:16:20:22) sts. of left sleeve, k. up 30 sts. down side of neck, (k.1, p.1) across 20(22:24:26:28) sts. on holder at front, k. up 30 sts. up side of neck, (k.1, p.1) across 18(22:16:20:22) sts. of right sleeve and across 48(50:52:54:56) sts. of back neck. [164(176:168:180:188) sts.]
Work in rounds of k.1, p.1 rib for 15 cm. (5¾ in.).
Cast off loosely in rib.

MAKING UP

Press lightly, avoiding rib.
Sew up side and sleeve seams.

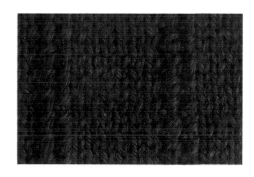

Wide-stripe Sweater

Hip-length, vertically-striped sweater with round neck, tight sleeves, ribbed welts and optional sewn-in shoulder pads

★★ Suitable for knitters with some previous experience

MATERIALS

Yarn
Patons Clansman 4 ply
3(4) × 50g. balls Col. A
4(5) × 50g. balls Col. B

Needles
1 pair 2¾mm.
1 pair 3¼mm.

Shoulder Pads (optional)
2

MEASUREMENTS

Bust
82/87(87/92) cm.
32/34(34/36) in.

Length
63(64) cm.
24¾(25) in.

Sleeve Seam
44(44) cm.
17¼(17¼) in.

TENSION

28 sts. and 36 rows = 10 cm. (4 in.) square over st. st. on 3¼mm. needles. If your tension square does not correspond to these measurements, see page 156 for adjustment instructions.

ABBREVIATIONS

k. = knit; p. = purl; st(s). = stitch(es); inc. = increas(ing) (see page 156); dec. = decreas(ing) (see page 157); beg. = begin(ning); rem. = remain(ing); rep. = repeat; alt. = alternate; tog. = together; sl. = slip (transfer one stitch from left needle, knitwise unless otherwise stated, to right hand needle.); cont. = continue; patt. = pattern; foll. = following; folls. = follows; mm. = millimetres; cm. = centimetres; in. = inches; st. st. = stocking st.: one row k., one row p.; g. st. = garter st.: every row k.; incs. = increases; decs. = decreases.

BACK

Beg. at side edge.

Smaller size only:
** Cast on 63 sts. with A and 3¼mm. needles.
1st row: k.
2nd row: cast on 6 sts., p. to end.
Rep. 1st and 2nd rows twice more.
7th row: inc. in 1st st., k. to end.

8th row: as 2nd.
Now rep. 1st and 2nd rows twice more, and then 7th row once.
Break yarn and leave sts. on spare needle.
Now cast on 8 sts. with A and 3¼mm. needles.
1st row: p.
2nd row: cast on 6 sts., k. to end.
Rep. 1st and 2nd rows 3 more times.
Next row: p. to end, cast on 14 sts., now p. across sts. left on spare needle. [147 sts.]

Larger size only:
** Cast on 65 sts. with B and 3¼mm. needles.
1st row: k.
2nd row: cast on 6 sts., p. to end.
Rep. 1st and 2nd rows twice more.
Join in A.
7th row: with A, inc. in 1st st., k. to end.
8th row: with A, as 2nd.
Now rep. 1st and 2nd rows twice more, and then 7th row once.
Break yarn and leave sts. on spare needle.
Cast on 10 sts. with 3¼mm. needles and B.
1st row: p.
Join in A.
2nd row: with A, cast on 6 sts., k. to end.
3rd row: with A, p.
Rep. 2nd and 3rd rows twice more, and then 2nd row once.
Next row: p. to end, cast on 14 sts., now p. across sts. left on spare needle.
Work 4 rows.
Next row: inc. in 1st st., k. to end.
Work 1 row. [152 sts.]

Both sizes:
Cont. in stripes of 14 rows in B and 14 rows in A.
Work 4 rows.
Inc. 1 st. at beg. of next row, and then on every 6th row until there are 152(157) sts.
Work 5 rows, ending at neck edge. **

Shape Back Neck
Dec. 1 st. at neck edge on the next 4 rows.
Work 51 rows, ending with the 5th row of a B stripe.
Inc. 1 st. at neck edge on the next 4 rows.
*** Work 5 rows.
Dec. 1 st. at beg. of next row, and then every 6th row until 147(151) sts. rem.
Work 3 rows.
Next row: k.101(103) sts., cast off 14 sts., k. to end.
Cont. on last set of 32(34) sts.
1st row: p.
2nd row: cast off 6 sts., k. to end.
Rep. 1st and 2nd rows 3 times more.
Cast off rem. 8(10) sts.
Rejoin yarn to rem. sts.

1st row: cast off 6 sts., p. to end.
2nd row: k.2 tog., k. to end.
3rd row: as 1st.
4th row: k.
Rep. 3rd and 4th rows once more.
7th row: as 1st.
8th row: as 2nd.
Now rep. 3rd and 4th rows twice more.
Cast off rem. 63(65) sts.

FRONT

Work as for back from ** to **.

Shape Neck
Next row: cast off 6 sts., k. to end.
Now dec. 1 st. at neck edge on every row until 138(143) sts. rem., and then on every alt. row until 133(138) sts. rem.
Work 21 rows, thus ending with the 4th row of an A stripe.
Inc. 1 st. at neck edge on the next row, and then every alt. row until there are 139(144) sts.
Now inc. 1 st. at neck edge on every row until there are 146(151) sts.
Next row: cast on 6 sts., k. to end.
Now foll. back instructions from *** to end.

SLEEVES

Beg. at side edge.
Cast on 16 sts. with 3¼mm. needles and A.
1st row: k.
2nd row: cast on 8 sts., p. to last st., inc. 1.
Rep. 1st and 2nd rows 3(4) times more.
Cont. in st. st. and stripes of 14 rows in B and 14 rows in A.
Rep. 1st and 2nd rows 7(6) times more. [115(115) sts.]
Now keeping cuff edge straight, cont. to inc. for sleeve top on every alt. row until there are 118(119) sts. and then every 4th row until there are 122(123) sts.
Work 27 rows, thus ending with the 7th row of a B stripe.
Now dec. for sleeve top on next row, and then every 4th row until 117(118) sts. rem., and then every alt. row until 115(115) sts. rem.
Work 1 row.
Cont. as folls.:
1st row: cast off 8 sts., p. to last 2 sts., p.2 tog.
2nd row: k.
Rep. 1st and 2nd rows 9 times more, and then 1st row once.
Cast off rem. 16 sts.

BACK WELT

With right side of work facing, 2¾mm.

needles and B, k. up 129(139) sts. evenly along lower edge, i.e. 8 sts. for each 9 rows.

1st row: * k.1, p.1, rep. from * to last st., k.1.

2nd row: k.2, * p.1, k.1, rep. from * to last st., k.1.

Rep. 1st and 2nd rows for 8 cm. (3¼ in.). Cast off loosely in rib.

Work front welt to match.

CUFFS

With right side facing, 2¾mm. needles and B, k. up 57(61) sts. across sleeve edge, i.e. approx. 7 sts. for each 9 rows.

Work 8 cm. (3¼ in.) in rib as welts.

Cast off in rib.

MAKING UP

Press each piece lightly.

Sew up right shoulder seam.

Neck Border

With right side facing, 2¾mm. needles and B, k. up 25 sts. down left side of front neck edge, 17 sts. evenly from the 21 rows straight, 24 sts. up right side of neck, and 49 sts. evenly along back neck edge.

Work 9 rows in rib as for welts.

Cast off loosely in rib.

Sew up left shoulder and neck border seam.

Place a marker 18(19) cm. 7(7½ in.) to each side of shoulder seams to mark depth of armholes.

Sew up side and sleeve seams.

Sew sleeves to armhole edges.

Press seams.

Sew shoulder pads into position.

Fold cuffs onto right side.

Sweater with Circular-ribbed Yoke

Simple, long-sleeved sweater in stocking stitch with stand-up collar, ribbed welts and circular-knitted yoke

★★ Suitable for knitters with some previous experience

MATERIALS

Yarn
Wendy Ascot DK
4(4:5:5) × 50g. balls.

Needles
1 pair 3¼mm.
1 pair 3¾mm.
1 set of 4 double-pointed 3¼mm.
1 set of 5 double-pointed 3¾mm.

MEASUREMENTS

Chest
51(56:61:66) cm.
20(22:24:26) in.
1/2(2/3:4/5:6/7) approx. age

Length
36(39:43:46) cm.
14(15¼:16¾:18) in.

Sleeve Seam
22(25:29:33) cm.
8½(9¾:11¼:13) in.

TENSION

24 sts. and 32 rows = 10 cm. (4 in.) square over st. st. on 3¾mm. needles. If your tension square does not correspond to these measurements, see page 156 for adjustment instructions.

ABBREVIATIONS

k. = knit; p. = purl; st(s). = stitch(es); inc. = increas(ing) (see page 156); dec. = decreas(ing) (see page 157); beg. = begin(ning); rem. = remain(ing); rep. = repeat; alt. = alternate; tog. = together; sl. = slip (transfer one stitch from left needle, knitwise unless otherwise stated, to right hand needle.); cont. = continue; patt. = pattern; foll. = following; folls. = follows; mm. = millimetres; cm. = centimetres; in. = inches; st. st. = stocking st.: one row k., one row p.; g. st. = garter st.: every row k.; incs. = increases; decs. = decreases; p.s.s.o. = pass the sl. st. over.

BACK

Cast on 66(72:78:84) sts. with 3¼mm. needles.

Work 14(14:16:18) rows in k.1, p.1 rib.

Change to 3¾mm. needles and beg. with a k. row, work straight in st. st. until work measures 21(23:25:28) cm. (8¼(9: 9¾:11) in.) from cast-on edge, ending with a p. row.

Shape Armholes

Cast off 2(3:4:5) sts. at beg. of next 2 rows.

Work 2 rows straight.

Dec. 1 st. at both ends of next row and every foll. 3rd row until 54(56:58:60) sts. rem.

Work 2(1:2:1) rows straight, thus ending with a p. row.

Leave sts. on spare needle.

FRONT

Work as for back until 58(60:62:64) sts. rem. in armhole shaping, ending with a p.(k.:p.:k.) row.

2nd and 4th sizes only: p. 1 row.

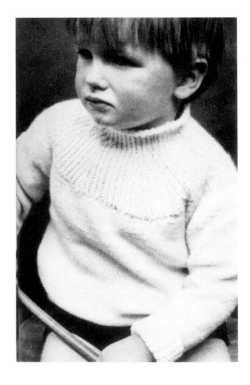

Shape Neck
All sizes:
1st row: k.18, turn.

** Still dec. 1 st. at armhole edge on every 3rd row, cast off 6 sts. at neck edge on next and foll. alt. row.

Work 1 row straight.

Cast off 2 sts. at beg. of next row.

Work 1(0:1:0) row straight then cast off rem. sts.

Sl. centre 22(24:26:28) sts. onto holder and rejoin yarn to first of rem. 18 sts. Work as for first side from ** to end.

SLEEVES

Cast on 36(38:40:42) sts. with 3¼mm. needles and work 14(14:16:18) rows in k.1, p.1 rib.

Change to 3¾mm. needles and beg. with a k. row, work 2 rows in st. st.

Cont. in st. st., inc. 1 st. at both ends of next and every foll. 6th row until there are 52(56:60:64) sts.

Cont. straight in st. st. until sleeve measures 22(25:29:33) cm. (8½(9¾:11¼: 13) in.).

Shape Top

Cast off 2(3:4:5) sts. at beg. of next 2 rows. Work 2 rows straight, then dec. 1 st. at both ends of next row and every foll. 3rd row until 40 sts. rem.

Work 2(1:2:1) rows straight.

Leave sts. on holder.

YOKE

Sew up all four armhole seams.

With right side facing and 3¾mm. double-pointed needles, k. up sts. around neck as folls.:

1st needle – 19 sts. down shaped edge of left front neck, 22(24:26:28) sts. from holder inc. 1 st. in centre, and 19 sts. up right side; 2nd needle – 40 sts. from sleeve inc. 1 st. in centre; 3rd needle – 54(56:58:60) from back, inc. 1 st. in centre; 4th needle – 40 sts. from left sleeve inc. 1 st. in centre. [198(202:206: 210) sts.]

Work 5 rounds in k.1, p.1 rib.

6th round: 1st needle – * sl. 1, k.2 tog., p.s.s.o., rib 17(17:17:19), k.3 tog. **, rib 15(17:19:17), rep. from * to **; 2nd needle – rib to end; 3rd needle – * sl. 1, k.2 tog., p.s.s.o., rib 15(15:15:17), k.3 tog. **, rib 13(15:17:15), rep. from * to **; 4th needle – rib to end.

Work 3 rounds in k.1, p.1 rib.

10th round: 1st needle – * sl.1, k.2 tog., p.s.s.o., rib 13(13:13:15), k.3 tog. **, rib 15(17:19:17), rep. from * to **; 2nd needle – rib 13, sl.1, k.2 tog., p.s.s.o., rib 9, k.3 tog., rib 13; 3rd needle – * sl.1, k.2 tog., p.s.s.o., rib 11(11:11:13), k.3 tog. **, rib 13(15:17:15), rep. from * to **; 4th needle – as 2nd.

Work 3 rounds in k.1, p.1 rib.

14th round: 1st needle – * sl. 1, k.2 tog., p.s.s.o., rib 9(9:9:11), k.3 tog. **, rib 15(17:19:17), rep. from * to **; 2nd needle – rib 11, sl. 1, k.2 tog., p.s.s.o., rib 9, k.3 tog., rib 11; 3rd needle – * sl. 1, k.2 tog., p.s.s.o., rib 7(7:7:9), k.3 tog. **, rib 13(15:17:15), rep. from * to **; 4th needle – as 2nd.

Work 3 rounds in k.1, p.1 rib.

18th round: 1st needle – * sl.1, k.2 tog., p.s.s.o., rib 5(5:5:7), k.3 tog. **, rib 15(17:19:17), rep. from * to **; 2nd needle – rib 9, sl. 1, k.2 tog., p.s.s.o., rib 9, k.3 tog., rib 9; 3rd needle – * sl. 1, k.2 tog., p.s.s.o., rib 3(3:3:5), k.3 tog. **, rib

13(15:17:15), rep. from * to **; 4th needle – as 2nd.

Work 3 rounds in k.1, p.1 rib.

22nd round: 1st needle – * sl. 1, k.2 tog., p.s.s.o., rib 5(5:5:7), k.3 tog. **, rib 7(9:11:9), rep. from * to **; 2nd needle – rib 7, sl.1, k.2 tog., p.s.s.o., rib 9, k.3 tog.,

rib 7; 3rd needle – * sl. 1, k.2 tog., p.s.s.o., rib 3(3:3:5), k.3 tog. **, rib 5(7:9:7), rep. from * to **; 4th needle – as 2nd.

Work 2 rounds in k.1, p.1 rib.

Change to double-pointed 3¼mm. needles.

Work 12 rounds in k.1, p.1 rib.

Cast off loosely in rib with 3¾mm. needle.

MAKING UP

Press.

Sew up side and sleeve seams.

Cable Alpaca Sweater

Fine, soft sweater in moss stitch with cable panels, V neckline, set-in sleeves and ribbed welts

★★ Suitable for knitters with some previous experience

MATERIALS

Yarn
Jaeger Alpaca
7(8:8:9:9:10) × 50g. balls

Needles
1 pair 2¼mm.
1 pair 3mm.
cable needle

MEASUREMENTS

Chest
92(97:102:107:112:117) cm.
36(38:40:42:44:46) in.

Length
65(66:66:67:67:69) cm.
25½(26:26:26¼:26¼:27) in.

Sleeve Seam
44(46:46:46:47:47) cm.
17¼(18:18:18:18½:18½) in.

TENSION

28 sts. and 36 rows = 10 cm. (4 in.) square over st. st. on 3mm. needles. If your tension square does not correspond to these measurements, see page 156 for adjustment instructions.

ABBREVIATIONS

k. = knit; p. = purl; st(s). = stitch(es); inc. = increas(ing) (see page 156); dec. = decreas(ing) (see page 157); beg. = begin(ning); rem. = remain(ing); rep. = repeat; alt. = alternate; tog. = together; sl. = slip (transfer one stitch from left needle, knitwise unless otherwise stated,

to right hand needle.); cont. = continue; patt. = pattern; foll. = following; folls. = follows; mm. = millimetres; cm. = centimetres; in. = inches; st. st. = stocking st.: one row k., one row p.; g. st. = garter st.: every row k.; incs. = increases; decs. = decreases; m.1 = make 1 st.: pick up horizontal loop lying before next st. and work into back of it; C8B = cable 8 back: sl. next 4 sts. onto cable needle and leave at back of work, k. next 4 sts., k. 4 sts. from cable needle.

BACK

** Cast on 117(125:133:141:149:157) sts. with 2¼mm. needles.

1st row (right side): k.1, * p.1, k.1, rep. from * to end.

2nd row: p.1, * k.1, p.1, rep. from * to end.

These 2 rows form rib patt.

Work 7 cm. (2¾ in.) in rib, ending with a 1st row. **

Next row: rib 7(3:7:2:6:2), m.1, * rib 6(7:7:8:8:9), m.1, rep. from * to last 8(3:7:3:7:2) sts., rib 8(3:7:3:7:2). [135(143: 151:159:167:175) sts.]

Change to 3mm. needles and st. st.

Beg. with a k. row, work straight until back measures 43 cm. (16¾ in.) from beg., ending with a p. row.

Shape Armholes

Cast off 4 sts. at beg. of next 2 rows, then dec. 1 st. at each end of next and every alt. row until 101(105:109:113:117:121) sts. rem.

Work straight until back measures 65(66:66:67:67:69) cm. (25½(26:26:26¼: 26¼:27) in.) from beg., ending with a wrong side row.

Shape Shoulders

Cast off 10(9:10:11:10:11) sts. at beg. of next 2 rows.

Cast off 9(10:10:10:11:11) sts. at beg. of next 4 rows.

Cast off rem. 45(47:49:51:53:55) sts.

FRONT

Work as for back from ** to **.

Next row: rib 8(2:6:10:4:8), m.1, * rib 5(6:6:6:7:7), m.1, rep. from * to last 9(3:7:11:5:9) sts., rib 9(3:7:11:5:9). [138(146:154:162:170:178) sts.]

Change to 3mm. needles and work in patt. as folls.:

1st row (right side): (k.1, p.1) 9(11:11:13:13:15) times, * k.10, (p.1, k.1) 6(6:7:7:8:8) times, p.1, rep. from * to last 28(32:32:36:36:40) sts., k.10, (p.1, k.1) 9(11:11:13:13:15) times.

2nd row: (k.1, p.1) 9(11:11:13:13:15) times, k.1, * p.8, (k.1, p.1) 7(7:8:8:9:9) times, k.1, rep. from * to last 27(31:31:35:35:39) sts., p.8, (k.1, p.1) 9(11:11:13:13:15) times, k.1.

3rd-6th rows: as 1st and 2nd, twice.

7th row: (k.1, p.1) 9(11:11:13:13:15) times, k.1, * C8B, (k.1, p.1) 7(7:8:8:9:9) times, k.1, rep. from * to last 27(31:31:35:35:39) sts., C8B, (k.1, p.1) 9(11:11:13:13:15) times, k.1.

8th row: as 2nd.

These 8 rows form patt.

Work straight in patt. until front matches back at side edge, ending with a wrong side row.

Shape Armhole and Divide for Neck

Next row: cast off 4, patt. 61(65:69:73:77:81), turn and leave rem. sts. on a spare needle.

Cont. on these 61(65:69:73:77:81) sts. for first side.

Work 1 row straight.

Dec. 1 st. at armhole edge on next and every alt. row and, AT THE SAME TIME, dec. 1 st. at neck edge on 3rd and every foll. 4th row until 40(42:45:47:50:52) sts. rem.

Now, keeping armhole edge straight, cont. dec. at neck edge on every foll. 6th row from last dec. until 30(32:34:36:38:40) sts. rem.

Work straight until front matches back armhole, ending with a wrong side row.

Shape Shoulder

Cast off 10(10:12:12:12:14) sts. at beg. of next row.

Cast off 10(11:11:12:13:13) sts. at beg. of foll. 2 alt. rows.

With right side facing, rejoin yarn to rem. 73(77:81:85:89:93) sts.

Next row: cast off centre 8 sts., patt. to end.

Complete to match first side.

SLEEVES

Cast on 61(63:63:69:69:75) sts. with 2¼mm. needles.

Work 7 cm. (2¾ in.) in k.1, p.1 rib as for back, ending with a 1st row.

Next row: rib 3(4:4:2:2:7), m.1, * rib 6(5:5:5:5:4), m.1, rep. from * to last 4(4:4:2:2:8) sts., rib 4(4:4:2:2:8). [71(75:75:83:83:91) sts.]

Change to 3mm. needles and st. st.

Beg. with a k. row, shape sides by inc. 1 st. at each end of 13th and every foll. 6th row until there are 103(107:107:115:115:123) sts.

Cont. straight until sleeve seam measures 44(46:46:46:47:47) cm. (17¼(18:18:18:18½:18½) in.), ending with a p. row.

Shape Top

Cast off 4 sts. at beg. of next 2 rows.

Now dec. 1 st. at each end of next and every alt. row until 63(63:63:71:71:79) sts. rem.

Next row: p.

Now dec. 1 st. at each end of every row until 27 sts. rem.

Cast off.

NECK BORDER

Sew up shoulder seams.

Cast on 15 sts. with 2¼mm. needles.

1st row (right side): k.2, * p.1, k.1, rep. from * to last st., k.1.

2nd row: k.1, * p.1, k.1, rep. from * to end.

Rep. last 2 rows until border fits from cast-off sts. at centre front all round neck to cast-off sts., sewing in position gradually while working, stretching band very slightly.

Cast off evenly in rib.

MAKING UP

Press work lightly on wrong side, omitting ribbing and taking care not to spoil patt.

Sew up side and sleeve seams.

Set in sleeves.

Overlap short ends of neck border and sew in position to cast-off sts. of front.

Press all seams.

Fair Isle Waistcoat 1982

Seven-colour, Fair Isle one-piece waistcoat with circular-knitted ribbed armhole welts, ribbed lower edge and borders

★★ Suitable for knitters with some previous experience

MATERIALS

Yarn

Pingouin Pingofine
1(1:2:2:3:3) × 50g. balls Main Col. A
1(1:2:2:3:3) × 50g. balls Col. B
1(1:1:1:1:1) × 50g. ball Col. C
1(1:1:1:1:1) × 50g. ball Col. D
1(1:1:1:1:1) × 50g. ball Col. E
1(1:1:1:1:1) × 50g. ball Col. F
1(1:1:1:1:1) × 50g. ball Col. G

Needles

1 pair 2¾mm.
1 pair 3¼mm.
1 circular 2¾mm. 40 cm. long

Buttons

4(4:5:5:6:6)

MEASUREMENTS

Chest

56(61:66:71:82) cm.
22(24:26:28:30:32) in.
1/2(2/3:4/5:6/7:7/8:9/10) approx. age

Length

31(34:37:41:44:49) cm.
12¼(13¼:14½:16:17¼:19¼) in.

TENSION

30 sts. and 27 rows = 10 cm. (4 in.) square over patt. on 3¼mm. needles. If your

tension square does not correspond to these measurements, see page 156 for adjustment instructions.

ABBREVIATIONS

k. = knit; p. = purl; st(s). = stitch(es); inc. = increas(ing) (see page 156); dec. = decreas(ing) (see page 157); beg. = begin(ning); rem. = remain(ing); rep. = repeat; alt. = alternate; tog. = together; sl. = slip (transfer one stitch from left needle, knitwise unless otherwise stated, to right hand needle.); cont. = continue; patt. = pattern; foll. = following; folls. = follows; mm. = millimetres; cm. = centimetres; in. = inches; st. st. = stocking st.: one row k., one row p.; g. st. = garter st.:

every row k.; incs. = increases; decs. = decreases.

NB Garment is knitted in one piece.

BODY

Cast on 140(156:170:180:190:210) sts. with 2¾mm. needles and A.
Work in k.1, p.1 rib for 5(5:6:8:9:9) cm. (2(2:2¼:3¼:3½:3½) in.), inc. 25(25:27:33: 37:33) sts. evenly across last row. [165(181:197:213:227:243) sts.]
Change to 3¼mm. needles and beg. patt. from chart.
Work rows 1 to 33.
Then rep. rows 2 to 33 throughout.
Cont. in patt. until work measures 18(21:23:26:28:31) cm. (7(8¼:9:10¼: 11:12¼) in.) from beg.

Shape Right Front

With right side facing, patt. across 41(45:49:53:56:60) sts., turn.
Cast off 6 sts., patt. to last 2 sts., p.2 tog.
Cont. to dec. at neck edge on every alt. row and on every row at armhole edge until 22(26:27:28:31:32) sts. rem.
Now, keeping armhole edge straight, cont. to dec. at neck edge on every alt. row until 17(20:22:23:24:26) sts. rem.
Cont. until armhole measures 13(13:14: 15:16:18) cm. (5(5:5½:5¾:6¼:7) in.) from beg.

Shape Right Shoulder

With wrong side facing, cast off 6(6:7:7: 8:8) sts. at beg. of next and foll. alt. row.
Work 1 row.

Cast off.
Rejoin yarn to rem. sts., cast off 6 sts., patt. across next 77(85:93:101:109:117) sts. including st. rem. on needle after casting off, turn.
Cast off 6 sts. at beg. of next row.
Dec. at both ends of every row until 55(63:67:71:79:83) sts. rem.
Cont. until armholes match front to shoulder shaping.

Shape Shoulders

With wrong side facing, cast off 6(6:7:7: 8:8) sts. at beg. of next 4 rows.
Cast off 5(8:8:9:8:10) sts. at beg. of next 2 rows, then cast off rem. sts.
Rejoin yarn to rem. sts. and complete left front to match right front, reversing all shapings.

BUTTON BAND

Sew up shoulder seams.
Cast on 9 sts. with 2¾mm. needles and A.
Work 4 rows in k.1, p.1 rib.

Make Buttonhole

Rib 4, cast off 2, rib to end.
Next row: rib 3, cast·on 2, rib to end.
Cont. in rib making more buttonholes 5 cm. (2 in.) apart, the last one 1 cm. (½ in.) below beg. of neck shaping.
Cont. in rib until band is long enough to fit fronts and back neck when slightly stretched.
Cast off in rib.

ARMBANDS

With 2¾mm. circular needle and A, pick up and k.80(84:88:98:108:110) sts. evenly around armhole.
Work in rounds of k.1, p.1 rib for 2(3:3:3: 3:3) cm. (¾(1¼:1¼:1¼:1¼:1¼) in.).
Cast off in rib.

MAKING UP

Sew on front bands with a flat seam.
Sew on buttons.

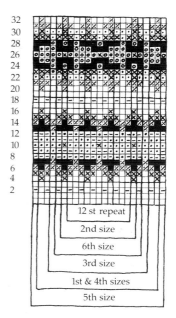

□ = Col. A
⊟ = Col. B
☒ = Col. C
◩ = Col. D
■ = Col. E
⊡ = Col. F
◙ = Col. G

12 st repeat
2nd size
6th size
3rd size
1st & 4th sizes
5th size

Long, Crew-necked Sweater

Fisherman's rib sweater with ribbed welts, doubled-over collar and dropped shoulder line

★★ Suitable for knitters with some previous experience

MATERIALS

Yarn
Patons Clansman 4 ply
11(12:12:13) × 50g. balls

Needles
1 pair 2¾mm.
1 pair 3¼mm.

MEASUREMENTS

Bust
87(92:97:102) cm.
34(36:38:40) in.

Length
63(64:65:66) cm.
24¾(25:25½:26) in.

Sleeve Seam
48(48:49:49) cm.
18¾(18¾:19¼:19¼) in.

TENSION

26 sts. and 52 rows = 10 cm. (4 in.) square over patt. on 3¼mm. needles. If your tension square does not correspond to these measurements, see page 156 for adjustment instructions.

ABBREVIATIONS

k. = knit; p. = purl; st(s). = stitch(es); inc. = increas(ing) (see page 156); dec. = decreas(ing) (see page 157); beg. = begin(ning); rem. = remain(ing); rep. = repeat; alt. = alternate; tog. = together; sl. = slip (transfer one stitch from left needle, knitwise unless otherwise stated, to right hand needle.); cont. = continue; patt. = pattern; foll. = following; folls. = follows; mm. = millimetres; cm. = centimetres; in. = inches; st. st. = stocking st.: one row k., one row p.; g. st. = garter st.: every row k.; incs. = increases; decs. = decreases; k.1b. = k. one below: k. into next st. one row below, at the same time sl. off st. above; p.s.s.o. = pass the sl. st. over.

FRONT

** Cast on 131(137:143:149) sts. with 2¾mm. needles.
1st row: k.2, * p.1, k.1, rep. from * to last st., k.1.
2nd row: * k.1, p.1, rep. from * to last st., k.1.
Rep. 1st and 2nd rows for 9 cm. (3½ in.), ending with a 2nd row.
Change to 3¼mm. needles and patt.
1st row (right side): k.
2nd row: k.1, * p.1, k.1b., rep. from * to last 2 sts., p.1, k.1.
These 2 rows form patt.
Work until front measures 42(42:43:43) cm. (16½(16½:16¾:16¾) in.) from beg., ending with a wrong side row.
Mark each end of last row to indicate beg. of armholes.

Shape Armholes
1st row: k.3, sl.1, k.2 tog., p.s.s.o., k. to last 6 sts., k.3 tog., k.3.
2nd to 4th rows: work in patt.
Rep. last 4 rows 4(5:5:6) times more. [111(113:119:121) sts.] **
Cont. until armholes measure 15(16:16: 17) cm. (5¾(6¼:6¼:6½) in.) from markers, ending with a right side row.

Shape Neck
Next row: patt. 45(46:48:49) sts., cast off 21(21:23:23) sts., patt. to end.
Cont. on last set of sts.
Work 1 row.
Dec. 1 st. at neck edge on next row and then on every alt. row until 33(34:36:37) sts. rem.
Work 6 rows, ending at armhole edge.

Shape Shoulder
Cast off 4(4:6:6) sts. at beg. of next row and 5(5:5:5) sts. at beg. of 5 foll. alt. rows.
Work 1 row.
Cast off rem. 4(5:5:6) sts.
Rejoin yarn to rem. sts. at neck edge and work to match first side, working one row more to end at armhole edge before shaping shoulder.

BACK

Work as for front from ** to **.
Cont. until armholes measure same as front to shoulder shaping, ending with a wrong side row.

Shape Shoulder and Back Neck
Cast off 4(4:6:6) sts. at beg. of next 2 rows and 5(5:5:5) sts. at beg. of 4 foll. rows.
Next row: cast off 5(5:5:5) sts., k. 19(20:20: 21) sts. including st. on needle, cast off 35(35:37:37) sts., k. to end.
Cont. on last set of sts.
1st row: cast off 5(5:5:5) sts., patt. to last 2 sts., k.2 tog.
2nd row: k.2 tog., k. to end.
Rep. 1st and 2nd rows once more and then 1st row again.
Work 1 row.
Cast off rem. 4(5:5:6) sts.
Rejoin yarn to rem. sts. at neck edge.
1st row: k.2 tog., patt. to end.
2nd row: cast off 5(5:5:5) sts., k. to last 2 sts., k.2 tog.
Rep. 1st and 2nd rows once more and then 1st row again.
Cast off rem. 4(5:5:6) sts.

SLEEVES

Cast on 61(65:65:69) sts. with 2¾mm. needles.
Work 8 cm. (3¼ in.) in rib as front, ending with a 2nd row.
Change to 3¼mm. needles and patt.
Work 4 rows.
Inc. 1 st. at each end of next and every 8th row until there are 109(113:113:117) sts., working inc. sts. into patt.
Work until sleeve measures 48(48:49:49) cm. (18¾(18¾:19¼:19¼) in.), ending with a wrong side row.

Shape Top

1st row: k.3, sl.1, k.2 tog., p.s.s.o., k. to last 6 sts., k.3 tog., k.3.
2nd to 4th rows: work in patt.
Rep. last 4 rows 4(5:5:6) times more.
Cast off.

MAKING UP

Press each piece lightly.
Sew up right shoulder seam.

Neck Border

With right side facing and 2¾mm. needles, k. up 31(31:31:31) sts. evenly down left side of front neck edge, 21(21:23:23) sts. from cast off sts., 30(30:30:30) sts. up right side of neck and 55(55:57:57) sts. evenly along back neck edge. [137(137:141:141) sts.]
1st to 4th rows: k.
5th row: * k.1, p.1, rep. from * to last st., k.1.

6th row: k.2, * p.1, k.1, rep. from * to last st., k.1.
Rep. 5th and 6th rows 8 more times.
Cast off loosely in rib.
Sew up left shoulder and neck border seam.
Fold ribbing of neck border in half onto wrong side and slip st. down.
Sew up side and sleeve seams.
Set in sleeves.
Press seams.

Vest with Garter-stitch Yoke

Vest knitted in one piece starting with the front, in stocking stitch with garter yoke pattern and back opening

★ Suitable for beginners

NB Vest is photographed on baby worn with back ribbon fastening at front.

MATERIALS

Yarn
Phildar Perle 5
2 × 50g. balls

Needles
1 pair 2¾mm.
2½mm. crochet hook

Satin Ribbon
40 cm. approx.
15¾ in. approx.

MEASUREMENTS

Chest
41 cm.
16 in. (1/3 months old)

Length
22 cm.
8½ in.

TENSION

30 sts. and 40 rows = 10 cm. (4 in.) square over st. st. on 2¾mm. needles. If your tension square does not correspond to these measurements, see page 156 for adjustment instructions.

ABBREVIATIONS

k. = knit; p. = purl; st(s). = stitch(es); inc. = increas(ing) (see page 156); dec. = decreas(ing) (see page 157); beg. = begin(ning); rem. = remain(ing); rep. = repeat; alt. = alternate; tog. = together; sl. = slip (transfer one stitch from left needle, knitwise unless otherwise stated, to right hand needle.); cont. = continue; patt. = pattern; foll. = following; folls. = follows; mm. = millimetres; cm. = centimetres; in. = inches; st. st. = stocking st.:

one row k., one row p.; g. st. = garter st.: every row k.; incs. = increases; decs. = decreases; ch. = chain (see page 162 for instructions); d.c. = double crochet (see page 162 for instructions); tr. = treble (see page 162 for instructions).

TO MAKE

Worked in one piece, beg. at lower edge of front.
Cast on 61 sts. with 2¾mm. needles.
K.13 rows.
Beg. with a k. row, work 37 rows in st. st., ending with a right side row.

Yoke

Next row: p.30, k.1, p.30.
Next row: k.
Next row: p.29, k.3, p.29.
Next row: k.
Next row: p.28, k.5, p.28.
Next row: k.
Cont. in st. st. with g. st. yoke patt. as set, taking 1 more st. on each side of yoke into g. st. on every wrong side row until there are 15 sts. in yoke patt., ending with a wrong side row.
Cont. working in yoke patt.:
Cast on 41 sts. at beg. of next 2 rows for sleeves. [143 sts.]
Now take the 8 sts. at each end of every

row into g. st. for cuff. AT THE SAME TIME when there are 21 sts. in g. st. for yoke work as folls.:
Next row (wrong side): k.8, p.42, k.43, p.42, k.8.
Next row: k.
Rep. last 2 rows 4 more times, then first of the rows again.

Shape Neck

Next row: work 69 sts., turn and leave rem. sts. on a spare needle.
Cast off 2 sts. at neck edge on next row.
Now dec. 1 st. at neck edge on the next 5 rows. [62 sts.]
Work 5 rows.
Inc. 1 st. at neck edge on next row.
Cast on 2 sts. at beg. of next row.
Work 1 row.
Cast on 13 sts. at beg. of next row. [78 sts.]
Cont. in g. st. and st. st. as set for 22 rows taking the centre back 28 sts. into g. st. for yoke, ending with a wrong side row.
Next row: cast off 41 sts., work to end.
Cont. straight on these 37 sts. for 50 rows, keeping 9 centre back sts. in g. st. and rem. in st. st.
Work 13 rows in g. st.
Cast off.
With right side facing rejoin yarn to rem. sts.
Cast off centre 5 sts. loosely and complete to match first side, reversing shapings.

MAKING UP

Press st. st. parts lightly on wrong side.
Work 1 row d.c. round neck, turn with 5 ch., work 1 tr. into the 3rd d.c. from end of last row, * work 2 ch., miss 2 d.c., work 1 tr. into next d.c., rep. from * to end.
Fasten off.
Sew up side and sleeve seams.
Join at centre back (or front as photographed) with satin ribbon.

Lacy, Flower-pattern Dress

*Allover-patterned dress with gathered skirt, fitted yoke,
puffed sleeves and back buttoning*

★ Suitable for beginners

MATERIALS

Yarn
Pingouin Fil d'Ecosse fin
4(4) × 50g. balls

Needles
1 pair 2¾mm. for 1st size
1 pair 3mm. for 2nd size

Buttons
5

MEASUREMENTS

Chest
51(56) cm.
20(22) in.
1/2(2/3) approx. age

Length
43(51) cm.
16¾(20) in.

Sleeve Seam
5(6) cm.
2(2¼ in.)

TENSION

32 sts. and 44 rows = 10 cm. (4 in.) square
over patt. on 2¾mm. needles.
30 sts. and 38 rows = 10 cm. (4 in.) square
over patt. on 3mm. needles. If your
tension does not correspond to these
measurements, see page 156 for adjustment instructions.

ABBREVIATIONS

k. = knit; p. = purl; st(s). = stitch(es);
inc. = increas(ing) (see page 156); dec. =
decreas(ing) (see page 157); beg. =
begin(ning); rem. = remain(ing); rep. =
repeat; alt. = alternate; tog. = together;
sl. = slip (transfer one stitch from left
needle, knitwise unless otherwise stated,
to right hand needle.); cont. = continue;
patt. = pattern; foll. = following; folls. =
follows; mm. = millimetres; cm. = centimetres; in. = inches; st. st. = stocking st.:
one row k., one row p.; g. st. = garter st.:
every row k.; incs. = increases; decs. =
decreases; y.fwd. = yarn forward; p.s.s.o.
= pass the sl. st. over.

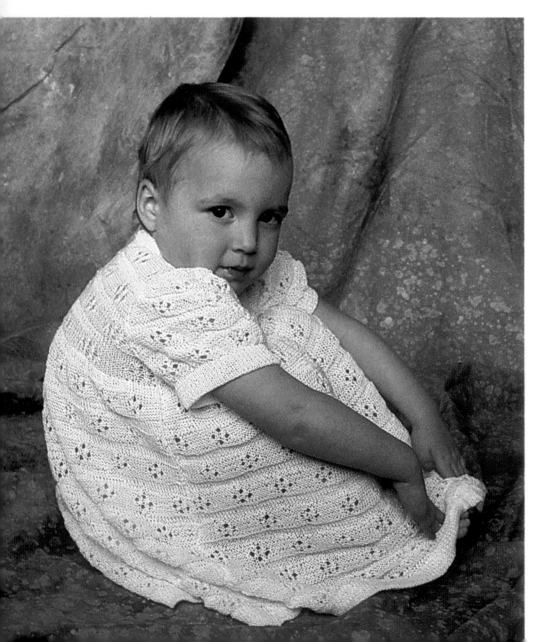

FRONT

Cast on 166 sts.

Beg. with a k. row, work 20 rows in st. st. Fold up cast-on edge behind sts. on needle and work 1 st. from cast-on edge tog. with 1 st. from needle all along row to form hem.

Now work in patt. as folls.:

1st row (wrong side): k.

2nd row: p.

3rd row: k.1, * k.10, y.fwd., sl.1, k.1, p.s.s.o., rep. from * to last 9 sts., k.9.

4th row: p.

5th row: k.8, * sl.1, k.1, p.s.s.o., y.fwd., k.3, y.fwd., sl.1, k.1, p.s.s.o., k.5, rep. from * to last 2 sts., k.2.

6th row: p.

7th row: as 3rd.

8th row: p.

9th row: k.

10th row: k.

11th row: p.

12th to 14th rows: rep. 10th and 11th once, then work 10th again.

15th row: k.

16th row: p.

17th row: k.5, * y.fwd., sl.1, k.1, p.s.s.o., k.10, rep. from * to last 5 sts., y.fwd., sl.1, k.1, p.s.s.o., k.3.

18th row: p.

19th row: k.2, * sl.1, k.1, p.s.s.o., y.fwd., k.3, y.fwd., sl.1, k.1, p.s.s.o., k.5, rep. from * to last 8 sts., sl.1, k.1, p.s.s.o., y.fwd., k.3, y.fwd., sl.1, k.1, p.s.s.o., k.1.

20th row: p.

21st row: as 17th.

22nd row: p.

23rd and 24th rows: k.

25th row: p.

26th row: k.

27th and 28th rows: as 25th and 26th.

These 28 rows form patt.

Rep. these 28 rows 3 times more, then rows 1 to 13 again.

Dec. row: k.2 tog. all across row.

Next row: k., working 41st and 42nd sts. tog. [82 sts.] **

Work 13 rows in patt.

Shape Armholes

Cast off 3 sts. at beg. of next 2 rows.

Cont. in patt., dec. 1 st. at each end of every row until 68 sts. rem.

Cont. in patt. for a further 26 rows.

Shape Neck

Next row: patt. 26, cast off 16, patt. 26.

Work on last 26 sts. only as folls.:

Work 1 row.

Cont. in patt., casting off 2 sts. at beg. of next and foll. 3 alt. rows. [18 sts.]

Shape Shoulder

Cast off 9 sts. at beg. of next and foll. alt. row.

Cast off.

Rejoin yarn to rem. 26 sts. and work to match first side, reversing all shapings.

BACK

Work as for front to **

NB
Use 2¾mm. needles for 1st size and 3mm. needles for 2nd size throughout.

Divide for Opening

16th row: p.38, k.6, turn. (Last 6 sts. are centre back border and will be in g. st. to neck.)

Work 2 rows.

* *Next row*: k.2, cast off 2, k.2 including st. rem. on needle after casting off, work to end.

Next row: patt., casting on 2 sts. over those cast off.

Work 9 rows, thus ending at side edge.

Shape Armhole

Cast off 3 sts. at beg. of next row.

Working buttonholes on every 13th and 14th row from previous buttonhole, dec. 1 st. at armhole edge on next 4 rows. [37 sts.]

Cont. until a total of 4 buttonholes have been worked, thus ending at centre back edge.

Shape Neck

Cast off 10 sts. at beg. of next row and 3 sts. at beg. of foll. 3 alt. rows.

Shape Shoulder

Cast off 9 sts. at beg. of next and foll. alt. row.

Rejoin yarn to rem. sts. and cast on 6 sts. for border (keep these 6 sts. in g. st. throughout).

Complete to match first side, omitting buttonholes and reversing shapings.

SLEEVES

Cast on 55 sts.

Beg. with a k. row, work 20 rows in st. st. Make a hem on next row as for front.

Inc. row: k.1, * inc. in next st., k.1, rep. from * to end. [82 sts.]

Beg. with a 2nd row, work 13 rows in patt.

Shape Top

Cast off 3 sts. at beg. of next 2 rows, then 1 st. at beg. of every row until 28 sts. rem. Cast off, working k.2 tog. all across row at the same time.

NECKBAND

Sew up side, shoulder and sleeve seams. Set in sleeves, gathering in fullness at the top.

Pick up and k. 19 sts. along left back neck, 36 sts. around front neck and 19 sts. along right back neck. [74 sts.]

Beg. with a p. row, work 3 rows in st. st.

* *Buttonhole row*: k. to last 4 sts., cast off 2, k. to end.

Next row: p.2, cast on 2 sts., p. to end. *

Work 4 rows.

Rep. from * to * once.

Work 3 rows.

Cast off VERY loosely.

MAKING UP

Fold neckband in half onto wrong side and hem so that the buttonholes correspond.

Buttonhole st. round buttonhole.

Sew down cast-on edge of button border neatly behind buttonhole border.

Sew on buttons.

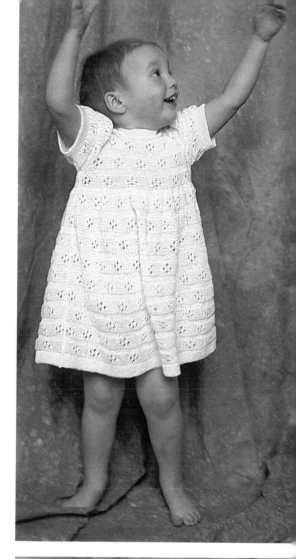

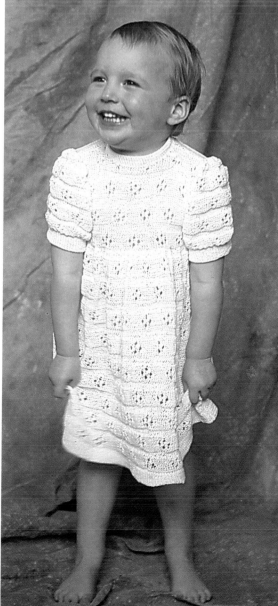

Woven-stitch Knitted Shirt

1955

Long-sleeved, woven-stitch sweater with collar, three-buttoned placket and ribbed welts

★ Suitable for beginners

MATERIALS

Yarn
Pingouin Corrida 3 4 ply
3(4:5) × 50g. balls

Needles
1 pair 2¾mm.
1 pair 3¼mm.

Buttons
3

MEASUREMENTS

Chest
51(56:61) cm.
20(22:24) in.
1/2(2/3:4/5) approx. age

Length
33(37:40) cm.
13(14½:15¾) in.

Sleeve Seam
21(23:27) cm.
8¼(9:10½) in.

TENSION

32 sts. and 44 rows = 10 cm. (4 in.) square over patt. on 3¼mm. needles. If your tension square does not correspond to these measurements, see page 156 for adjustment instructions.

ABBREVIATIONS

k. = knit; p. = purl; st(s). = stitch(es); inc. = increas(ing) (see page 156); dec. = decreas(ing) (see page 157); beg. = begin(ning); rem. = remain(ing); rep. = repeat; alt. = alternate; tog. = together; sl. = slip (transfer one stitch from left needle, knitwise unless otherwise stated, to right hand needle.); cont. = continue; patt. = pattern; foll. = following; folls. = follows; mm. = millimetres; cm. = centimetres; in. = inches; st. st. = stocking st.: one row k., one row p.; g. st. = garter st.: every row k.; incs. = increases; decs. = decreases; y.fwd. = yarn forward; y.b. = yarn back; m.1 = make 1 st.: pick up horizontal loop lying before next st. and work into back of it; sl.1p. = sl. 1 st. purlwise.

FRONT

** Cast on 78(86:94) sts. with 2¾mm. needles.
Work in rib as folls.:
1st row (right side): k.2, * p.2, k.2, rep. from * to end.
2nd row: p.2, * k.2, p.2, rep. from * to end.
Rep. these 2 rows until work measures 5 cm. (2 in.), ending with a 1st row.
Next row: rib 4(3:2), * m.1, rib 7(8:9), rep. from * to last 4(3:2) sts., m.1, rib to end. [89(97:105) sts.]
Change to 3¼mm. needles and work in patt. as folls.:
1st row (right side): k.1, * y.fwd., sl.1p., y.b., k.1, rep. from * to end.
2nd row: p.
3rd row: k.2, * y.fwd., sl.1p., y.b., k.1, rep. from * to last st., k.1.
4th row: p.
These 4 rows form patt.
Cont. in patt. until front measures 23(26:27) cm. (9(10¼:10½) in.), ending with a wrong side row.

Shape Armholes

Keeping patt. straight, cast off 4 sts. at beg. of next 2 rows.
Dec. 1 st. at each end of next 5 rows.
Work 1 row.
Dec. 1 st. at each end of next and every alt. row until 63(71:77) sts. rem. **
Work 1(3:7) rows.

Divide for Front Opening

Next row: patt. 29(33:36), turn and leave rem. sts. on a spare needle.
Work on left side of front as folls.:
Next row: cast on 5 sts., p. across these sts., p. to end. [34(38:41) sts.]
Work 15 rows in patt., thus ending with a right side row.

Shape Neck

Cast off 6 sts. at beg. of next row.
Cast off 3 sts. at beg. of foll. alt. row.

Dec. 1 st. at neck edge on every row until 15(18:20) sts. rem.
Work 0(1:2) rows, thus ending with a wrong side row.

Shape Shoulder

Cast off 5(6:7) sts. at beg. of next and foll. alt. row.
Work 1 row.
Cast off rem. 5(6:6) sts.
Next row: with right side facing rejoin yarn to 34(38:41) sts. from spare needle, patt. to end.
Next row: p. to last st., k.1.

Make Buttonholes

Next row: patt. 2, cast off 2, patt. to end.
Next row: p. to last 2 sts., cast on 2, p.1, k.1.
Work 4 rows in patt., working k.1 at end of wrong side rows.
Rep. last 6 rows once more, then first 2 rows again.
Finish to match left side, reversing shapings.

BACK

Work as for front from ** to **
Work straight until back measures same as front to beg. of shoulder shaping, ending with a wrong side row.

Shape Shoulders

Cast off 5(6:7) sts. at beg. of next 4 rows.
Cast off 5(6:6) sts. at beg. of next 2 rows.
Cast off rem. 33(35:37) sts.

SLEEVES

Cast on 42(42:46) sts. with 2¾mm. needles and work 5 cm. (2 in.) in rib as given for front, ending with a 1st row.
Next row: rib 3(3:2), * m.1, rib 9(6:7), rep. from * to last 3(3:2) sts., m.1, rib to end. [47(49:53) sts.]
Change to 3¼mm. needles and work in patt. as given for front, shaping sides by inc. 1 st. at each end of 7th(3rd:9th) and every foll. 6th(8th:8th) row until there are 63(67:73) sts., taking inc. sts. into patt.
Work straight until sleeve seam measures 21(23:27) cm. (8¼(9:10½) in.), ending with a wrong side row.

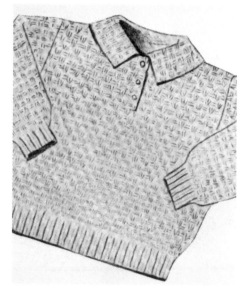

Shape Top

Keeping patt. straight, cast off 4 sts. at beg. of next 2 rows.

Dec. 1 st. at each end of next and every alt. row until 35(37:39) sts. rem.

Work 1 row.

Dec. 1 st. at each end of every row until 19(19:21) sts. rem.

Cast off.

COLLAR

Cast on 61(67:73) sts. with 3¼mm. needles and work in patt. as folls.:

1st row (right side): k.2, * y.fwd., sl.1p., y.b., k.1, rep. from * to last st., k.1.

2nd and every alt. row: k.2, p. to last 2 sts., k.2.

3rd row: k.2, m.1, * k.1, y.fwd., sl.1p., y.b., rep. from * to last 3 sts., k.1, m.1, k.2.

5th row: k.2, * k.1, y.fwd., sl.1p., y.b., rep. from * to last 3 sts., k.3.

7th row: k.2, m.1, * y.fwd., sl.1p., y.b., k.1, rep. from * to last 3 sts., y.fwd., sl.1p., y.b., m.1, k.2.

8th row: as 2nd.

Rep. these 8 rows once more, then 1st to 4th rows again. [71(77:83) sts.]

K.3 rows.

Cast off.

MAKING UP

Sew up shoulder, side and sleeve seams.

Set in sleeves.

Sew cast-on edge of collar to neck edge, beg. and ending at centre front.

Catch down underwrap at base of opening.

Sew on buttons.

Sleeveless Pullover in Brick Stitch 1942

Hip-length, sleeveless pullover with V-neck in brick stitch with garter stitch neck border and bias, garter stitch sleeve borders

★★ Suitable for knitters with some previous experience

MATERIALS

Sirdar Country Style 4 ply
4(4:5:5) × 50g. balls

Needles
1 pair 2¾mm.
1 pair 3¼mm.

MEASUREMENTS

Chest
97(102:107:112) cm.
38(40:42:44) in.

Length
59(61:63:65) cm.
23¼(24:24¾:25½) in.

TENSION

28sts. and 36 rows = 10 cm. (4 in.) square over patt. with 3¼mm. needles. If your tension square does not correspond to these measurements, see page 156 for adjustment instructions.

ABBREVIATIONS

k. = knit; p. = purl; st(s). = stitch(es); inc. = increas(ing) (see page 156); dec. = decreas(ing) (see page 157); beg. = begin(ning); rem. = remain(ing); rep. = repeat; alt. = alternate; tog. = together; sl. = slip (transfer one stitch from left needle, knitwise unless otherwise stated, to right hand needle.); cont. = continue; patt. = pattern; foll. = following; folls. = follows; mm. = millimetres; cm. = centimetres; in. = inches; st. st. = stocking st.: one row k., one row p.; g. st. = garter st.: every row k.; incs. = increases; decs. = decreases; m.1 = make 1 st.: pick up horizontal loop lying before next st. and k. into back of it.

BACK

*** Cast on 128(131:134:137) sts. with 2¾mm. needles and work in rib as folls.:
1st row (right side): * k.2, p.1, rep. from * to last 2 sts., k.2.
2nd row: p.2, * k.1, p.2, rep. from * to end.
Rep. these 2 rows until rib measures 8 cm. (3¼ in.) from cast-on edge, ending

with a 2nd row.
Next row: rib 4(8:2:10), m.1, (rib 6(5:5:4), m.1) 20(23:26:29) times, rib to end. [149(155:161:167) sts.]
Change to 3¼mm. needles.
K. 1 row.
Cont. in patt.:
1st row (right side): * p.5, k.1, rep. from * to last 5 sts., p.5.
2nd row: k.5, * p.1, k.5, rep. from * to end.
3rd and 5th rows: as 1st.
4th and 6th rows: as 2nd.
7th row: p.2, * k.1, p.5, rep. from * to last 3 sts., k.1, p.2.
8th row: k.2, p.1, * k.5, p.1, rep. from * to last 2 sts., k.2.
9th and 11th rows: as 7th.
10th and 12th rows: as 8th.
These 12 rows form patt.
Cont. straight in patt. until back measures 38(39:40:41) cm. (15(15¼:15¾: 16) in.) from cast-on edge, ending with a wrong side row. ***

Shape Armholes
Cast off 8(10:11:12) sts. at beg. of next 2 rows.
Dec. 1 st. at each end of next and every foll. alt. row until 117(121:125:129) sts. rem.
Cont. on rem. sts. in patt. until armholes measure 21(22:23:24) cm. (8¼(8½:9:9½) in.) from beg. of armhole shaping, ending with a wrong side row.

Shape Shoulders
Cast off 18(19:20:21) sts. at beg. of next 2 rows.
Cast off 18(18:17:17) sts. at beg. of foll. 2 rows.
Cast off rem. 45(47:51:53) sts.

FRONT

Work as for back from *** to ***

Shape Armholes
Cast off 8(10:11:12) sts. at beg. of next 2 rows.
Dec. 1 st. at each end of next row and foll. 2 alt. rows, then work 1 row. [127(129: 133:137) sts.]

Shape Neck
Next row: patt. 2 tog., patt. 61(62:64:66) sts., turn, leave rem. sts. on a spare needle.

Dec. 1 st. at neck edge on next and every foll. 3rd row 22(23:25:26) times in all, AT THE SAME TIME cont. to shape armhole until 8(7:7:7) decs. in all have been worked. [36(37:37:38) sts.]

Work straight on rem. sts. until the same number of rows have been worked as for back to shoulder shaping, ending at armhole edge.

Shape Shoulder
Cast off 18(19:20:21) sts. at beg. of next row.
Work 1 row.
Cast off rem. sts.
Return to sts. on spare needle, cast off centre st., rejoin yarn and complete right half of neck line as left half, reversing all shapings.

NECKBAND

Sew up shoulder seams.
Cast on 1 st. with 2¾mm. needles.
1st row (right side): k.1.
2nd row: k. into front and back of st.
3rd row: k.2.
4th row: inc. 1 st., k.1.
Cont. in g. st., inc. 1 st. at same edge on every alt. row until there are 12 sts.
Work straight on all sts. in g. st. until band fits left side of neck to centre back neck, with point to centre front, and band slightly stretched.
Count number of rows worked on all sts., and work that number of rows again.
Dec. 1 st. at shaped edge on every alt. row until 1 st. rem.
Fasten off.

ARMHOLE BANDS

Cast on 12 sts. with 2¾mm. needles and k. 1 row.
Work as folls.:
1st row: inc. 1 st., k.9, k.2 tog.
2nd row: k.2 tog., k. to last st., m.1, k.1.
Rep. these 2 rows until bias band fits armhole when slightly stretched.
Cast off.
Make another band in the same way.

MAKING UP

Using a flat seam, neatly sew on armhole bands.
Sew up side and armhole band seams.
Sew on neckband with a flat seam.
Do not press.

Casual, Aran-style Sweater

Long, thick sweater with aran pattern on front, back and wide, drop-shoulder sleeves, slit pockets and ribbed welts

★★★ Suitable for experienced knitters only

MATERIALS

Yarn
Lister-Lee Pure Wool Aran
15(16:17:18) × 50g. balls

Needles
1 pair 5mm.
1 pair 5½mm.
1 cable needle

MEASUREMENTS

Bust
82(87:92:97) cm.
32(34:36:38) in.

Length
63(63:70:70) cm. approx.
24¾(24¾:27½:27½) in. approx.

Sleeve Seam
41 cm.
16 in.

TENSION

16 sts. and 20 rows = 10 cm. (4 in.) square over st. st. on 5½mm. needles. If your tension square does not correspond to these measurements, see page 156 for adjustment instructions.

ABBREVIATIONS

k. = knit; p. = purl; st(s). = stitch(es); inc. = increas(ing) (see page 156); dec. = decreas(ing) (see page 157); beg. = begin(ning); rem. = remain(ing); rep. = repeat; alt. = alternate; tog. = together; sl. = slip (transfer one stitch from left needle, knitwise unless otherwise stated, to right hand needle.); cont. = continue; patt. = pattern; foll. = following; folls. = follows; mm. = millimetres; cm. = centimetres; in. = inches; st. st. = stocking st.: one row k., one row p.; g. st. = garter st.: every row k.; incs. = increases; decs. = decreases; Cr.5 = sl. next 3 sts. onto cable needle, hold at back, k.2, replace last st. from cable needle onto left hand needle, bring cable needle to front, p.1, then k.2 from cable needle; C4B = cable 4 back: sl. next 2 sts. onto cable needle and hold at back, k. next 2 sts., then k.2 from cable needle; C4F = sl. next 2 sts. onto cable needle, hold at front, k. next 2 sts., then k.2 from cable needle; Cr.3R = cross 3 right: sl. next st. onto cable needle, hold at back, k.2, then p.1 from cable needle; Cr.3L = cross 3 left: sl. next 2 sts. onto cable needle, hold at front, p.1, then k.2 from cable needle; MB = make bobble: (k.1, p.1, k.1, p.1, k.1) into next st; PB = p. bobble sts.; p.s.s.o. = pass the sl. st. over.

BACK

Cast on 73(77:81:85) sts. with 5mm. needles and work in k.1, p.1 rib for 8 cm. (3¼ in.).
Change to 5½mm. needles and patt.:
1st row (right side): k.23(25:27:29), p.1, C4B, p.6, Cr.5, p.6, C4F, p.1, k.23 (25:27:29).
2nd row: p.23(25:27:29), k.1, p.4, k.6, p.2, k.1, p.2, k.6, p.4, k.1, p.23(25:27:29).
3rd row: k.23(25:27:29), p.1, C4B, p.5, Cr.3R, p.1, Cr.3L, p.5, C4F, p.1, k.23 (25:27:29).
4th row: work sts. as set.
5th row: k.23(25:27:29), p.1, C4B, p.4, Cr.3R, p.3, Cr.3L, p.4, C4F, p.1, k.23 (25:27:29).
6th row: work sts. as set.
7th row: k.23(25:27:29), p.1, C4B, p.3, Cr.3R, p.2, MB, p.2, Cr.3L, p.3, C4F, p.1, k.23(25:27:29).
8th row: work sts. as set, PB at centre.
9th row: k.23(25:27:29), p.1, C4B, p.2, Cr.3R, p.1, MB, p.1, sl.1, k.4 tog., p.s.s.o., p.1, MB, p.1, Cr.3L, p.2, C4F, p.1, k.23 (25:27:29).
10th row: as set, with PB, k.3, PB at centre.
11th row: k.23(25:27:29), p.1, C4B, p.2, k.2, p.2, sl.1, k.4 tog., p.s.s.o., p.1, MB, p.1, sl.1, k.4 tog., p.s.s.o., p.2, k.2, p.2, C4F, p.1, k.23(25:27:29).
12th row: as set, with PB at centre.
13th row: k.23(25:27:29), p.1, C4B, p.2, Cr.3L, p.3, sl.1, k.4 tog., p.s.s.o., p.3, Cr.3R, p.2, C4F, p.1, k.23(25:27:29).
14th row: as set.
15th row: k.23(25:27:29), p.1, C4B, p.3, Cr.3L, p.5, Cr.3R, p.3, C4F, p.1, k.23 (25:27:29).
16th row: as set.
17th row: k.23(25:27:29), p.1, C4B, p.4, Cr.3L, p.3, Cr.3R, p.4, C4F, p.1, k.23 (25:27:29).
18th row: as set.
19th row: k.23(25:27:29), p.1, C4B, p.5,

Shape Shoulders

Cast off 10 sts. at beg. of next 2 rows and 10(10:12:13) sts. at beg. of foll. 2 rows. [33(37:37:39) sts.].
Leave rem. sts. on a spare needle for back of neck.

FRONT

Work as for back to shoulder shaping, then rep. 1st row again.

Shape Shoulder and Neck.

Next row: p.26(28:30:32), cast off 21 sts., p.26(28:30:32).
Next row: cast off 10 sts. and k. to neck edge.
Next row: cast off 6(8:8:9) sts., p. to end.
Next row: cast off rem. 10(10:12:13) sts.
Return to rem. sts. and complete to match first side.

SLEEVES

Cuff

Cast on 33 sts. with 5½mm. needles.
Work 2 rows in k.1, p.1 rib.
Change to patt., beg. and ending rows with k.3 on right side and p.3 on wrong side.
Work patt. 3 times, then rep. 1st and 2nd rows.
Work 2 rows in k.1, p.1 rib.
Cast off.

Shoulder Band

Work as for cuff, but work patt. 4 times.

Main Sleeve

Cast on 56 sts. with 5½mm. needles and work in st. st. inc. 1 st. at each end of 9th and every foll. 6th row until there are 70 sts.
Cont. straight until work measures 27 cm. (10½ in.).
Cast off.

MAKING UP

Press work.
Sew side edge of shoulder bands to top of main sleeves.
Sew cuffs to lower edge of sleeves with wrong side facing, for turnback.

Neckband

Sew up right shoulder seam.
With right side facing and 5mm. needles, pick up and k.37(41:41:45) sts. evenly around front neck and 33(37:37:39) sts. from back neck.
Work 6 rows in k.1, p.1 rib.
Cast off loosely in rib.
Sew up left shoulder seam.
Set in sleeves and sew up side seams, leaving 13 cm. (5 in.) unstitched from ribbing at lower edge for insertion of pockets.
Sew up sleeve seams.
Turn back cuffs and press seams.

Pocket Edge

Pick up and k.24 sts. along open edge of front with 5mm. needles.
Work 4 rows in k.1, p.1 rib.
Cast off in rib.

Pockets

Cast on 20 sts. with 5½mm. needles.
Work 5 cm. (2 in.) in st. st.
Dec. 1 st. at beg. of next 14 rows.
Work 2 rows straight.
Now inc. 1 st. at beg. of next 14 rows.
Work 5 cm. (2 in.) straight.
Cast off.
Make another pocket to match.
Fold in half with right side inside, and join row-ends.
Insert into pocket slit.
Sew pocket opening edges to garment openings.

Cr.3L, p.1, Cr.3R, p.5, C4F, p.1, k.23 (25:27:29).
20th row: as set.
These 20 rows form patt.
Rep. them 5(5:6:6) times more, thus ending with a wrong side row.

Three-coloured Striped Socks

Simple socks in stocking stitch stripes with ribbed welts and adjustable length

1952

★★ Suitable for knitters with some previous experience

MATERIALS

Yarn

Rowan 3 ply Botany
4 × 25g. hanks Main Col. A
1 × 25g. hank Col. B
1 × 25g. hank Col. C

Needles

1 pair 2¾mm.
1 set of 4 double-pointed 2¾mm.
3 st. holders

MEASUREMENTS

Foot Length (adjustable)

from 24 cm.
9½ in.

Length from Top to Base of Heel

28 cm. approx.
11 in. approx.

TENSION

36 sts. and 44 rows = 10 cm. (4 in.) square over st. st. on 2¾mm. needles. If your tension square does not correspond to these measurements, see page 156 for adjustment instructions.

ABBREVIATIONS

k. = knit; p. = purl; st(s). = stitch(es); inc. = increas(ing) (see page 156); dec. = decreas(ing) (see page 157); beg. = begin(ning); rem. = remain(ing); rep. = repeat; alt. = alternate; tog. = together; sl. = slip (transfer one stitch from left needle, knitwise unless otherwise stated, to right hand needle.); cont. = continue; patt. = pattern; foll. = following; folls. =

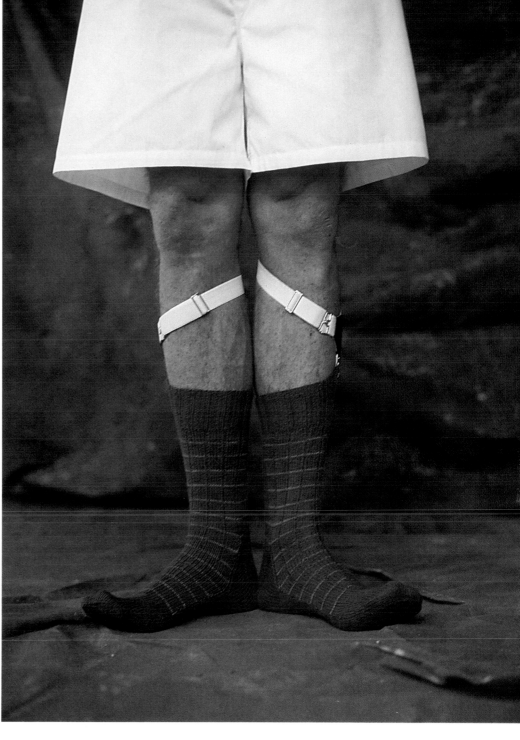

follows; mm. = millimetres; cm. = centimetres; in. = inches; st. st. = stocking st.: one row k., one row p.; g. st. = garter st.: every row k.; incs. = increases; decs. = decreases; p.s.s.o. = pass the sl. st. over; sl.1p. = sl. 1 purlwise.

Cast on 64 sts. with 2¾mm. needles and A.
Work in k.2, p.2 rib for 8 cm. (3¼ in.)
Inc. row: k.3, * k. twice into next st., k.6, rep. from * to last 5 sts., k. twice into next st., k.4. [73 sts.]
Work in patt. as folls., carrying yarns not in use loosely up sides of work.
1st row (wrong side): p.
2nd row: * p.1, k.5, rep. from * to last st., p.1.
3rd row: * k.1, p.5, rep. from * to last st., k.1.
Rep. last 2 rows twice more.
8th row: with B, as 2nd.
9th row: with C, p.
10th row: with A, k.
11th row: with A, as 3rd.
12th row: with A, as 2nd.
Rep. last 2 rows twice more.
17th row: with B, as 3rd.
18th row: with C, k.
These 18 rows form patt.
Work until sock measures approx. 23 cm. (9 in.) from beg., ending with a 10th row.
Break off all 3 colours.

Divide for Heel
Next row (wrong side): sl. first 18 sts. onto a holder for heel, join in A and k.1, * p.5, k.1, rep. from * 5 times more.
Sl. rem. 18 sts. onto 2nd holder for heel.

Instep
Cont. working in patt. on rem. 37 instep sts. for 18 cm. (7 in.), ending on wrong side with A.
Break yarn and sl. sts. onto a holder.

Shape Heel
With wrong side facing, sl. 36 heel sts. onto one needle.
Join in A.
1st row: sl.1p., p. to end.
2nd row: * keeping yarn at back, sl.1p., k.1, rep. from * to end.
Rep. last 2 rows 17 times more.

Turn Heel
1st row: sl.1, p.20, p.2 tog., p.1, turn.
2nd row: sl.1, k.7, sl.1, k.1, p.s.s.o., k.1, turn.
3rd row: sl.1, p.8, p.2 tog., p.1, turn.
4th row: sl.1, k.9, sl.1, k.1, p.s.s.o., k.1, turn.
5th row: sl.1, p.10, p.2 tog., p.1, turn.
Cont. to dec. in this way, working 1 more st. before the dec. on each row until 22 sts. rem.
Pick up 18 sts. down each side of heel and arrange these sts. and heel sts. onto 1 needle.
1st row: k.1, sl.1, k.1, p.s.s.o., k. to last 3 sts., k.2 tog., k.1.
2nd row: p.
Rep. last 2 rows until 36 sts. rem.
Cont. in st. st. until sole measures same as instep ending with a p. row.
With set of 4 double-pointed needles divide sole sts. onto 2 needles.

With 3rd needle, k. across instep sts., dec. 1 st. in centre of row. [72 sts.]
Work in the round until foot measures 19 cm. (7½ in.) or 5 cm. (2 in.) less than desired length.

Shape Toe
Next round: 1st needle – k.1, sl.1, k.1, p.s.s.o., k. to end, 2nd needle – k. to last 3 sts., k.2 tog., k.1, 3rd needle – k.1, sl.1, k.1, p.s.s.o., k. to last 3 sts., k.2 tog., k.1.
K. 1 round.
Rep. last 2 rounds until 20 sts. rem.
Sl. sts. from first needle onto second needle.
Cast off sts. from two needles tog.: hold 2 needles parallel and cast off 1 st. from each needle alternately to end.

MAKING UP

Sew up back and foot seams.

Flower-pattern, Fair Isle Sweater

1960

Three-colour Fair Isle sweater with round neck, long, set-in sleeves, shoulder opening for two smallest sizes, and ribbed welts

★ Suitable for adventurous beginners

MATERIALS

Yarn
Rowan Yarns Light Tweed
5(5:5:5:6) × 25g. hanks Main Col. A
2(2:2:2:3) × 25g. hanks Col. B
2(2:2:2:3) × 25g. hanks Col. C

Needles
1 pair 2¾mm.
1 pair 3¼mm.
st. holder

Buttons
1st and 2nd sizes only: 2

MEASUREMENTS

Chest
51(56:61:66:71) cm.
20(22:24:26:28) in.
1/2(2/3:4/5:6/7:8/9) approx. age

Length
26(31:37:42:47) cm.
10¼(12¼:14½:16½:18½) in.

Sleeve Seam
15(20:25:31:35) cm.
5¾(7¾:9¾:12¼:13¾) in.

TENSION

28 sts. and 36 rows = 10 cm. (4 in.) square over st. st. on 3¼mm. needles. If your tension square does not correspond to these measurements, see page 156 for adjustment instructions.

ABBREVIATIONS

k. = knit; p. = purl; st(s). = stitch(es); inc. = increas(ing) (see page 156); dec. = decreas(ing) (see page 157); beg. = begin(ning); rem. = remain(ing); rep. = repeat; alt. = alternate; tog. = together; sl. = slip (transfer one stitch from left needle, knitwise unless otherwise stated, to right hand needle.); cont. = continue; patt. = pattern; foll. = following; folls. = follows; mm. = millimetres; cm. = centimetres; in. = inches; st. st. = stocking st.: one row k., one row p.; g. st. = garter st.: every row k.; incs. = increases; decs. = decreases.

BACK

Cast on 76(84:90:98:104) sts. with 2¾mm. needles and A.
Work in k.1, p.1 rib for 2 cm. (¾ in.), inc. 1 st. at end of last row. [77(85:91:99:105) sts.]
Change to 3¼mm. needles.
Joining in and breaking off colours as required, cont. in st. st., working in patt. from chart.
NB When working from chart, read odd rows k. from right to left and even rows p. from left to right.

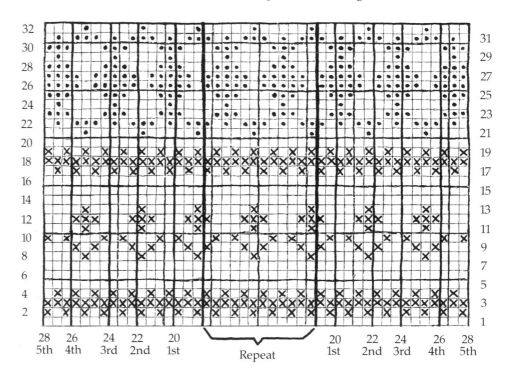

28 26 24 22 20
5th 4th 3rd 2nd 1st

Repeat

20 22 24 26 28
1st 2nd 3rd 4th 5th

□ = Col A
☒ = Col B
⊡ = Col C

Cont. until work measures 15(19:23: 27:31) cm. (5¾(7½:9:10½:12¼) in.) from beg., ending with a p. row. [46(60:74: 90:104) patt. rows]

Shape Armholes
Keeping patt. straight, cast off 4 sts. at the beg. of next 2 rows.
Now dec. 1 st. at each end of next row, and 0(1:2:3:3) foll. alt rows. [67(73:77: 83:89) sts.]
** Cont. straight until armholes measure 11(12:14:15:16) cm. (4¼(4¾:5½:5¾:6¼) in.). [40(44:50:54:58) patt. rows from beg. of armhole shaping.]

Shape Shoulders
Cast off 9(10:11:12:13) sts. at beg. of next 2 rows.
Cast off 9(10:10:11:12) sts. at beg. of foll. 2 rows.
Sl. rem. 31(33:35:37:39) sts. onto holder.

FRONT

Work as for back to **.
Cont. straight until armholes measure 7(8:9:10:10) cm. (2¾(3¼:3½:4:4) in.), ending with a right side row. [25(29:31:35:35) patt. rows from beg. of armhole shaping.]

Shape Neck
Next row: patt. 26(28:30:33:35) sts., leave these sts. on a spare needle until required for right front shoulder, cast off 15(17:17: 17:19) sts., work to end and cont. on these 26(28:30:33:35) sts. for left front shoulder.
Dec. 1 st. at neck edge on next 8(8:9:10:10 rows. [18(20:21:23:25) sts.]
Work 6(6:9:8:12) rows.

Shape Shoulder
Cast off 9(10:11:12:13) sts. at beg. of next row.
Work 1 row.
Cast off rem. 9(10:10:11:12) sts.
Cast off.

Right front shoulder:
With right side facing, rejoin yarn to inner edge of sts. left on spare needle.
Next row: dec. 1 st., work to end of row.
Work as for left front shoulder to end, but work 1 extra row before shaping shoulder.

SLEEVES

Cast on 48(48:48:54:54) sts. with 2¾mm. needles and A.
Work in k.1, p.1 rib for 2 cm. (¾ in.), inc. 1 st. at end of last row. [49(49:49:55:55) sts.]
Change to 3¼mm. needles.
Joining in and breaking off colours as required, cont. in st. st., working in patt. from chart as folls.:
1st size: beg. with the 1st patt. row, placing sts. as for 2nd size on chart.
2nd size: beg. with 2 rows A, then foll. chart from 1st row, placing sts. as for 2nd size on chart.
3rd size: beg. with 23rd patt. row, placing sts. as for 2nd size on chart.
4th and 5th sizes: beg. with 2 rows A., then foll. chart from 21st row, placing sts. as for 3rd size on chart.
Keeping patt. correct as set and working extra sts. into patt. as they occur, inc. 1 st. at each end of 5th and every foll. 6th(6th: 6th:12th:12th) row until there are 63(67:71:73:77) sts.
Cont. straight until sleeve measures 15(20:25:31:35) cm. (5¾(7¾:9¾:12¼: 13¾) in.) from beg., ending with a p. row.
(Patt. at this point should correspond to patt. at armhole shaping of back and front).

Shape Sleeve Top
Cont. in patt. as set.
Cast off 4 sts. at beg. of next 2 rows.

Dec. 1 st. at each end of next and foll. 6(7:12:13:15) alt. rows, then dec. 1 st. at each end of next 5(6:3:3:1) rows. [31(31: 31:31:35) sts.]
Cast off 3(3:3:3:4) sts. at beg. of next 6 rows.
Now cast off 4(4:4:4:3) sts. at beg. of foll. 2 rows.
Cast off rem. 5 sts.
Sew up right shoulder seam.

NECKBAND

With 2¾mm. needles and A, pick up and k. 82(88:96:100:108) sts., including sts. on holder.
Work in k.1, p.1 rib for 2 cm. (¾ in.)
Cast off loosely in rib.

LEFT SHOULDER EDGING

(1st and 2nd sizes only)

Sew up shoulder seam for 1 cm. (½ in.) at armhole edge.
With 2¾mm. needles and A, pick up and k.18(20) sts. from left back shoulder (including neckband), then 18(20) sts. from left front shoulder.
K.1 row.
Next row: k.20(22), cast off 2, k. next 10(12) sts., cast off 2, k. to end.
Next row: k. across row, casting on 2 sts. over cast off sts.
Cast off.

MAKING UP

Press all pieces except ribbing with a warm iron over a damp cloth.
Sew up left shoulder seam for 3rd, 4th and 5th sizes.
Set in sleeves.
Sew up side and sleeve seams.
Sew on buttons for 1st and 2nd sizes.
Press all seams.

Ridge-pattern Cardigan 1953

Rugged, hip-length sports cardigan buttoning to a V neckline, with set-in sleeves, ribbed welts and borders

★★ Suitable for knitters with some previous experience

MATERIALS

Yarn
Sunbeam St Ives 4 ply
21(21:22:23:23) × 25g. balls.

Needles
1 pair 3mm.
1 pair 3¾mm.

Buttons
5

MEASUREMENTS

Chest
92(97:102:107:112) cm.
36(38:40:42:44) in.

Length
64(66:68:70:71) cm.
25(26:26¾:27½:27¾) in.

Sleeve Seam
52(53:55:55:56) cm.
20½(20¾:21½:21½:22) in.

TENSION

28 sts. and 36 rows = 10 cm. (4 in.) square over patt. slightly stretched on 3¾mm. needles. If your tension square does not correspond to these measurements, see page 156 for adjustment instructions.

ABBREVIATIONS

k. = knit; p. = purl; st(s). = stitch(es); inc. = increas(ing) (see page 156); dec. = decreas(ing) (see page 157); beg. = begin(ning); rem. = remain(ing); rep. = repeat; alt. = alternate; tog. = together; sl. = slip (transfer one stitch from left needle, knitwise unless otherwise stated, to right hand needle.); cont. = continue; patt. = pattern; foll. = following; folls. = follows; mm. = millimetres; cm. = centimetres; in. = inches; st. st. = stocking st.: one row k., one row p.; g. st. = garter st.: every row k.; incs. = increases; decs. = decreases.

BACK

Cast on 155(161:170:176:182) sts. with 3mm. needles.
Work 9 cm. (3½ in.) in rib as folls., ending with a 2nd patt. row:
1st row (right side): * k.2, p.1, rep. from * to last 2 sts., k.2.
2nd row: * p.2, k.1, rep. from * to last 2 sts., p.2.
Next row: inc. 1(2:0:1:2) sts. across the row. [156(163:170:177:184) sts.]
Change to 3¾mm. needles and work as folls.:
1st row (wrong side): * k.2, p.5, rep. from * to last 2 sts., k.2.
2nd row: ** p.2, k.1, * k.2 tog., then k. again into first st. before slipping sts. off needle, rep. from * once more, rep. from ** to last 2 sts., p.2.
These 2 rows form patt.
Rep. 1st and 2nd rows until back measures 43(44:46:47:48) cm. (16¾(17¼: 18:18½:18¾) in.).

Shape Armholes
Cast off 6(7:8:9:10) sts. at beg. of next 2 rows.
Dec. 1 st. at each end of every alt. row until 126(131:134:137:140) sts. rem.
Work until armholes measure 21(22:22: 23:23) cm. (8¼(8½:8½:9:9) in.) measured on the straight.

Shape Shoulders
Cast off at beg. of next and foll. rows 12(12:10:10:11) sts. twice and 10(10:11:11: 11) sts. 6 times.
Cast off rem. sts.

LEFT FRONT

Cast on 74(77:83:89:92) sts. with 3mm. needles.
Work 9 cm. (3½ in.) in rib as for back ending with 2nd patt. row.
Next row: inc. 5(2:3:4:1) sts. evenly across the row. [79(79:86:93:93) sts.]
Change to 3¾mm. needles and work in patt. as for back until front measures same as back to armholes, ending with right side facing.

Shape Armhole and Neck
1st row: cast off 7(7:9:9:10) sts., work to last 2 sts., k.2 tog.
Dec. 1 st. at armhole edge on every alt. row 8(9:9:11:11) times, at the same time dec. at neck edge on every 3rd row until 45(48:46:56:55) sts. rem.
Now dec. at neck edge on every 4th(4th: 2nd:2nd:2nd) row until 42(42:43:43:44) sts. rem.
Work until armhole measures same as back.

Shape Shoulder
Cast off at armhole edge 12(12:10:10:11) sts. once and 10(10:11:11:11) sts. 3 times.

RIGHT FRONT

Work as for left front, reversing all shapings.

SLEEVES

Cast on 77(77:80:83:86) sts. with 3mm. needles.

Work 9 cm. (3½ in.) in rib as for back, ending with a 2nd patt. row.
Next row: inc. 2(2:6:3:0) sts. across the row. [79(79:86:86:86) sts.]
Change to 3¾mm. needles and work in patt. as back.
Inc. 1 st. at each end of every 6th row, working all inc. sts. into patt., until there are 119(123:128:132:136) sts.
Work until sleeve measures 52(53:55:55: 56) cm. (20½(20¾:21½:21½:22) in.)

Shape Top
Cast off 7(8:9:10:11) sts. at beg. of next 2 rows.
Dec. 1 st. at each end of every alt. row 12 times.
Cast off 5 sts. at beg. of next 12 rows.
Cast off rem. sts.

FRONT BORDER

Cast on 17 sts. with 3mm. needles, and work in rib as given for back.
Work 2 cm. (¾ in.)
Make buttonhole as folls.:
Next row (right side): rib 6 sts., cast off 6 sts., rib to end.
Next row: cast on 6 sts. above cast-off sts. of preceding row.
Work 4 more buttonholes 9(9:9:10:10) cm. (3½(3½:3½:4:4) in.) apart.
Work until border is same length as fronts and back neck when slightly stretched.
Cast off.

MAKING UP

Sew up shoulder seams.
Set in sleeves.
Sew up side and sleeve seams.
Sew up front border to fronts and back neck with buttonholes on left side.
Sew on buttons.
Press lightly.

Twinset with Round or V Neckline   1957

Classic twinsets in stocking stitch with raglan sleeves, sweater with long or short sleeves, cardigan with high or V-neck buttoning

★ Suitable for beginners

NB twinset cardigan was photographed without buttons

MATERIALS

Yarn
Rowan botany wool 3 ply
Long Sleeved Sweater:
6(6:8:8:9:10) × 25g. hanks
Short Sleeved Sweater:
5(5:6:7:8:9) × 25g. hanks
Cardigan:
6(6:8:8:9:10) × 25g. hanks

Needles
1 pair 2¼mm.
1 pair 3mm.
1 set of 4 double-pointed 2¼mm. for sweater
safety pin
st. holders

Buttons
7 for round-neck cardigan
or
6 for v-neck cardigan

MEASUREMENTS

Chest
61(66:71:76:82:87) cm.
24(26:28:30:32:34) in.
4/5(6/7:8/9:10/11:12/13:14/15) approx. age

Length
Sweater:
37(40:44:46:51:54) cm.
14½(15¾:17¼:18:20:21¼) in.
Cardigan:
39(43:46:48:53:57) cm.
15¼(16¾:18:18¾:20¾:22¼) in.

Sleeve Seam
Short-sleeved sweater:
8(9:10:11:12:13) cm.
3¼(3½:4:4¼:4¾:5) in.
Long-sleeved sweater:
23(27:31:36:41:42) cm.
9(10½:12¼:14:16:16½) in.
Cardigan Sleeve Seam:
24(28:32:37:42:43) cm.
9½(11:12½:14½:16½:16¾) in.

TENSION

32 sts. and 40 rows = 10 cm. (4 in.) square over st. st. on 3mm. needles. If your tension square does not correspond to these measurements, see page 156 for adjustment instructions.

ABBREVIATIONS

k. = knit; p. = purl; st(s). = stitch(es); inc. = increas(ing) (see page 156); dec. = decreas(ing) (see page 157); beg. = begin(ning); rem. = remain(ing); rep. = repeat; alt. = alternate; tog. = together; sl. = slip (transfer one stitch from left needle, knitwise unless otherwise stated, to right hand needle.); cont. = continue; patt. = pattern; foll. = following; folls. = follows; mm. = millimetres; cm. = centimetres; in. = inches; st. st. = stocking st.: one row k., one row p.; g. st. = garter st.: every row k.; incs. = increases; decs. = decreases; p.s.s.o. = pass the sl. st. over.

SWEATER BACK

Cast on 104(112:120:128:136:144) sts. with 2¼mm. needles.
Work 6 cm. (2¼ in.) in k.1, p.1 rib.
Change to 3mm. needles and st. st.
Cont. straight until work measures 23(25:28:29:33:35) cm. (9(9¾:11:11¼:13:13¾) in.), ending with a p. row.

Shape Raglans
Cast off 4(5:6:7:8:9) sts. at beg. of next 2 rows.
Dec. 1 st. at each end of next 7 rows.
Next row: p.
11th row: k.2, k.2 tog., k. to last 4 sts., sl.1, k.1, p.s.s.o., k.2.
12th row: p.
Rep. last 2 rows until 36(38:40:42:44:46)

sts. rem., ending with a p. row.
Leave sts. on holder.

SWEATER FRONT

Work as for back until 56(58:60:62:64:66) sts. rem., ending with a k. row.

Shape Neck
Next row: p.22, turn.
Finish this side first.
** Cont. dec. 1 st. at raglan edge on every alt. row, AT THE SAME TIME dec. 1 st. at neck edge on next 5 rows, then on every alt. row 3 times, then on every 3rd row until 3 sts. rem.
Next row: p.3.
Next row: k.1, k.2 tog.
Next row: p.2.
Cast off.
Sl. centre 12(14:16:18:20:22) sts. onto st. holder for neck.
Rejoin yarn to rem. sts. and p. to end.
Work to match first side from ** to end.

SWEATER SHORT SLEEVES

Cast on 66(70:74:78:82:86) sts. with 2¼mm. needles.
Work 3 cm. (1¼ in.) in k.1, p.1 rib.
Change to 3mm. needles and st. st.
Inc. 1 st. at each end of next and every 4th row until there are 78(84:90:96:102:108) sts.
Work 1 row.

Shape Raglan
Cast off 4(5:6:7:8:9) sts. at beg. of next 2 rows.
3rd row: k.2, k.2 tog., k. to last 4 sts., sl.1, k.1, p.s.s.o., k.2.
4th row: p.
Rep. last 2 rows until 16 sts. rem.
Leave sts. on holder.

SWEATER LONG SLEEVES

Cast on 48(50:54:56:58:60) sts. with 2¼mm. needles.
Work 5 cm. (2 in.) in k.1, p.1 rib.
Change to 3mm. needles and st. st.
Inc. 1 st. at each end of next and every foll. 4th(5th:5th:5th:6th:6th) row until there are 78(84:90:96:102:108) sts.
Cont. straight until sleeve measures 23(27:31:36:41:42) cm. (9(10½:12¼:14:16: 16½) in.), ending with a p. row.

Shape Raglan
Cast off 4(5:6:7:8:9) sts. at beg. of next 2 rows.
3rd row: k.2, k.2 tog., k. to last 4 sts., sl.1, k.1, p.s.s.o., k.2.
4th row: p.
Rep. last 2 rows until 16 sts. rem.
Leave sts. on holder.

SWEATER NECKBAND

Sew up raglan seams.
With right side facing and set of 2¼mm. needles, pick up and k.36(38:40:42:44:46) sts. from holder at back, 16 sts. from left sleeve, 20 sts. down left front, 12(14:16: 18:20:22) sts. from holder at front, 20 sts. up right front and 16 sts. from right sleeve. [120(124:128:132:136:140) sts.]

Work 5 cm. (2 in.) in k.1, p.1 rib.
Cast off loosely in rib.

SWEATER MAKING UP

Press work lightly with warm iron over damp cloth.
Sew up side and sleeve seams.
Press seams.
Turn neckband in half onto wrong side and sl. st. loosely down.

ROUND-NECK CARDIGAN BACK

Cast on 108(116:124:132:140:148) sts. with 2¼mm. needles.
Work 8 cm. (3¼ in.) in k.1, p.1 rib.
Change to 3mm. needles and st. st.
Cont. straight until work measures 24(27:29:30:34:37) cm. (9½(10½:11¼:11¾: 13¼:14½) in.), ending with a p. row.

Shape Raglans
Cast off 5(6:7:8:9:10) sts. at beg. of next 2 rows.
Now dec. 1 st. at each end of next 7 rows.
Next row: p.
11th row: k.2, k.2 tog., k. to last 4 sts., sl.1, k.1, p.s.s.o., k.2.
12th row: p.
Rep. last 2 rows until 36(38:40:42:44:46) sts. rem., ending with a p. row.
Leave sts. on holder.

ROUND-NECK CARDIGAN LEFT FRONT

Cast on 51(55:59:63:67:71) sts. with 2¼mm. needles.
Work 8 cm. (3¼ in.) in k.1, p.1 rib, beg. alt. rows p.1.
Change to 3mm. needles and st. st.
Work until front measures same as back to armholes, ending with a p. row (end with a k. row on right front). **

Shape Raglan
Cast off 5(6:7:8:9:10) sts. at beg. of next row.
P. 1 row (omit this row on right front).
Dec. 1 st. at armhole edge on next 7 rows.
P. 1 row.
11th row: k.2, k.2 tog., k. to end.
12th row: p.
Rep. last 2 rows until 26(27:28:29:30:31) sts. rem., ending with a p. row.

Shape Neck
1st row: k.2, k.2 tog., k.19, turn, sl. rem. 3(4:5:6:7:8) sts. onto holder.
Still dec. at armhole edge as before, dec. 1 st. at neck edge on next 4 rows then at neck edge of every alt. row 3 times, then every 3rd row until 3 sts. rem., ending with a p. row.
Next row: k.1, k.2 tog.
Next row: p.2.
Cast off.

ROUND-NECK CARDIGAN RIGHT FRONT

Work as for left front, reversing all shapings.
Work raglan shaping as folls.:
Work to last 4 sts., sl.1, k.1, p.s.s.o., k.2.

ROUND-NECK CARDIGAN SLEEVES

Cast on 52(54:56:58:60:62) sts. with 2¼mm. needles.
Work 5 cm. (2 in.) in k.1, p.1 rib.
Change to 3mm. needles and st. st.
Inc. 1 st. at each end of next and every foll. 5th(5th:5th:5th:6th:6th) row until there are 82(88:94:100:106:112) sts.
Work until sleeve measures 24(28:32:37: 42:43) cm. (9½(11:12½:14½:16½:16¾) in.), ending with a p. row.

Shape Raglan
Cast off 5(6:7:8:9:10) sts. at beg. of next 2 rows.
3rd row: k.2, k.2 tog., k. to last 4 sts., sl.1, k.1, p.s.s.o., k.2.
4th row: p.
Rep. last 2 rows until 16 sts. rem.
Leave sts. on holder.

ROUND-NECK CARDIGAN BUTTON BAND

Cast on 12 sts. with 2¼mm. needles.
Work in k.1, p.1 rib until band is long enough, when slightly stretched, to fit up front to beg. of neck.
Sl. sts. onto a safety pin.
Break off yarn.
Sew in place.
Mark positions for 7 buttons, placing 1st hole 1 cm. (½ in.) from lower edge and allowing for last one to be in the centre of 2 cm. (¾ in.) neckband which is worked later.

ROUND-NECK CARDIGAN BUTTONHOLE BAND

Work as for button band, working buttonholes to correspond with positions marked for buttons as folls.:
1st buttonhole row: rib 4, cast off 4, rib to end.
Next row: rib to cast-off sts., cast on 4, rib to end.

ROUND-NECK CARDIGAN NECKBAND

Sew up raglan seams.
With right side of work facing and 2¼mm. needles, rib 15(16:17:18:19:20) sts. from holders at right front (including 12 sts. from front band), pick up and k.16 sts. from right front, 16 sts. from right sleeve, 36(38:40:42:44:46) sts. from holder at back, 16 sts. from left sleeve, 16 sts. down left front and rib 15(16:17:18:19:20) sts. from holders at left front (including 12 sts. from front band). [130(134:138:142: 146:150) sts.]
Work 5 rows in k.1, p.1 rib.
Work buttonhole on next 2 rows.
Rib 10 rows.
Work buttonhole on next 2 rows.
Rib 5 rows.
Cast off loosely in rib.

ROUND-NECK CARDIGAN MAKING UP

Sew up side and sleeve seams.
Fold neckband in half onto wrong side

and sew in place.
Neaten double buttonhole on neckband.
Sew on buttons.
Press seams.

V-NECK CARDIGAN BACK AND SLEEVES

Work as for round-necked cardigan, but cast off rem. sts.

V-NECK CARDIGAN LEFT FRONT

Work as for round-necked cardigan to **.

Shape Raglan and Neck
1st row: cast off 5(6:7:8:9:10) sts., k. to last 2 sts., k.2 tog.
2nd row: work to end.
3rd row: k.2 tog., work to end.
4th row: work to last 2 sts., p.2 tog.
5th row: k.2 tog., work to last 2 sts., k.2 tog.
6th row: as 4th.
7th row: as 3rd.
8th row: as 4th.
9th row: k.2, k.2 tog., k. to last 2 sts., k.2 tog.
10th row: work to end.
11th row: k.2, k.2 tog., work to end.
12th row: as 10th.
Rep. 9th to 12th rows until 6 sts. rem., ending with a 10th row.
Dec. at raglan edge only until 2 sts. rem., ending with a p. row.
Cast off.

V-NECK CARDIGAN RIGHT FRONT

Work as for left front, reversing all shapings.
Work raglan shaping as folls.:
Work to last 4 sts., sl.1, k.1, p.s.s.o., k.2.

V-NECK CARDIGAN FRONT BAND

Sew up raglan seams.
Sew up side and sleeve seams.
Cast on 12 sts. with 2¼mm. needles and work in k.1, p.1 rib until band is long enough, when slightly stretched, to fit up left front, across back neck and down front to first front dec., sewing in place as you k.
1st buttonhole row: rib 4, cast off 4, rib to end.
Next row: rib to cast off sts., cast on 4 sts., rib to end.
Mark position for buttons on button band, first to match with buttonhole already worked, the last to come 1 cm. (½ in.) from lower edge, rem. 4 equally spaced between.
Cont. in rib, working buttonholes as before to match with positions marked for buttons.
Cast off in rib.

V-NECK CARDIGAN MAKING UP

Sew on buttons.
Press seams.

Thick Cotton Sleeveless Pullover

Horizontal rib sleeveless pullover with ribbed lower welt, armholes and V-neck

★ Suitable for beginners

MATERIALS

Yarn
Christian de Falbe Studio Yarns
Paradise Cotton
4(4:5:6) × 50g. balls.

Needles
1 pair 3mm.
1 pair 3¾mm.

MEASUREMENTS

Chest
61(66:71:76) cm.
24(26:28:30) in.
4/5(6/7:8/9:10/12) approx. age

Length
34(37:39:41) cm.
13¼(14½:15¼:16) in.

TENSION

23 sts. and 28 rows = 10 cm. (4 in.) square with double yarn over st. st. on 3¾mm. needles. If your tension square does not correspond to these measurements, see page 156 for adjustment instructions.

ABBREVIATIONS

k. = knit; p. = purl; st(s). = stitch(es); inc. = increas(ing) (see page 156); dec. = decreas(ing) (see page 157); beg. = begin(ning); rem. = remain(ing); rep. = repeat; alt. = alternate; tog. = together; sl. = slip (transfer one stitch from left needle, knitwise unless otherwise stated, to right hand needle.); cont. = continue; patt. = pattern; foll. = following; folls. = follows; mm. = millimetres; cm. = centimetres; in. = inches; st. st. = stocking st.: one row k., one row p.; g. st. = garter st.: every row k.; incs. = increases; decs. = decreases; t.b.l. = through back of loops.

NB Use yarn double throughout.

BACK

Cast on 72(78:86:92) sts. with 3mm. needles.
Work 5(5:6:6) cm. (2(2:2¼:2¼) in.) in k.1, p.1 rib.
Change to 3¾mm. needles and patt. as folls.:
1st and 2nd rows: k.
3rd and 4th rows: p.
These 4 rows form patt.
Cont. in patt. until work measures 23(24:26:27) cm. (9(9½:10¼:10½) in.)

Shape Armholes

Cast off 2(2:3:3) sts. at beg. of next 2 rows.
Dec. 1 st. at each end of next 4 rows.
Dec. 1 st. at each end of next and foll. alt. rows until 56(60:68:70) sts. rem. **

Cont. without shaping until work measures 34(37:39:41) cm. (13¼(14½: 15¼:16) in.)

Shape Shoulders

Cast off 5(5:6:6) sts. at beg. of next 2 rows.

Cast off 5(6:6:6) sts. at beg. of next 2 rows.
Cast off 6(6:7:7) sts. at beg. of next 2 rows.
Cast off rem. 24(26:30:32) sts.

FRONT

Work as for back to **.

Shape Neck

Next row: patt. 26(28:32:33), work 2 tog., turn.

Working on 27(29:33:34) sts., cont. in patt., dec. at neck edge on alt. rows until 16(17:19:19) sts. rem.

Cont. without shaping until work measures same as back to shoulder shaping, ending at armhole edge.

Shape Shoulder

Cast off 5(5:6:6) sts., patt. to end.
Work 1 row.
Cast off 5(6:6:6) sts., patt. to end.
Work 1 row.
Cast off rem. 6(6:7:7) sts.
Rejoin yarn to rem. sts. at neck edge.
Next row: work 2 tog., patt. to end.
Work to match other side.

NECKBAND

Sew up right shoulder seam.

With 3mm. needles pick up and k. 40(42:42:44) sts. from left side front neck, 1 st. from centre front neck, 40(42:42:44) sts. from right front neck and 24(26:30:32) sts. from back neck. [105(111:115:121) sts.]

1st row: * k.1, p.1, rep. from * 30(32:34:36) times, k.2 tog.t.b.l., p.1, k.2 tog., * p.1, k.1, rep. from * 18(19:19:20) times.

2nd row: rib as set to within 2 sts. of centre front st., k.2 tog. t.b.l., k.1, k.2 tog., rib as set to end.

3rd row: rib to within 2 sts. of centre front st., k.2 tog. t.b.l., p.1, k.2 tog., rib to end.

Rep. 2nd and 3rd rows once, then 2nd row again.

Cast off loosely in rib.

ARMBANDS

Sew up left shoulder and neckband seam.
With 3mm. needles pick up and k.76(80:84:88) sts. evenly around armhole.
Work 6 rows in k.1, p.1 rib.
Cast off in rib.

MAKING UP

Sew up side and armband seams.

Long, Lean Angora Sweater 1948

Long, fine sweater in stocking stitch with raised rib yoke, set-in sleeves and pocket

★★ Suitable for knitters with some previous experience

MATERIALS

Yarn
Christian de Falbe Studio Yarns Watership
13(14:15:16) × 20g. balls

Needles
1 pair 2¾mm.
1 pair 3¾mm.

MEASUREMENTS

Bust
87(92:97:102) cm.
34(36:38:40) in.

Length
60(61:62:63) cm.
23¾(24:24¼:24¾) in.

Sleeve Seam
43(44:45:46) cm.
16¾(17¼:17¾:18) in.

TENSION

27 sts. and 32 rows = 10 cm. (4 in.) square

over st. st. using 3¾mm. needles. If your tension square does not correspond to these measurements, see page 156 for adjustment instructions.

ABBREVIATIONS

k. = knit; p. = purl; st(s). = stitch(es); inc. = increas(ing) (see page 156); dec. = decreas(ing) (see page 157); beg. = begin(ning); rem. = remain(ing); rep. = repeat; alt. = alternate; tog. = together; sl. = slip (transfer one stitch from left needle, knitwise unless otherwise stated, to right hand needle.); cont. = continue; patt. = pattern; foll. = following; folls. = follows; mm. = millimetres; cm. = centimetres; in. = inches; st. st. = stocking st.: one row k., one row p.; g. st. = garter st.: every row k.; incs. = increases; decs. = decreases.

BACK

Cast on 120(128:136:144) sts. with 2¾mm. needles.
Work 5 cm. (2 in.) in k.1, p.1 rib.
Change to 3¾mm. needles and st. st.
Cont. until work measures 41(42:42:43)

cm. (16(16½:16½:16¾) in.), ending with a p. row.

Shape Armholes

Cast off 5(6:7:8) sts. at beg. of next 2 rows.
Dec. 1 st. at each end of next 4 rows.

Dec. 1 st. at each end of next and every foll. alt. row until 92(96:100:104) sts. rem. Work 1 row.

Change to rib patt. as folls.:
1st row (right side): k.
2nd row: k.3(2:1:0), * p.2, k.4, rep. from * to last 5(4:3:2) sts., p.2, k.3(2:1:0).
These 2 rows form rib patt.
Cont. in patt. until work measures 60(61:62:63) cm. (23¾(24:24¼:24¾) in.)

Shape Shoulders

Cast off 6 sts. at beg. of next 2 rows.
Cast off 6(6:7:7) sts. at beg. of next 2 rows.
Cast off 6(7:7:7) sts. at beg. of next 2 rows.
Cast off 7(7:7:8) sts. at beg. of next 2 rows.
Cast off rem. 42(44:46:48) sts.

FRONT

Work as for back until work measures 36 cm. (14 in.), ending with a p. row.
Cont. as folls.:
1st row: k.
2nd row: p.58(62:66:70), k.1, p.2, k.1, p.58(62:66:70).
3rd and alt. rows: k.
4th row: p.57(61:65:69), k.2, p.2, k.2, p.57(61:65:69).
6th row: p.56(60:64:68), k.3, p.2, k.3, p.56(60:64:68).
8th row: p.55(59:63:67), k.4, p.2, k.4, p.55(59:63:67).
10th and 12th rows: as 8th.
14th row: p.52(56:60:64), k.1, p.2, k.4, p.2, k.4, p.2, k.1, p.52(56:60:64).
Cont. inc. rib patt. by one st. on each side, on alt. rows until work measures same as back to armhole.

Shape Armholes

Work as for back, keeping rib patt. enlarging correct.
Cont. until armhole shapings are completed. [92(96:100:104) sts.]
Change to rib patt. across all sts.
Cont. in rib patt. until work measures 53(54:54:55) cm. (20¾(21¼:21¼:21½) in.).

Shape Neck

1st row: patt. 36(38:39:41), cast off 20(20:22:22) sts., patt. to end.
Now work on 2nd set of 36(38:39:41) sts.
Dec. 1 st. at neck edge on next 6 rows.
Now dec. 1 st. at neck edge on alt. rows until 25(26:27:28) sts. rem.
Cont. without shaping until work measures same as back to shoulder, ending at armhole edge.

Shape Shoulder

Cast off 6 sts. at beg. of next row.
Work 1 row.
Cast off 6(6:7:7) sts. at beg. of next row.
Work 1 row.
Cast off 6(7:7:7) sts. at beg. of next row.
Work 1 row.
Cast off rem. 7(7:7:8) sts.
Rejoin yarn to neck edge of rem. 36(38:39:41) sts. and work to match first side.

SLEEVES

Cast on 52(52:58:58) sts. with 2¾mm.

needles.
Work 7 cm. (2¾ in.) in k.1, p.1 rib.
Change to 3¾mm. needles and rib patt.:
1st row: k.
2nd row: * k.4, p.2, rep. from * to last 4 sts., k.4.
Cont. in patt., inc. 1 st. at each end of 5th and every foll. 6th row until there are 94(94:100:100) sts., working inc. sts. into patt.
Cont. without shaping until work measures 43(44:45:46) cm. (16¾(17¼: 17¾:18) in.).

Shape Top
Cast off 5(3:3:3) sts. at beg. of next 2(4:4:4) rows.
Dec. 1 st. at each end of next 4 rows.

Dec. 1 st. at each end of next and every foll. alt. row until 46(44:48:46) sts. rem.
Dec. 1 st. at each end of next 4 rows.
Cast off 4 sts. at beg. of next 6 rows.
Cast off.

POCKET

Cast on 46 sts. with 3¾mm. needles.
Work in rib patt. as folls.:
1st row: k.
2nd row: * k.4, p.2, rep. from * to last 4 sts., k.4.
Cont. until work measures 15 cm. (5¾ in.).
Cast off.

NECKBAND

Sew up right shoulder seam.

With 2¾mm. needles, pick up and k.30(32:34:36) sts. from side front neck, 20(20:22:22) sts. from centre front neck, 30(32:34:36) sts. from side front neck and 44(44:46:46) sts. from back neck. [124(128:136:140) sts.].
Work 5 cm. (2 in.) in k.1, p.1 rib.
Cast off loosely in rib.

MAKING UP

Sew up left shoulder and neckband seam.
Sew up side and sleeve seams.
Set in sleeves.
Fold neckband in half to inside and slip st. into place.
Place pocket at desired position and slip st. into place.

Three-colour Norwegian Twin Set 1959

Stocking stitch twinset with allover Norwegian design, cardigan with patterned collar, all with ribbed welts

★★★ Suitable for experienced knitters

MATERIALS

Yarn
Templeton's H & O Shetland Fleece
9(10:10:11:12) × 25g. balls Main Col. A
2(2:2:2:2) × 25g. balls Col. B
2(2:2:2:2) × 25g. balls Col. C

Needles
1 pair 2¾mm.
1 pair 3¼mm.
1 crochet hook 2.5mm.

Buttons
5(6:6:6:6)

MEASUREMENTS

Chest
54(56:59:61:64) cm.
21(22:23:24:25) in.
1/2(2:3:4:5) approx. age

Length
Sweater:
35(38:40:42:45) cm.
13¾(15:15¾:16½:17) in.
Cardigan:
37(40:42:44:47) cm.
14½(15¾:16½:17¼:18½) in.

Sleeve Seam
Sweater:
23(25:27:28:30) cm.
9(9¾:10½:11:11¾) in.
Cardigan:
24(26:28:29:31) cm.
9½(10¼:11:11¼:12¼) in.

TENSION

28 sts. and 32 rows = 10 cm. (4 in.) square over patt. on 3¼mm. needles. If your tension square does not correspond to these measurements, see page 156 for adjustment instructions.

ABBREVIATIONS

k. = knit; p. = purl; st(s). = stitch(es); inc. = increas(ing) (see page 156); dec. = decreas(ing) (see page 157); beg. = begin(ning); rem. = remain(ing); rep. = repeat; alt. = alternate; tog. = together; sl. = slip (transfer one stitch from left needle, knitwise unless otherwise stated, to right hand needle.); cont. = continue; patt. = pattern; foll. = following; folls. = follows; mm. = millimetres; cm. = centimetres; in. = inches; st. st. = stocking st.: one row k., one row p.; g. st. = garter st.: every row k.; incs. = increases; decs. = decreases; d.c. = double crochet (see page 162 for instructions); ch. = chain st. (see page 162 for instructions).

SWEATER BACK

Cast on 76(84:90:98:104) sts. with 2¾mm. needles and A.
Work 5 cm. (2 in.) in k.1, p.1 rib, inc. 1 st. at beg. of last row. [77(85:91:99:105) sts.]
Change to 3¼mm. needles and st. st.
Work in patt. from chart 1, reading from 1(2:3:4:5) to dotted line, working st. to left of dotted line (centre st.), and working from dotted line back to 1(2:3:4:5).

These 44 rows form the patt. which is rep. throughout.
Work until back measures 23(25:27:28:30) cm. (9(9¾:10½:11:11¾) in.), ending with a wrong side row.

Shape Armholes
Cast off 3(3:4:4:5) sts. at beg. of next 2 rows.
Dec. 1 st. at each end of next 2 right side rows. [67(75:79:87:91) sts.]
Work straight until armholes measure 12(13:13:14:15) cm. (4¾(5:5:5½:5¾) in.), ending with a wrong side row.

Shape Shoulders

Cast off 4(4:5:5:5) sts. at beg. of next 2 rows.
Cast off 4(5:5:5:6) sts. at beg. of next 2 rows.
Cast off 5(5:5:6:6) sts. at beg. of next 2 rows.
Cast off 5(5:6:6:6) sts. at beg. of next 2 rows.
Leave rem. 31(37:37:43:45) sts. on holder.

SWEATER FRONT

Work as for back until armholes measure 7(8:8:9:10) cm. (2¾(3¼:3¼:3½:4) in.), ending with a wrong side row.

Shape Neck

1st row: patt. 22(23:25:28:29), turn.
Work left side on these sts., leaving rem. sts. on holder.
** Keeping patt. straight, dec. 1 st. at neck edge on every right side row until 18(19:21:22:23) sts. rem.
Work straight until armhole matches back to shoulder, ending at armhole edge.

Shape Shoulder

Cast off 4(4:5:5:5) sts. at beg. of next row.
Work 1 row.
Cast off 4(5:5:5:6) sts. at beg. of next row.
Work 1 row.
Cast off 5(5:5:6:6) sts. at beg. of next row.
Work 1 row.
Cast off rem. 5(5:6:6:6) sts. **
With right side of rem. sts. facing, sl. centre 23(29:29:31:33) sts. onto holder.
1st row: rejoin yarn to neck edge of rem. 22(23:25:28:29) sts., patt. to end.
Work as for left side from ** to **.

SLEEVES

Cast on 46(48:50:52:54) sts. with 2¾mm. needles and A.
Work 5 cm. (2 in.) in k.1, p.1 rib, inc. 1 st. at beg. of last row. [47(49:51:53:55) sts.]
Change to 3¼mm. needles and st. st.
Work in patt. from chart 2, inc. 1 st. at

each end of 4th row and every foll. 6th row until there are 63(65:67:69:71) sts., working inc. sts. into patt.
Work straight until sleeve measures same length as back to armholes, ending with same patt. row as back to match patt. stripes.

Shape Top

Cast off 3(3:4:4:5) sts. at beg. of next 2 rows.
Dec. 1 st. at each end of every right side row until 35(35:37:37:37) sts. rem.
Work 1 row.
Cast off 3 sts. at beg. of next 4 rows.
Cast off rem. sts.

NECKBAND

Sew up left shoulder seam.
With A and 2¾mm. needles and right side facing, k. across 31(37:37:43:45) sts. from back holder, k. up 19 sts. from left side, k. across 23(29:29:31:33) sts. from front holder and k. up 19 sts. up other side of neck. [92(104:104:112:116) sts.]
Work 3 cm. (1¼ in.) in k.1, p.1 rib.
Cast off loosely in rib.

CARDIGAN BACK

Work as for sweater back, making sides 1 cm. (½ in.) longer, and armholes 1 cm. (½ in.) longer.

CARDIGAN LEFT FRONT

Cast on 39(43:46:50:53) sts. with 2¾mm. needles and A.
Work 5 cm. (2 in.) in k.1, p.1 rib, beg. alt. rows p.1 on 1st, 2nd and 5th sizes only.
Change to 3¼mm. needles and st. st.
Work from chart 1, reading from 1(2:3:4:5) to st. beyond dotted line on k. rows, then on p. rows reading from left to right, work st. before dotted line, then work to 1(2:3:4:5).
Work until front matches back to armhole, ending at side edge.

Shape Armhole

Cast off 3(3:4:4:5) sts. at beg. of next row.
Dec. 1 st. at armhole edge on next 2 right side rows. [34(38:40:44:46) sts.]
Work straight until armhole measures 3 cm. (1¼ in.) less than cardigan back to shoulder, ending at centre front.

Shape Neck

Next row: cast off 10(10:10:10:11) sts., patt. to end.
Work 1 row.
Cast off 2(3:3:4:4) sts. at neck edge on next and foll. 2 alt. rows. [18(19:21:22:23) sts.]
Work straight until armhole measures same as cardigan back to shoulder, ending at armhole edge.

Shape Shoulder

Work as for sweater front shoulder.

CARDIGAN RIGHT FRONT

Work as for cardigan left front, reading patt. chart from st. before dotted line to 1(2:3:4:5) on k. rows, and in reverse on p. rows.

SLEEVES

Cast on 48(50:52:54:56) sts. with 2¾r.m. needles and A.
Work 5 cm. (2 in.) in k.1, p.1 rib, inc. 1 st. on last row. [49(51:53:55:57) sts.]
Change to 3¼mm. needles and st. st.
Work in patt. from chart 2, noting that there is 1 more st. at each side, therefore reading from 1 st. before 1(2:3:4:5) to dotted line, working centre st. and reading from dotted line to 1 st. after 1(2:3:4:5), AT THE SAME TIME inc. 1 st. at each end of 4th row and every foll. 6th row until there are 65(67:69:71:73) sts., working inc. sts. into patt.
Work straight until sleeve measures same length as back to armholes, ending with same patt. row as back to match patt. stripes.

Chart 1

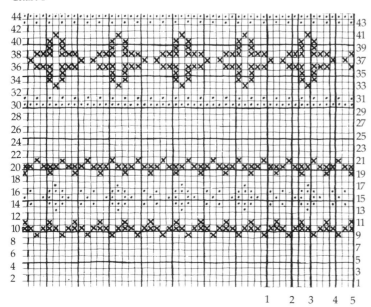

☐ = Col A
☒ = Col B
⊡ = Col C

Chart 2

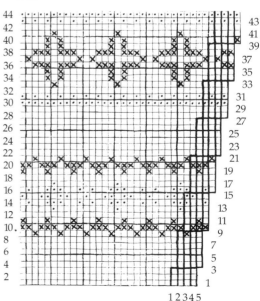

Shape Top

Cast off 3(3:4:4:5) sts. at beg. of next 2 rows.
Dec. 1 st. at each end of every right side row until 35(35:37:37:37) sts. rem.
Cast off 2 sts. at beg. of next 4 rows.
Cast off rem. sts.

NECKBAND

Sew up both shoulder seams.
With A, 2¾mm. needles and right side facing, k. up 24(27:28:29:30) sts. up right front neck, k. across sts. of back neck, then k. up 24(27:28:29:30) sts. down left front neck. [79(91:93:101:105) sts.]
Work 3 cm. (1¼ in.) in k.1, p.1 rib.

Cast off loosely in rib.

MAKING UP

Sweater

Sew up right shoulder and neckband seam.
Set in sleeves.
Sew up side and sleeve seams.

Cardigan

Set in sleeves.
Sew up side and sleeve seams.

Button Band

With right side facing and A, work 6 rows in d.c. along front edge, left side for girl and right side for boy.

Mark positions for buttons, first to come 1 cm. (½ in.) from lower edge and last to come 1 cm. (½ in.) from top edge, with remainder spaced evenly between.
Sew on buttons.

Buttonhole Band

With right side facing and A, work 3 rows in d.c.
Next row: work across, missing 2 d.c. at position for each buttonhole and working 2 ch. in their place.
Next row: work across, working 2 d.c. into each set of 2 ch.
Work 1 more row.
Press both garments under a damp cloth with a warm iron, omitting ribbing.

Striped Summer Sweater 1939

Stocking stitch sweater in two-colour stripe, with long or short, set-in sleeves, narrow collar and slit front opening

★ Suitable for beginners

MATERIALS

Yarn

Yarnworks Cotton
Short Sleeve Version:
6(7:7:8) × 50g. balls Main Col. A
3(3:3:3) × 50g. balls Col. B
Long Sleeve Version:
7(8:8:9) × 50g. balls Main Col. A
4(4:4:4) × 50g. balls Col. B

Needles

1 pair 3¼mm.
1 pair 4mm.

MEASUREMENTS

Bust

82(87:92:97) cm.
32(34:36:38) in.

Length

61(61:63:63) cm.
24(24:24¾:24¾) in.

Short Sleeve Seam

13 cm.
5 in.

Long Sleeve Seam

42 cm.
16½ in.

TENSION

20 sts. and 28 rows = 10 cm. (4 in.) square over st. st. using 4mm. needles. If your tension square does not correspond to these measurements, see page 156 for adjustment instructions.

ABBREVIATIONS

k. = knit; p. = purl; st(s). = stitch(es); inc. = increas(ing) (see page 156); dec. = decreas(ing) (see page 157); beg. = begin(ning); rem. = remain(ing); rep. = repeat; alt. = alternate; tog. = together; sl. = slip (transfer one stitch from left needle, knitwise unless otherwise stated, to right hand needle.); cont. = continue; patt. = pattern; foll. = following; folls. = follows; mm. = millimetres; cm. = centimetres; in. = inches; st. st. = stocking st.: one row k., one row p.; g. st. = garter st.: every row k.; incs. = increases; decs. = decreases.

BACK

Cast on 80(86:90:96) sts. with 4mm. needles and A.
Work 4 rows st. st. for hem.
Work in st. st., making stripe patt. as folls.:
6 rows A, 2 rows B, 2 rows A, 2 rows B, 6 rows A, and 2 rows B.
These 20 rows form stripe patt.
Work in stripe patt. until back measures 21 cm. (8¼ in.) from beg., ending with a wrong side row.
Change to 3¼mm. needles and work 10 rows in stripe patt.
Change to 4mm. needles and work in stripe patt., inc. 1 st. at each end of foll. 9th and every foll. 16th row twice more. [86(92:96:102) sts.]
Work straight in stripe patt. until back measures 43 cm. (16¾ in.) from beg., ending with a wrong side row.

Armhole Shaping

Cast off 3(3:4:4) sts. at beg. of next 2 rows, 2(3:3:4) sts. at beg. of foll. 4 rows. [72(74:76:78) sts.]
Dec. 1 st. at each end of next and every foll. alt. row twice more. [66(68:70:72) sts.] **
Work straight in patt. until armholes measure 19(19:21:21) cm. (7½(7½:8¼:8¼) in.), ending with a wrong side row.

Shoulder Shaping

Cast off 8 sts. at beg. of next 4 rows, then 7(8:8:9) sts. at beg. of foll. 2 rows.
Cast off rem. 20(20:22:22) sts.

FRONT

Work as for back to **.
P. 1 row.

Shape Neck

Next row (right side): k.31(32:33:34), k.2 tog., join in a 2nd ball of yarn and k.2 tog., then k. to end.
Working both sides of neck at same time with separate balls of yarn, dec. 1 st. at neck edge on every 4th row 9(9:10:10) times. [23(24:24:25) sts. each side].
Work straight until armholes measure same as back to shoulder, ending with a wrong side row.

Shoulder Shaping

Cast off 8 sts. at each armhole edge twice, then 7(8:8:9) sts. once.

SHORT SLEEVES

Cast on 56(58:60:62) sts. with 4mm. needles and A.
Work 4 rows in st. st. for hem.
Work in st. st. and stripe patt. as for back, inc. 1 st. at each end of foll. 5th row and every foll. 6th row twice more. [62(64:66: 68) sts.]
Work straight in stripe patt. until sleeve measures 14 cm. (5½ in.) from beg., ending with same stripe as back to armhole.

Shape Top

Cast off 3(3:4:4) sts. at beg. of next 2 rows.
Dec. 1 st. at each end of next and every foll. alt. row 10(9:13:12) times more. [34(38:30:34) sts.]
Dec. 1 st. at each end of next 9(11:7:9) rows.
Cast off rem. 16 sts.

LONG SLEEVES

Cast on 40(42:44:46) sts. with 4mm. needles and A.
Work 4 rows in st. st. for hem.
Work in st. st. stripe patt. as for back, inc. 1 st. at each end of foll. 15th row and every foll. 8th row 10 times more. [62(64:66:68) sts.]
Work straight in stripe patt. until sleeve measures 43 cm. (16¾ in.) from beg., ending with same stripe as back to armhole.

Shape Top

Work as for short sleeves.

REVERS

Right Side

Cast on 31(31:36:36) sts. with 4mm. needles and A.
Work 4 rows in st. st. for hem.
Now cont. in stripe patt. as for back as folls.:
Work 2 rows straight.
Next row: cast off 3 sts., k. to end.
Next row: p.
Next row: cast off 3 sts., k. to last 2 sts., inc. in next st., k.1.
Next row: p.
Rep. last 4 rows 4(4:5:5) times more, then first 2 rows once more.
Cast off rem. 3 sts.

Left Side

Cast on 31(31:36:36) sts. with 4mm. needles and A.
Work 4 rows in st. st. for hem.
Now work in stripe patt. as for back as folls.:
Work 3 rows straight.
Next row: cast off 3 sts., p. to end.
Next row: k.
Next row: cast off 3 sts., p. to last 2 sts., inc. in next st., p.1.
Next row: k.
Rep. last 4 rows 4(4:5:5) times more, then first 2 rows once more.
Cast off rem. 3 sts.

COLLAR

Cast on 55(55:57:57) sts. with 4mm. needles and A.

Work 4 rows in st. st. for hem.
Work in stripe patt. as for back but always work 8 sts. at each end of every row in A, (4 sts. for hem and 4 sts. for border).
It will be necessary to use a 2nd ball of A at end of k. rows for border and yarns must be twisted round each other at each change of colour.
Work 18 rows in this way.
Cast off.

MAKING UP

Sew up side, shoulder and sleeve seams.
Set in sleeves.
Sew shaped edge of revers to neck edges of front.
Sew end of collar to back neck and top of revers.
Turn up all hems and sew in position.

Fisherman's-rib, Round-neck Sweater 1982

Traditional fisherman's-ribbed sweater with round neck, raglan sleeves and ribbed welts

★★ Suitable for knitters with some previous experience

MATERIALS

Yarn
Sunbeam Pure New Wool 4 ply
4(5:5:6) × 50g. balls

Needles
1 pair 2¾mm.
1 pair 3¼mm.

MEASUREMENTS

Chest
51(56:61:66) cm.
20(22:24:26) in.
1(2/3:4/5:6/7) approx. age

Length
33(38:42:46) cm.
13(15:16½:18) in.

Sleeve Seam
21(23:27:31) cm.
8¼(9:10½:12¼) in.

TENSION

26 sts. and 52 rows = 10 cm. (4 in.) square over patt. on 3¼mm. needles. If your tension square does not correspond to these measurements, see page 156 for adjustment instructions.

ABBREVIATIONS

k. = knit; p. = purl; st(s). = stitch(es); inc. = increas(ing) (see page 156); dec. = decreas(ing) (see page 157); beg. = begin(ning); rem. = remain(ing); rep. = repeat; alt. = alternate; tog. = together; sl. = slip (transfer one stitch from left needle, knitwise unless otherwise stated, to right hand needle.); cont. = continue; patt. = pattern; foll. = following; folls. = follows; mm. = millimetres; cm. = centimetres; in. = inches; st. st. = stocking st.: one row k., one row p.; g. st. = garter st.: every row k.; incs. = increases; decs. = decreases; p.s.s.o. = pass the sl. st. over; k.1b. = k. 1 below: k. into next st. one row below, at the same time sl. off st. above.

BACK

** Cast on 73(79:85:91) sts. with 2¾mm. needles.
1st row: k.2, * p.1, k.1, rep. from * to last st., k.1.
2nd row: * k.1, p.1, rep. from * to last st., k.1.
Rep. 1st and 2nd rows 6(8:10:12) times more.

Change to 3¼mm. needles and patt.
1st row (right side): k.
2nd row: k.1, * p.1, k.1b., rep. from * to last 2 sts., p.1, k.1.
These 2 rows form patt.
Work until back measures 22(25:28:31) cm. (8½(9¾:11:12¼) in.) from beg., ending with a wrong side row.
Mark each end of last row to indicate start of armholes.

Shape Raglans
1st row: k.3, sl.1, k.2 tog., p.s.s.o., k. to last 6 sts., k.3 tog., k.3.
2nd to 4th rows: work in patt.
5th row: as 1st.
Work 5 rows. **
Cont. dec. in this way at each end of next row and every foll. 6th row until 37(39: 41:43) sts. rem., and then every 4th row until 25(27:29:31) sts. rem.
Work 3 rows.
Cast off.

FRONT

Work as for back from ** to **.
Cont. dec. in this way at each end of next row and every foll. 6th row until 41(43:45: 47) sts. rem.
Work 4(4:2:2) rows.

Shape Neck
Next row: patt. 16(16:17:17) sts., cast off 9(11:11:13) sts., patt. to end.
Cont. on last set of sts.
3rd and 4th sizes only:
Next row: k.
Next row: k.2 tog., patt. to end.
All sizes:
Next row: k.3, sl.1, k.2 tog., p.s.s.o., k. to end.
Now dec. for raglan on 2 foll. 6th rows, AND AT THE SAME TIME dec. 1 st. at neck edge on next row, and then every alt. row until 3 sts. rem.
Work 1 row.
Next row: k.2 tog., k.1.
Next row: k.2 tog., fasten off.
Rejoin yarn to rem. sts. at neck edge and complete to match first side.

SLEEVES

Cast on 39(43:43:47) sts. with 2¾mm. needles.
Work 14(18:22:26) rows in rib as back.
Change to 3¼mm. needles and patt.
Work 6 rows.
Inc. 1 st. at each end of next row, and then every 10th row until there are 55(59:63:67) sts., working inc. sts. into patt.
Work until sleeve measures 21(23:27:31)

cm. (8¼(9:10½:12¼) in.) from beg., ending with a wrong side row.
Mark each end of last row to indicate start of sleeve top.

Shape Top
1st row: k.3, sl.1, k.2 tog., p.s.s.o., k. to last 6 sts., k.3 tog., k.3.
2nd to 4th rows: work in patt.
5th row: as 1st.
Work 5 rows.
Cont. to dec. in this way at each end of next row and every foll. 6th row until 11 sts. rem.
Work 3 rows.
Cast off.

NECK BORDER

Press each piece lightly.
Sew up front and right back raglan seams.
With 2¾mm. needles and right side facing, k. up to 13 sts. evenly along left sleeve top, 14(14:15:15) sts. down left side of neck, 9(11:11:13) sts. from the cast off sts., 14(14:15:15) sts. up right side of neck, 12 sts. along right sleeve top, and 30(32:34:36) sts. evenly along back neck edge.
1st-4th rows: k.
Now work 8 rows in k.1, p.1, rib.
Cast off in rib.

MAKING UP

Sew up left back raglan and neck border seam.
Sew up side and sleeve seams.
Press seams lightly.

V-neck, Sleeveless Cabled Pullover 1957

Long slipover with front and back cable panels,
V-neck and ribbed welts

★★ Suitable for knitters with some previous experience

MATERIALS

Yarn
Wendy Pampas
4(5:5:5) × 50g. balls

Needles
1 pair 3mm.
1 pair 3¾mm.
cable needle

MEASUREMENTS

Chest
92(97:102:107) cm.
36(38:40:42) in.

Length
63(65:67:68) cm.
24¾(25½:26¼:26¾) in.

TENSION

24 sts. and 32 rows = 10 cm. (4 in.) square over st. st. on 3¾mm. needles. If your tension square does not correspond to these measurements, see page 156 for adjustment instructions.

ABBREVIATIONS

k. = knit; p. = purl; st(s). = stitch(es); inc. = increas(ing) (see page 156); dec. = decreas(ing) (see page 157); beg. = begin(ning); rem. = remain(ing); rep. = repeat; alt. = alternate; tog. = together; sl. = slip (transfer one stitch from left needle, knitwise unless otherwise stated, to right hand needle.); cont. = continue; patt. = pattern; foll. = following; folls. = follows; mm. = millimetres; cm. = centimetres; in. = inches; st. st. = stocking st.: one row k., one row p.; g. st. = garter st.: every row k.; incs. = increases; decs. = decreases; C8F = cable 8 front: sl. the next 4 sts. onto cable needle and hold at front of work, k. 4 sts., k. sts. from cable needle; t.b.l. = through back of loops; m.1 = make 1 st.: pick up horizontal loop lying before next st. and k. into the front of it.

BACK

Cast on 118(124:130:136) sts. with 3mm. needles.
Work 8 cm. (3¼ in.) in k.1, p.1 rib, ending with a right side row.
Inc. row (wrong side): rib 23(25:27:29), m.1, rib 2, m.1, rib 5, m.1, rib 2, m.1, rib 5, m.1, rib 2, m.1, rib 40(42:44:46), m.1, rib 2, m.1, rib 5, m.1, rib 2, m.1, rib 5, m.1, rib 2, m.1, rib 23(25:27:29) sts. [130(136: 142:148) sts.]
Change to 3¾mm. needles.
Work in reverse st. st. with cable panels as folls.:

1st row (right side): p.21(23:25:27), k.8, p.1, k.8, p.1, k.8, p.36(38:40:42), k.8, p.1, k.8, p.1, k.8, p.21(23:25:27).
2nd row: k.21(23:25:27), p.8, k.1, p.8, k.1, p.8, k.36(38:40:42), p.8, k.1, p.8, k.1, p.8, k.21(23:25:27).
3rd row: p.21(23:25:27), C8F, p.1, k.8, p.1, C8F, p.36(38:40:42), C8F, p.1, k.8, p.1, C8F, p.21(23:25:27).
4th row: as 2nd.
5th and 6th rows: as 1st and 2nd.
7th row: p.21(23:25:27), C8F, p.1, C8F, p.1, C8F, p.36(38:40:42), C8F, p.1, C8F, p.1, C8F, p.21(23:25:27).
8th row: as 2nd.
These 8 rows form patt.
Cont. straight in patt. until work measures 36(38:39:40) cm. (14(15:15¼: 15¾) in.), ending with a wrong side row.

Shape Armholes
Cast off 7(8:10:11) sts. at beg. of next 2 rows.
Cast off 2 sts. at beg. of foll. 2 rows.
Dec. 1 st. at both ends of next and foll. 9 right-side rows. [92(96:98:102) sts.]
Cont. straight in patt. until armholes measure 27(27:28:28) cm. (10½(10½:11: 11) in.), ending with a wrong side row.

Shape Shoulders
Cast off 10(11:11:11) sts. at beg. of next 4 rows.
Cast off 10(10:10:11) sts. at beg. of foll. 2 rows. [32(32:34:36) sts.]
Change to 3mm. needles.
Work 10 rows in k.1, p.1 rib.
Cast off in rib.

FRONT

Work as for back until 108(112:114:118) sts. rem. in armhole shaping, ending with a wrong side row.

Shape Neck
1st row: p.2 tog., patt. 50(52:53:55), p.2 tog., turn and work on these 52(54:55:57) sts.
Leave rem. 54(56:57:59) sts. on a spare needle.
** Work 1 row straight.
Dec. 1 st. at armhole edge on next row.
Work 1 row straight.
Dec. 1 st. at both ends of next row.
Work 1 row straight.
Dec. 1 st. at armhole edge on next row.

Work 1 row straight.
Rep. last 4 rows twice. [42(44:45:47) sts.]
Dec. 1 st. at neck edge on next and every foll. 4th row until 30(32:32:33) sts. rem.
Cont. straight until work measures same as back to shoulders, ending at armhole edge.

Shape Shoulder
Cast off 10(11:11:11) sts. at beg. of next and foll. alt. row.
Work 1 row straight.
Cast off rem. 10(10:10:11) sts.
With right side of work facing, rejoin yarn to first of rem. 54(56:57:59) sts.
1st row: p.2 tog., patt. 50(52:53:55), p.2 tog.
Now work from ** to end as for first side.

FRONT NECKBAND

With right side facing and 3mm. needles, beg. at left front shoulder, pick up and k.61(61:65:65) sts. down neck edge to centre, pick up and k. 1 st. from centre V, then pick up and k.61(61:65:65) sts. to right front shoulder. [123(123:131:131) sts.]
1st row: k.1, * p.1, k.1 * rep. from * to * to centre V, p. centre st., k.1, then rep. from * to * to end.
2nd row: p.1, * k.1, p.1 *, rep. from * to * to 2 sts. before centre st., k.2 tog. t.b.l., k. centre st., k.2 tog., p.1, rep. from * to * to end.
3rd row: * k.1, p.1 *, rep. from * to * to centre st., p.1, ** p.1, k.1, rep. from ** to end.
4th row: * p.1, k.1 *, rep. from * to * to 2 sts. before centre st., p.2 tog. t.b.l., p.2 tog., then rib to end.
Rep. last 4 rows once and 1st row again.
Cast off loosely in rib, dec. as before.

ARMBANDS

Sew up shoulder seams, carrying seams across neckband.
With right side facing and 3mm. needles, pick up and k.152(152:158:158) sts. around armhole.
Work 9 rows in k.1, p.1 rib.
Cast off loosely in rib.

MAKING UP

Press work.
Sew up side seams, carrying seams across armbands.

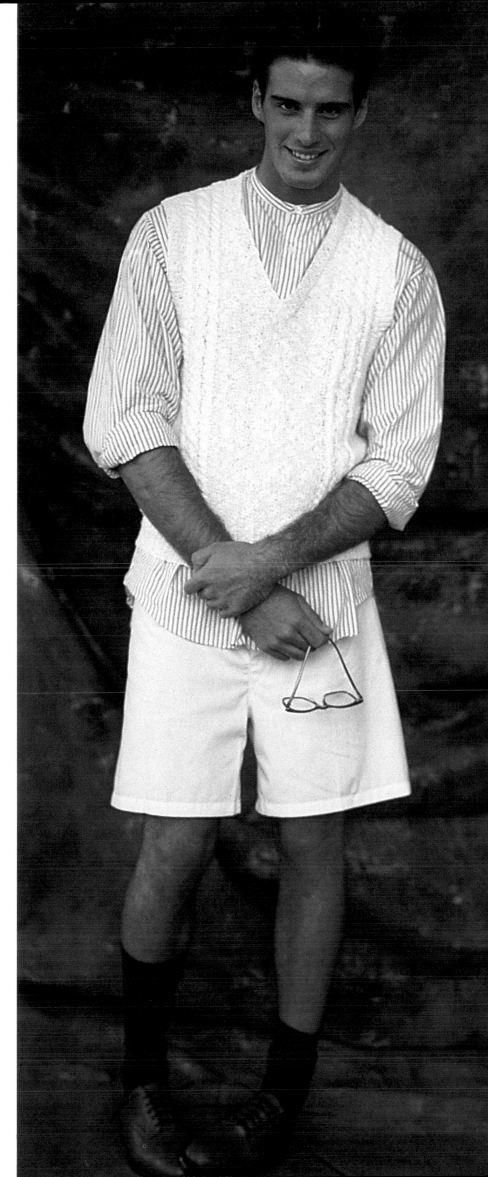

Lacy-yoked Sweater

Long-sleeved sweater with dropped shoulderline, squared neck, triangular lacy sections on yoke and shoulder buttoning

★ Suitable for beginners

MATERIALS

Yarn
Wendy Ascot 4 ply
2(3) × 50g. balls

Needles
1 pair 3mm.
1 pair 3¼mm.

Buttons
2

MEASUREMENTS

Chest
46(51) cm.
18(20) in.
6 months/1(1/2) approx. age

Length
24(27) cm.
9½(10½) in.

Sleeve Seam
15(19) cm.
5¾(7½) in.

TENSION

28 sts. and 36 rows = 10 cm. (4 in.) square over st. st. on 3¼mm. needles. If your tension square does not correspond to these measurements, see page 156 for adjustment instructions.

ABBREVIATIONS

k. = knit; p. = purl; st(s). = stitch(es); inc. = increas(ing) (see page 156); dec. = decreas(ing) (see page 157); beg. = begin(ning); rem. = remain(ing); rep. = repeat; alt. = alternate; tog. = together; sl. = slip (transfer one stitch from left needle, knitwise unless otherwise stated, to right hand needle.); cont. = continue; patt. = pattern; foll. = following; folls. = follows; mm. = millimetres; cm. = centimetres; in. = inches; st. st. = stocking st.: one row k., one row p.; g. st. = garter st.: every row k.; incs. = increases; decs. = decreases; y.fwd. = yarn forward.

BACK

Cast on 68(76) sts. with 3mm. needles.
Work 3 cm. (1¼ in.) in k.2, p.2 rib.
Change to 3¼mm. needles.
Beg. with a k. row, work straight in st. st. until work measures 15(17) cm. (5¾(6½) in.) from cast-on edge, ending with a p. row.

Shape Armholes

Cast off 4 sts. at beg. of next 2 rows. [60(68) sts.]
Cont. straight in st. st. until armholes measure 5 cm. (2 in.), ending with a p. row.
Now work triangle patt. as folls.:
1st row (right side): k.8(9), * y.fwd., k.2 tog., k.12(14), rep. from * twice, y.fwd., k.2 tog., k.8(9).
2nd row and all even rows: p.
3rd row: k.7(8), * (y.fwd., k.2 tog.) twice, k.10(12), rep. from * twice, (y.fwd., k.2 tog.) twice, k.7(8).

5th row: k.6(7), * (y.fwd., k.2 tog.) 3 times, k.8(10), rep. from * twice, (y.fwd., k.2 tog.) 3 times, k.6(7).
7th row: k.5(6), * (y.fwd., k.2 tog.) 4 times, k.6(8), rep. from * twice, (y.fwd., k.2 tog.) 4 times, k.5(6).
9th row: k.4(5), * (y.fwd., k.2 tog.) 5 times, k.4(6), rep. from * twice, (y.fwd., k.2 tog.) 5 times, k.4(5).
11th row: k.3(4), * (y.fwd., k.2 tog.) 6 times, k.2(4), rep. from * twice, (y.fwd., k.2 tog.) 6 times, k.3(4).
1st size only:
P.1 row.
13th row: k.2, * y.fwd., k.2 tog., rep. from * to end.
K. 5 rows.
Cast off.
2nd size only:
P. 1 row.
13th row: k.3, * (y.fwd., k.2 tog.) 7 times, k.2, rep. from * twice, (y.fwd., k.2 tog.) 7 times, k.3.
P. 1 row.
15th row: k.2, * y.fwd., k.2 tog., rep. from * to end.
K. 5 rows.
Cast off.

FRONT

Work as for back until end of armhole shaping. [60(68) sts.]
Work 2(0) rows straight.
Now work triangle patt. as folls.:
1st row (right side): k.22(25), y.fwd., k.2 tog., k.12(14), y.fwd., k.2 tog., k.22(25).
2nd row: p.

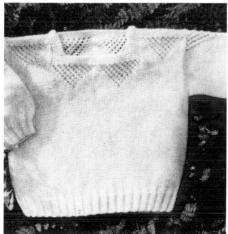

3rd row: k.21(24), (y.fwd., k.2 tog.) twice, k.10(12), (y.fwd., k.2 tog.) twice, k.21(24).
4th row: p.
These 4 rows set patt.
Cont. to work these 2 centre triangles, keeping the rest of the front in st. st. until rows 12(14) have been worked.
Next row: k.16(18), (y.fwd., k.2 tog.) 14(16) times, k.16(18).
Next row: p.16(18), k.28(32), p.16(18).
Now work triangles on shoulders as folls.:
1st row: k.8(9), y.fwd., k.2 tog., k.40(46), y.fwd., k.2 tog., k.8(9).
2nd row: p.16(18), k.28(32), p.16(18).
3rd row: k.7(8), (y.fwd., k.2 tog.) twice, k.38(44), (y.fwd., k.2 tog.) twice, k.7(8).
4th row: as 2nd.

Shape Neck

Next row: patt. 20(22) sts. and leave on holder until required, cast off next 20(24) sts., then patt. to end. [20(22) sts.]
Cont. on these last 20(22) sts.
Keeping the 4 sts. at neck edge in g. st., patt. 8(10) more rows.
K. 5 rows.
Cast off.
Rejoin yarn to wrong side of rem. 20(22) sts. and work as for first side to end.

SLEEVES

Beg. at top edge.
Cast on 60(64) sts. with 3¼mm. needles.
P. 1 row.
Now work in patt. as folls.:
1st row: k.23(24), (y.fwd., k.2 tog.) 7(8) times, k.23(24).
2nd and all even rows: p.
3rd row: k.24(25), (y.fwd., k.2 tog.) 6(7) times, k.24(25).
5th row: k.25(26), (y.fwd., k.2 tog.) 5(6) times, k.25(26).
7th row: k.26(27), (y.fwd., k.2 tog.) 4(5) times, K.26(27).
9th row: k.27(28), (y.fwd., k.2 tog.) 3(4) times, k.27(28).
11th row: k.28(29), (y.fwd., k.2 tog.) 2(3) times, k.28(29).
13th row: k.29(30), (y.fwd., k.2 tog.) once (twice), k.29(30).
2nd size only:
15th row: k.31, y.fwd., k.2 tog., k.31.
Both sizes:
Beg. with a p. row, work straight in st. st. until work measures 13(17) cm. (5(6½) in.).
Dec. row: k.0(2), * k.1, k.2 tog., rep. from * 19 times, k.0(2). [40(44) sts.]
Change to 3mm. needles.
Work 3 cm. (1¼ in.) in k.2, p.2 rib.
Cast off loosely in rib.

MAKING UP

Sew up shoulder seams for 3 cm. (1¼ in.) from shoulder edges.
Set in sleeves, sewing last 5 rows of sides of sleeves to cast-off sts. of armhole shaping.
Sew up side and sleeve seams.
Make buttonloop on each front shoulder.
Sew a button to each back shoulder to correspond.

Diagonal-stitch Cardigan

V-neck cardigan in diagonal stitch, with set-in sleeves,
two knitted-in pockets and moss stitch borders

★ Suitable for beginners

NB Garment was photographed without buttons.

MATERIALS

Yarn
Christian de Falbe Studio Yarns
Watership
4(4:5:6) × 20g. balls

Needles
1 pair 2¾mm.
1 pair 3¾mm.

Buttons
4

MEASUREMENTS

Chest
46(51:56:61) cm.
18(20:22:24) in.
6 months/1(1/2:2/3:4/5) approx. age

Length
25(28:31:36) cm.
9¾(11:12¼:14) in.

Sleeve Seam
15(18:21:27) cm.
5¾(7:8¼:10½) in.

TENSION

25 sts. and 36 rows = 10 cm. (4 in.) square over patt. on 3¾mm. needles. If your tension square does not correspond to these measurements, see page 156 for adjustment instructions.

ABBREVIATIONS

k. = knit; p. = purl; st(s). = stitch(es); inc. = increas(ing) (see page 156); dec. = decreas(ing) (see page 157); beg. = begin(ning); rem. = remain(ing); rep. = repeat; alt. = alternate; tog. = together; sl. = slip (transfer one stitch from left needle, knitwise unless otherwise stated, to right hand needle.); cont. = continue; patt. = pattern; foll. = following; folls. = follows; mm. = millimetres; cm. = centimetres; in. = inches; st. st. = stocking st.: one row k., one row p.; g. st. = garter st.: every row k.; incs. = increases; decs. = decreases.

BACK

Cast on 65(70:75:80) sts. with 2¾mm. needles.
1st row: * k.1, p.1, rep. from * to last 1(0:1:0) st., k.1(0:1:0) st.
2nd row: k.1(0:1:0) st., * p.1, k.1, rep. from * to end.
These 2 rows form moss st. patt.
Rep. 1st and 2nd rows 3 times.
Change to 3¾mm. needles and patt. as folls.:
1st row (right side): * k.3, p.2, rep. from * to end.
2nd row: * p.1, k.2, p.2, rep. from * to end.
3rd row: * k.1, p.2, k.2, rep. from * to end.
4th row: * p.3, k.2, rep. from * to end.
5th row: * p.1, k.3, p.1, rep. from * to end.
6th row: * k.2, p.3, rep. from * to end.
7th row: * k.2, p.2, k.1, rep. from * to end.

8th row: * p.2, k.2, p.1, rep. from * to end.
9th row: * p.2, k.3, rep. from * to end.
10th row: * k.1, p.3, k.1, rep. from * to end.
These 10 rows form patt.
Cont. in patt. until work measures 14(15:17:19) cm. (5½(5¾:6½:7½) in.).
Shape Armholes
Cast off 2(2:2:3) sts. at beg. of next 2 rows.
Dec. 1 st. at each end of next and every foll. alt. row until 53(58:61:64) sts. rem.
Cont. without shaping until work measures 25(28:31:36) cm. (9¾(11: 12¼:14) in.).

Shape Shoulders
Cast off 4(5:5:5) sts. at beg. of next 2 rows.
Cast off 5 sts. at beg. of next 2 rows.
Cast off 5(5:5:6) sts. at beg. of next 2 rows.
Cast off rem. 25(28:31:32) sts.

LEFT FRONT

Cast on 31(33:35:37) sts. with 2¾mm. needles.
Work 8 rows in moss st. as for 1st size of back.
Change to 3¾mm. needles and work as folls.:
1st row: * k.3, p.2, rep. from * to last 1(3:0:2) sts., k.1(3:0:2).
2nd row: k.0(1:0:0), p.1(2:0:2), * p.1, k.2, p.2, rep. from * to end.
3rd row: * k.1, p.2, k.2, rep. from * to last 1(3:0:2) sts., k.1(1:0:1), p.0(2:0:1).
4th row: p.0(1:0:0), k.1(2:0:2), * p.3, k.2, rep. from * to end.
These 4 rows set patt.

Cont. in patt. to match back until work measures same as back to armholes, ending with a wrong side row.

Shape Armhole and V-neck

1st row: cast off 2(2:2:3) sts., patt. to last 2 sts., k.2 tog.

Dec. 1 st. at each end of next 4(4:5:5) alt. rows.

Dec. 1 st. at neck edge only on every foll. 2nd(2nd:2nd:3rd) row until 14(15:15:16) sts. rem.

Cont. without shaping until work measures same as back to shoulders.

Shape Shoulder

Cast off 4(5:5:5) sts. at beg. of next row.
Work 1 row.
Cast off 5 sts. at beg. of next row.
Work 1 row.
Cast off rem. 5(5:5:6) sts.

RIGHT FRONT

Work as for left front, reversing all shapings.

SLEEVES

Cast on 40(40:40:40) sts. with 2¾mm. needles.

Work 8 rows in moss st. as folls.:

1st row: * k.1, p.1, rep. from * to end.
2nd row: * p.1, k.1, rep. from * to end.

Change to 3¾mm. needles and work in patt. as for back, inc. 1 st. at each end of every 5th row until there are 52(54:56:60) sts., working extra sts. into patt.

Cont. without shaping until work measures 15(18:21:27) cm. (5¾(7:8¼: 10½) in.).

Shape Top

Cast off 2(2:2:3) sts. at beg. of next 2 rows.
Dec. 1 st. at each end of next and every foll. alt. row until 34 sts. rem.
Cast off 6 sts. at beg. of next 2 rows.
Cast off.

FRONT BAND

Sew up shoulder seams.

Cast on 7 sts. with 2¾mm. needles.

Work 4 rows in moss st. as given for 1st size at beg. of back.

5th row: moss st. 3, cast off 1 st., moss st. to end.

6th row: moss st. 3, cast on 1 st., moss st. 3.

Cont. in moss st., making 3 further buttonholes as on 5th and 6th rows at the foll. intervals:

1st size: 5,9,13 cm. (2,3½,5 in.).
2nd size: 6,10,15 cm. (2¼,4,5¾ in.).
3rd size: 6,11,17 cm. (2¼,4¼,6½ in.).
4th size: 7,13,19 cm. (2¾,5,7½ in.).

Cont. in moss st., sewing band onto fronts gradually, until band fits all around front edge when slightly stretched.

Cast off.

MAKING UP

Sew up side and sleeve seams.
Set in sleeves.
Sew on buttons.

Giant Cable-stitch Sweater

Warm sweater with cable bands on moss stitch, set-in sleeves, ribbed turtle neck and welts

★★ Suitable for knitters with some previous experience

MATERIALS

Yarn
Sirdar Talisman DK
13(13:14:14) × 50g. balls

Needles
1 pair 3¼mm.
1 pair 4mm.
1 cable needle
st. holder

MEASUREMENTS

Chest
97(102:107:112) cm.
38(40:42:44) in.

Length
62(64:66:68) cm.
24¼(25:26:26¾) in.

Sleeve Seam
47(48:49:50) cm.
18½(18¾:19¼:19½) in.

TENSION

23 sts. and 34 rows = 10 cm. (4 in.) square over m.st. on 4mm. needles. If your tension square does not correspond to these measurements, see page 156 for adjustment instructions.

ABBREVIATIONS

k. = knit; p. = purl; st(s). = stitch(es); inc. = increas(ing) (see page 156); dec. = decreas(ing) (see page 157); beg. = begin(ning); rem. = remain(ing); rep. = repeat; alt. = alternate; tog. = together; sl. = slip (transfer one stitch from left needle, knitwise unless otherwise stated, to right hand needle.); cont. = continue; patt. = pattern; foll. = following; folls. = follows; mm. = millimetres; cm. = centimetres; in. = inches; st. st. = stocking st.: one row k., one row p.; g. st. = garter st.: every row k.; incs. = increases; decs. = decreases; m.1 = make 1 st.: pick up horizontal loop lying before next st. and

k. into the back of it; C6B = cable 6 back: sl. next 6 sts. onto cable needle and leave at back, k. 6 sts., then k.6 from cable needle.

BACK

Cast on 112(116:120:124) sts. with 3¼mm. needles.
Work 8(9:10:11) cm. (3¼(3½:4:4¼) in.) in k.2, p.2 rib, ending with a right side row.
Next row: rib 9(1:3:5), m.1, (rib 5(6:5:5), m.1) 19(19:23:23) times, rib to end. [132(136:144:148) sts.]
Change to 4mm. needles and work in patt. as folls.:
1st row (right side): m. st. 25(25:27:27), (k.12, m. st. 23(25:27:29)) twice, k.12, m. st. 25(25:27:27).
2nd row: m. st. 25(25:27:27), (p.12, m. st. 23(25:27:29)) twice, p.12, m. st. 25(25:27:27).
Rep. 1st and 2nd rows three more times.
9th row: m. st. 25(25:27:27), (C6B, m. st. 23(25:27:29)) twice, C6B, m. st. 25(25:27:27).
10th row: as 2nd.
11th, 13th and 15th rows: as 1st.
12th, 14th and 16th rows: as 2nd.
These 16 rows form the patt. and are repeated throughout.
Cont. straight in patt. until back measures 42(43:44:45) cm. (16½(16¾:17¼:17¾) in.) from cast-on edge, ending with a wrong side row.

Shape Armholes
Cast off 5 sts. at beg. of next 2 rows.
Dec. 1 st. at each end of next and every foll. alt. row until 110(114:122:126) sts. rem. **
Cont. straight in patt. on rem. sts. until armholes measure 20(21:22:23) cm. (7¾(8¼:8½:9) in.) from beg. of armhole shaping, ending with a wrong side row.

Shape Shoulders
Cast off 36(37:40:41) sts. at beg. of next 2 rows, in patt.
Leave rem. 38(40:42:44) sts. on holder.

FRONT

Work as for back to **.
Cont. straight in patt. on rem. sts. until armholes measure 13(14:14:15) cm. (5(5½:5½:5¾) in.) from beg. of armhole shaping, ending with a wrong side row.

Shape Neck
Next row: patt. 46(47:50:51) sts., cast off centre 18(20:22:24) sts., patt. to end.
Now work on last group of sts. only, sl. rem. sts. onto spare needle.
Dec. 1 st. at neck edge on next and every

foll. alt. row 10 times in all. [36(37:40:41) sts.]
Cont. straight on rem. sts. until armhole measures 20(21:22:23) cm. (7¾(8¼:8½:9) in.) from beg. of armhole shaping, ending with a right side row.

Shape Shoulder
Cast off in patt.
Return to sts. on spare needle, rejoin yarn and complete left side of neck as for right side, reversing shapings.

SLEEVES

Cast on 56(56:60:60) sts. with 3¼mm. needles.
Work 8(9:10:11) cm. (3¼(3½:4:4¼) in.), in k.2, p.2 rib, ending with a right side row.
Next row: rib 8(8:12:12), m.1, (rib 2, m.1) 20(20:18:18) times, rib to end. [77(77:79:79) sts.]
Change to 4mm. needles and work in patt. as folls.:
1st row (right side): m. st. 15, k.12, m. st. 23(23:25:25), k.12, m. st. 15.
2nd row: m. st. 15, p.12, m. st. 23(23:25:25), p.12, m. st. 15.
Cont. on sts. as set, foll. patt. as given for back.
Inc. 1 st. at each end of 15th and every foll. 16th row until there are 93(93:95:95) sts. on needle, working extra sts. into m. st. patt.
Cont. straight on all sts. until sleeve measures 47(48:49:50) cm. (18½(18¾:19¼:19½) in.) from cast-on edge, ending with a wrong side row.

Shape Top
Cast off 5 sts. at beg. of next 2 rows.
Dec. 1 st. at each end of every foll. alt. row until 41 sts. rem.
Cast off 3 sts. at beg. of next 6(6:8:8) rows.
Cast off rem. sts.

POLO COLLAR

Sew up right shoulder seam.
With 4mm. needles, pick up and k. 32(32:34:34) sts. from left side front, 18(20:22:24) sts. from centre front, 32(32:34:34) sts. from right side front and 38(40:42:44) sts. from centre back. [120(124:132:136) sts.]
Work 15 cm. (5¾ in.) in k.2, p.2 rib.
Cast off in rib.

MAKING UP

Do not press.
Sew up rem. shoulder seam and polo collar seam.
Sew up side and sleeve seams.
Set in sleeves.

Mock Cable Rib Sweater

Raglan-sleeved sweater in mock cable rib with ribbed welts and plain round neck or shawl collar option

★★ Suitable for knitters with some previous experience

MATERIALS

Yarn
Argyll Ambridge DK
Round-neck version:
4(5:5:5) × 50g. balls
Shawl-neck version:
5(5:5:6) × 50g. balls

Needles
1 pair 3¼mm.
1 pair 4mm.
Round-neck version:
1 set of 4 double-pointed 3¼mm.

MEASUREMENTS

Chest
46/48(51/53:56/58:61/63) cm.
18/19(20/21:22/23:24/25) in.
6 months/1(1/2:2/3:4/5) approx. age

Length (excluding neckband or collar)
32(34:38:40) cm.
12¾(13½:15:16) in.

Sleeve Seam
20(23:27:29) cm.
7¾(9:10½:11¼) in.

TENSION

26 sts. and 32 rows = 10 cm. (4 in.) square over unstretched patt. on 4mm. needles.

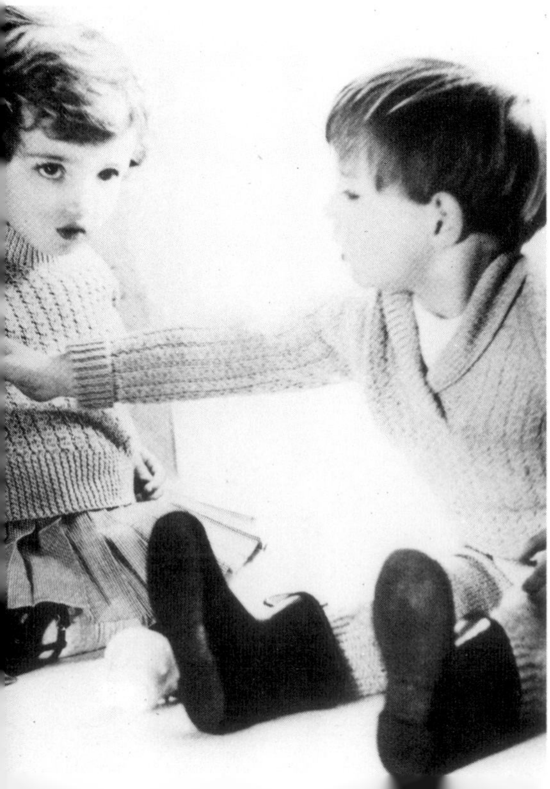

If your tension square does not correspond to these measurements, see page 156 for adjustment instructions.

ABBREVIATIONS

k. = knit; p. = purl; st(s). = stitch(es); inc. = increas(ing) (see page 156); dec. = decreas(ing) (see page 157); beg. = begin(ning); rem. = remain(ing); rep. = repeat; alt. = alternate; tog. = together; sl. = slip (transfer one stitch from left needle, knitwise unless otherwise stated, to right hand needle.); cont. = continue; patt. = pattern; foll. = following; folls. = follows; mm. = millimetres; cm. = centimetres; in. = inches; st. st. = stocking st.: one row k., one row p.; g. st. = garter st.: every row k.; incs. = increases; decs. = decreases; k.b. = k. into back of next st.; p.b. = p. into back of next st.; C1F = miss first st. on left needle, now k. into front of second st., k. the missed st., sl. both sts. off left needle; C1B = miss first st. on left needle, taking needle behind missed st., k. into front of next st., k. the missed st., sl. both sts. off left needle; t.b.l. = through back of loop; p.s.s.o. = pass the slipped st. over.

ROUND-NECK VERSION

BACK

Cast on 49(55:63:69) sts. with 3¼mm. needles.
1st row (right side): k.1, (k.b., p.1) to last 2 sts., k.b., k.1.
2nd row: k.1, (p.b., k.1) to end.
Rep. these 2 rows for 5(5:6:6) cm. (2(2:2¼:2¼) in.), ending after a 1st row.
Next row: rib 2(1:5:4), (inc. in next st., rib 3) 11(13:13:15) times, inc. in next st., rib to end. [61(69:77:85) sts.]
Change to 4mm. needles and patt. as folls.:
1st row: p.1, * C1F, k.1, p.1, rep. from * to end.
2nd row: p.
3rd row: p.1, * k.1, C1B, p.1, rep. from * to end.
4th row: p.
These 4 rows form patt.
Cont. in patt. until work measures 21(22:24:25) cm. (8¼(8½:9½:9¾) in.) from beg., ending with a p. row.

Shape Raglan
Keeping patt. correct, work as folls.:

1st and 2nd rows: cast off 2 sts., work to end.
3rd row: k.2, p.1, k.1, k.2 tog. t.b.l., patt. to last 6 sts., k.2 tog., k.1, p.1, k.2.
4th row: p.4, p.2 tog., p. to last 6 sts., p.2 tog. t.b.l., p.4.
Rep. 3rd and 4th rows 0(1:2:3) times.
Next row: as 3rd.
Next row: p.
Rep. the last 2 rows until 21(23:25:27) sts. rem., ending after a p. row.
Leave sts. on a spare needle.

FRONT

Work as for back until 31(35:37:41) sts. rem. on raglan shaping, ending with a p. row.

Shape Neck
Next row: k.2, p.1, k.1, k.2 tog. t.b.l., patt. 3(5:5:7), turn.
Cont. on this group of sts.
Still dec. at raglan edge as before, at the same time dec. 1 st. at neck edge on next 2(3:3:4) rows. [5(6:6:6) sts.].
1st and 4th sizes only: p.1 row.
All sizes: dec. 1 st. at neck edge only on every right side row until 2 sts. rem.
Work 1 row.
K.2 tog., fasten off.
With right side facing, sl. centre 13(13:15:15) sts. onto a spare needle.
Rejoin yarn to rem. sts. and work 1 row, dec. at raglan edge as before.
Complete as for first side of neck.

SLEEVES

Cast on 29(31:33:35) sts. with 3¼mm. needles.
Work in rib as on welt for 5(5:6:6) cm. (2(2:2¼:2¼) in.), ending with a 2nd row and inc. 8(6:8:6) sts. evenly on last row. [37(37:41:41) sts.]
Change to 4mm. needles.
Patt. as on back, shaping sleeve by inc. 1 st. at each end of the 9th row, and then on every foll. 8th(6th:6th:6th) row until there are 47(51:57:61) sts., taking extra sts. into the patt.
Work straight until sleeve measures 20(23:27:29) cm. (7¾(9:10½:11¼) in.) from beg., ending with a p. row.

Shape Raglan
1st and 2nd rows: cast off 2 sts., work to end.
Rep. 3rd and 4th rows of raglan shaping as given for back 0(0:1:1) times each.

Next row: k.2, p.1, k.1, k.2 tog. t.b.l., patt. to last 6 sts., k.2 tog., k.1, p.1, k.2.
Next row: p.
Rep. the last 2 rows until 11 sts. rem.
Next row: p.
Next row: k.2, p.1, k.1, sl.1, k.2 tog., p.s.s.o., k.1, p.1, k.2.
Next row: p.
Sl. final 9 sts. onto spare needle.

NECKBAND

Sew up raglan shapings.
With set of 3¼mm. needles and right side facing, k. across sts. of right sleeve, back, then left sleeve, k. up 9(11:11:13) sts. down left front neck, k. across centre sts., finally k. up 9(11:11:13) sts. up right front neck. [70(76:80:86) sts.]
Working into the back of every k. st., work 16(18:18:20) rounds in k.1, p.1 rib.
Cast off VERY loosely.

MAKING UP

Omitting rib, press lightly.
Sew up side and sleeve seams.
Fold neckband in half to wrong side and hem in position.
Press seams.

SHAWL-NECK VERSION

BACK AND SLEEVES

Work as for round-neck version, but cast off final sts. instead of leaving on spare needles.

FRONT

Work as for back to raglan shaping.

Shape Raglan and Neck

1st row: cast off 2 sts., patt. 20(23:26:29) sts. including st. on needle after casting off, cast off centre 17(19:21:23) sts., patt. to end.
Cont. on last group of sts.
Next row: cast off 2 sts., p. to end.
Next row: patt. to last 6 sts., k.2 tog., k.1, p.1, k.2.
Next row: p.4, p.2 tog., p. to end.
Rep. the last 2 rows 0(1:2:3) times.
Next row: patt. to last 6 sts., k.2 tog., k.1, p.1, k.2.
Next row: p.
** Rep. the last 2 rows until 5 sts. rem.
Now dec. 1 st. at neck edge on every right side row until 2 sts. rem.
Work 1 row.
K.2 tog., fasten off.**

With wrong side facing, rejoin yarn to rem. sts. and p.1 row.
Next row: k.2, p.1, k.1, k.2 tog. t.b.l., patt. to end.
Next row: p. to last 6 sts., p.2 tog. t.b.l., p.4.
Rep. the last 2 rows 0(1:2:3) times.
Next row: k.2, p.1, k.1, k.2 tog. t.b.l., patt. to end.
Next row: p.
Work as for first half from ** to **

COLLAR

Cast on 117(127:137:147) sts.
Work in rib as on back welt until side edge fits across centre front cast-off sts., allowing for the front to be very slightly stretched.

Shape Neck

Keeping rib correct, work as folls.:
1st and 2nd rows: rib to last 10 sts., turn.
3rd and 4th rows: rib to last 20 sts., turn.
5th and 6th rows: rib to last 30 sts., turn.
7th and 8th rows: rib to last 40 sts., turn.
9th row: rib to end.
Cast off all sts.

MAKING UP

Press as for round-neck version.
Sew up raglan, side and sleeve seams.
Sew shaped edge of collar to neck edge, stitching side edges to centre front cast-off sts., overlapping right side over left for traditional girl's style, and left over right for traditional boy's style.
Press seams.

Twisted-stitch Slipover

Shaped, twisted-stitch sleeveless sweater with round neck and moss stitch bands, ribbed neck and hem

★ Suitable for beginners

MATERIALS

Yarn
Sunbeam St Ives 4 ply
5(5:6:6) × 25g. balls

Needles
1 pair 2¼mm.
1 pair 3mm.

Buttons
2

MEASUREMENTS

Chest
56(61:66:72) cm.
22(24:26:28) in.
2/3(4/5:6/7:8/9) approx. age

Length
34(38:42:46) cm.
13¼(15:16½:18) in.

TENSION

32 sts. and 36 rows = 10 cm. (4 in.) square over rib patt. (slightly stretched) on 3mm. needles. If your tension square does not correspond to these measurements, see page 156 for adjustment instructions.

ABBREVIATIONS

k. = knit; p. = purl; st(s). = stitch(es); inc. = increas(ing) (see page 156); dec. = decreas(ing) (see page 157); beg. = begin(ning); rem. = remain(ing); rep. = repeat; alt. = alternate; tog. = together; sl. = slip (transfer one stitch from left needle, knitwise unless otherwise stated, to right hand needle.); cont. = continue; patt. = pattern; foll. = following; folls. = follows; mm. = millimetres; cm. = centimetres; in. = inches; st. st. = stocking st.: one row k., one row p.; g. st. = garter st.: every row k.; incs. = increases; decs. = decreases; Tw.2R = k. into front of 2nd st. on left hand needle, then k. into front of first st. on left hand needle and sl. both sts. off needle tog.

BACK

Cast on 90(98:106:114) sts. with 2¼mm. needles.
1st row: k.2, * p.2, k.2, rep. from * to end.
2nd row: p.2, * k.2, p.2, rep. from * to end.
Rep. these 2 rows for 5 cm. (2 in.), ending with a 2nd row and inc. 8(10:12:14) sts. evenly across last row. [98(108:118:128) sts.]

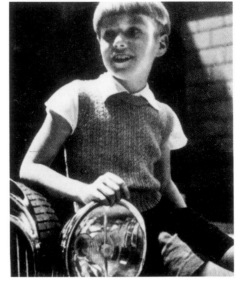

Change to 3mm. needles and cont. in patt. as folls.:
1st row (right side): p.1, k.1, p.1, * k.2, p.1, k.1, p.1, rep. from * to end.
2nd row: k.1, p.1, k.1, * p.2, k.1, p.1, k.1, rep. from * to end.
3rd row: p.1, k.1, p.1, * Tw.2R, p.1, k.1, p.1, rep. from * to end.
4th row: as 2nd.
These 4 rows form the patt. and are rep. throughout.
Cont. in patt. until work measures 20(22: 24:26) cm. (7¾(8½:9½:10¼) in.) from beg., ending with a wrong side row.

Shape Armholes

Keeping patt. straight, cast off 6(6:8:8) sts. at beg. of next 2 rows, 3 sts. at beg. of next 2 rows and 2 sts. at beg. of next 2 rows.
Now dec. 1 st. at each end of next and foll. 1(3:3:5) alt. rows. [72(78:84:90) sts.]
Cont. without shaping until armholes measure 14(16:18:20) cm. (5½(6¼:7:7¾) in.), ending with a wrong side row.

Shape Shoulders

Cast off 4(5:5:6) sts. at beg. of next 4 rows and 5(5:7:7) sts. at beg. of next 2 rows.
Cast off rem. 46(48:50:52) sts.

FRONT

Work as for back until armholes measure 9(11:11:12) cm. (3½(4¼:4¼:4¾) in.), ending with a wrong side row.

Shape Neck

Next row: patt. 31(33:36:38), turn and leave rem. sts. on spare needle.

Cast off 4 sts. at beg. of next row, 3 sts. at beg. of foll. 2 alt. rows and 2 sts. at beg. of foll. 2 alt. rows.
Cast off 1 st. at beg. of foll. 4(4:5:5) alt. rows. [13(15:17:19) sts.]
Cont. without shaping until armhole measures same as back, ending with a wrong side row.

Shape Shoulder

Cast off 4(5:5:6) sts. at beg. of next and foll. alt. row.
Work 1 row.
Cast off rem. 5(5:7:7) sts.
Return to sts. on spare needle, with right side facing rejoin yarn.
Next row: cast off 10(12:12:14) sts., patt. to end.
Work 1 row.
Cont. to match first side, reversing all shapings.

NECKBAND

Sew up right shoulder seam, then sew up left shoulder for about half its length, starting from armhole edge.
Cast on 9 sts. with 2¼mm. needles.
1st row: k.1, * p.1, k.1, rep. from * to end.
Rep. this row until band is long enough to fit round neck edge, when slightly stretched.
Cast off.

Armhole Bands

Work as for neckband, making bands long enough to fit round armholes, when slightly stretched.

MAKING UP

Press work very lightly taking care not to flatten the patt.
Sew on bands overlapping them slightly over the edge of work.
Sew up side seams.
Sew 2 buttons to left back shoulder and make loops on left front to correspond.
Press seams.

Stripe-bordered Cardigan

Thick cotton cardigan in two lengths, with set-in sleeves, round neck, buttonband, cuffs and hem in contrast stripes

1955

★ Suitable for beginners

NB Short version photographed

MATERIALS

Yarn
Christian de Falbe Studio Yarns
Paradise Cotton
Short Cardigan:
9(10:10:11:11) × 50g. balls Main Col. A
2(2:2:2:2) × 50g. balls Col. B
Long Cardigan:
11(12:12:13:13) × 50g. balls Main Col. A
2(2:2:2:2) × 50g. balls Col. B

Needles
1 pair 3mm.
1 pair 3¾mm.
st. holders

Buttons
Short Cardigan:
8
Long Cardigan:
10

MEASUREMENTS

Bust
82(87:92:97:102) cm.
32(34:36:38:40) in.

Length
Short Cardigan:
58(59:59:60:60) cm.
22¾(23¼:23¼:23¾:23¾) in.
Long Cardigan:
71(72:72:73:73) cm.
27¾(28¼:28¼:28½:28½) in.

Sleeve Seam
43(44:45:45:46) cm.
16¾(17¼:17¾:17¾:18) in.

TENSION

23 sts. and 28 rows = 10 cm. (4 in.) square over st. st. on 3¾mm. needles. If your tension square does not correspond to these measurements, see page 156 for adjustment instructions.

ABBREVIATIONS

k. = knit; p. = purl; st(s). = stitch(es); inc. = increas(ing) (see page 156); dec. = decreas(ing) (see page 157); beg. = begin(ning); rem. = remain(ing); rep. = repeat; alt. = alternate; tog. = together; sl. = slip (transfer one stitch from left needle, knitwise unless otherwise stated, to right hand needle.); cont. = continue; patt. = pattern; foll. = following; folls. = follows; mm. = millimetres; cm. = centimetres; in. = inches; st. st. = stocking st.: one row k., one row p.; g. st. = garter st.: every row k.; incs. = increases; decs. = decreases.

NB Use yarn double throughout.

BACK

Cast on 103(109:115:121:127) sts. with 3mm. needles and A.
Work in stripe rib as folls.:
1st row: with A, * k.1, p.1, rep. from * to last st., k.1.
2nd row: with A, k.1, * k.1, p.1, rep. from * to last 2 sts., k.2.
3rd and 4th rows: as 1st and 2nd.
5th and 6th rows: with B, as 1st and 2nd.
These 6 rows form patt.
Cont. until 34 patt. rows have been worked.
Change to 3¾mm. needles and st. st.
With A, cont. until work measures 38 cm. (15 in.) for short version or 51 cm. (20 in.) for long version.

Shape Armholes
Cast off 5(6:6:7:8) sts. at beg. of next 2 rows.
Dec. 1 st. at each end of next 4 rows.
Dec. 1 st. at each end of next and every foll. alt. row until 75(77:79:81:83) sts. rem.
Cont. without shaping until work measures 48 cm. (18¾ in.) for short version or 61 cm. (24 in.) for long version.
Inc. 1 st. at each end of next and every foll. 6th row 4 times. [83(85:87:89:91) sts.]
Cont. without shaping until work measures 58(59:59:60:60) cm. (22¾(23¼: 23¼:23¾:23¾) in.) for short version or 71(72:72:73:73) cm. (27¾(28¼:28¼: 28½:28½) in.) for long version.

Shape Shoulders
Cast off 7 sts. at beg. of next 6 rows.
Cast off 5(6:6:7:7) sts. at beg. of next 2 rows.
Leave 31(31:33:33:35) sts. on holder.

POCKET LININGS

Short version only:
Cast on 31 sts. with 3mm. needles and A.
Work 33 rows in striped rib as for back.
Leave sts. on holder.
Fasten off.

LEFT FRONT

Short version:
Cast on 67(70:73:76:79) sts. with 3mm. needles and A.
Work 32 rows in striped rib as for back.
Pocket row: rib 6(8:8:10:12) sts., cast off 31 sts., rib 30(31:34:35:36).
34th row: rib to cast off section, rib across pocket lining, rib to end.
Long version:
Work as for short version, but work 34 rows in striped rib and omit pocket opening.
Both versions:
Change to 3¾mm. needles, with A work as folls.:
Next row: k.43(46:49:52:55) sts., turn, leave 24 sts. on holder for button band.
Cont. in st. st. until work measures same as back to armhole, ending at side edge.

Shape Armhole
Cast off 5(6:6:7:8) sts. at beg. of next row.
Work 1 row.
Dec. 1 st. at armhole edge on next 4 rows.
Dec. 1 st. at armhole edge on next and foll. alt. rows until 29(30:31:32:33) sts. rem.
Cont. without shaping until work measures 48 cm. (18¾ in.) for short version or 61 cm. (24 in.) for long version.

Inc. 1 st. at armhole edge on next and every foll. 6th row 4 times in all, AT THE SAME TIME, when work measures 53(54:54:55:55) cm. (20¾(21¼:21¼: 21½: 21½) in.) for short version or 66(67:67: 68:68) cm. (26(26¼:26¼: 26¾:26¾) in.) for long version, work as folls.:

Shape Neck
Dec. 1 st. at neck edge on next 4 rows.
Dec. 1 st. at neck edge on next and foll. alt. rows until 26(27:27:28:28) sts. rem. Cont. until work measures same as back to shoulder shaping, ending at armhole edge.

Shape Shoulder
Cast off 7 sts. at beg. of next and foll. 2 alt. rows.
Work 1 row.
Cast off.

BUTTON BAND
Rejoin yarns to 24 sts. on holder and with 3mm. needles, work in striped rib as for back until band measures same as work to neck shaping when slightly stretched, ending with 2 rows of B.
Leave sts. on holder.
Fasten off.
Sew in place.

Mark positions for buttons evenly along band, first to come 1 cm. (½ in.) from lower edge of band, last to be worked on third and fourth rows from top of band, and rem. buttons spaced evenly between.

RIGHT FRONT
Work as for left front, reversing all shapings and pocket row. Work button-holes to correspond with positions marked on left front for buttons, each hole to be worked as folls.:
1st buttonhole row (right side): rib 10, cast off 3 sts., rib to end.
2nd buttonhole row: rib, casting on 3 sts. over those cast off.

SLEEVES
Cast on 51(53:55:57:59) sts. with 3mm. needles and A.
Work 33 rows in stripe patt. as for back.
34th row: rib 4(1:3:3:4), * inc. 1 st., rib 5(6:6:6:6) sts., rep. from * 6 times more, inc. 1 st., rib 4(2:2:4:5) sts. [59(61:63: 65:67) sts.]
Change to 3¾mm. needles and with A, work in st. st., inc. 1 st. at each end of every 7th row until there are 83(85:87: 89:91) sts.
Cont. without shaping until work

measures 43(44:45:45:46) cm. (16¾(17¼: 17¾:17¾:18) in.)

Shape Top
Cast off 5(6:6:7:8) sts. at beg. of next 2 rows.
Dec. 1 st. at each end of next 4 rows.
Dec. 1 st. at each end of foll. alt. rows until 39 sts. rem.
Cast off 3 sts. at beg. of next 8 rows.
Cast off.

NECKBAND
Sew up shoulder seams.
With 3mm. needles and A, rib across right front band, pick up and k. 15(16:17:18:19) sts. from right front neck, k. across back neck sts. from holder, pick up and k. 15(16:17:18:19) sts. across left front neck and rib across 24 sts. of button band. [109(111:115:117:121) sts.]
Work 3 rows in rib.
Cast off in rib.

MAKING UP
Sew up side and sleeve seams.
Set in sleeves.
Sew down pocket linings (short version).
Press lightly, excluding ribbing, with warm iron over damp cloth.
Sew on buttons.

Ridged Stocking Stitch Sweater

Hemmed, ridge-pattern sweater with raglan sleeves, ribbed welts and back placket buttoning

★ Suitable for beginners

MATERIALS

Yarn
Georges Picaud Coton Canelle
3 × 50g. balls

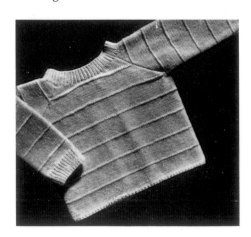

Needles
1 pair 2¼mm.
1 pair 2¾mm.
st. holder.

Buttons
4 small

MEASUREMENTS

Chest
48 cm.
18¾ in. (6/9 months approx. age)

Length
21 cm.
8¼ in.

Sleeve Seam
15 cm.
5¾ in.

TENSION
33 sts. and 51 rows = 10 cm. (4 in.) square over patt. on 2¾mm. needles. If your

tension square does not correspond to these measurements, see page 156 for adjustment instructions.

ABBREVIATIONS
k. = knit; p. = purl; st(s). = stitch(es); inc. = increas(ing) (see page 156); dec. = decreas(ing) (see page 157); beg. = begin(ning); rem. = remain(ing); rep. = repeat; alt. = alternate; tog. = together; sl. = slip (transfer one stitch from left needle, knitwise unless otherwise stated, to right hand needle.); cont. = continue; patt. = pattern; foll. = following; folls. = follows; mm. = millimetres; cm. = centi-metres; in. = inches; st. st. = stocking st.: one row k., one row p.; g. st. = garter st.: every row k.; incs. = increases; decs. = decreases; p.s.s.o. = pass the sl. st. over; y.r.n. = yarn round needle.

FRONT
Cast on 88 sts. with 2¼mm. needles.

Work 5 rows in k.1, p.1 rib.
Change to 2¾mm. needles.
Work 9 rows in st. st., beg. with a p. row.
10th row (right side): p.
These 10 rows form ridge patt., worked throughout.
Cont. in ridge patt. until a total of 63 rows have been worked from top of rib.

Shape Raglan
Cast off 5 sts. at beg. of next 2 rows.
Next row: sl.1, k.1, p.s.s.o., patt. to last 2 sts., patt. 2 tog.
Next row: p.
Rep. the last 2 rows until 48 sts. rem., ending with a p. row.

Shape Neck
Next row: sl.1, k.1, p.s.s.o., k.16, and leave these 17 sts. on a spare needle, k. next 12 sts. then leave these 12 sts. on holder, k. to last 2 sts., k.2 tog.
Work each side separately.
1st, 3rd, 5th and 7th rows: p.
2nd row: cast off 4 sts., k. to last 2 sts., k.2 tog.
4th row: cast off 4 sts., p. to last 2 sts., p.2 tog.
6th row: cast off 2 sts., k. to last 2 sts., k.2 tog.
8th row: k.2 tog. twice.
9th row: p.2 tog., break yarn and fasten off.
Rejoin yarn to neck edge of other side and work as for first side, reversing all shapings.

BACK

Work as for front until there are 62 sts., ending with 8th ridge.

Work Back Opening
Next row (wrong side): p. 33 sts., turn, leave rem. sts. on spare needle.
1st row: p.4, k. to last 2 sts., k.2 tog.
2nd row: p.
Rep. last 2 rows 3 times.
9th row: p.2, y.r.n., p.2 tog., p. to last 2 sts., p.2 tog.
Cont. working 2nd and 1st rows, making another buttonhole on 17th row, keeping to ridge patt., until 21 sts. rem.
Work 1 row, thus ending at neck edge, do not break yarn.
Leave sts. on a spare needle.
Join separate yarn to inner edge of rem. sts.
Work 2nd side as folls.:
Cast on 4 sts., p. to end.
1st row: sl.1, k.1, p.s.s.o., k. to last 4 sts., p.4.
2nd row: p.
Keeping to ridge patt., cont. working 1st and 2nd rows until 21 sts. rem.
Work 1 row.
Break yarn and leave sts. on spare needle.

SLEEVES

Cast on 48 sts. with 2¼mm. needles.
Work 5 rows in k.1, p.1 rib.
Change to 2¾mm. needles and work in ridge patt. as for front.
Inc. 1 st. at each end of every 6th row until there are 72 sts. and 73 rows have

been worked.

Shape Top
Cast off 5 sts. at beg. of next 2 rows.
Dec. 1 st. at each end of next and every alt. row until 26 sts. rem.
Now dec. 1 st. at each end of every row until 16 sts. rem.
Leave on spare needle.

NECKBAND

With 2¼mm. needles, work from left side of back, using yarn still attached as folls.:
1st row: across sts. of left back work p.2, y.r.n., p.2 tog., k.15, k.2 tog., across sts. of left sleeve work k.2 tog., k.12, k.2 tog., pick up and k. 14 sts. down left front neck, k. across 12 sts. at centre front, pick up and k. 14 sts. up right front neck, work across right sleeve as for left sleeve then,

across sts. of right back, work k.17, p.4. [109 sts.]
2nd row: p.4, * p.1, k.1, rep. from * to last 5 sts., p.5.
3rd row: p.4, rib to last 4 sts., p.4.
Rep. 3rd row 3 times.
7th row: p.2, y.r.n., p.2 tog., rib to last 4 sts., p.4.
Work 1 more row.
Cast off in rib.

MAKING UP

Sew up raglan seams.
Sew up side and sleeve seams with small back-st., ensuring that ridges meet neatly.
Sew cast-on edge of button border neatly behind buttonhole border.
Sew on buttons.

Cable Sweater with Shirt Collar

Garter stitch and cable pattern sweater with set-in sleeves, ribbed welts and shirt-style collar

★ Suitable for adventurous beginners

MATERIALS

Yarn
Pingouin Pingoperle 4 ply
3(4:4:5:6) × 50g. balls

Needles
1 pair 2¾mm.
1 pair 3¼mm.
1 set of 4 double-pointed 2¾mm.
1 cable needle

MEASUREMENTS

Chest
51(56:61:66:72) cm.
20(22:24:26:28) in.
1/2(2/3:4/5:6/7:8/9) approx. age

Length
33(37:39:43:46) cm.
13(14½:15¼:16¾:18) in.

Sleeve Seam
21(23:27:31:35) cm.
8¼(9:10½:12¼:13¾) in.

TENSION

32 sts. and 48 rows = 10 cm. (4 in.) square over patt. on 3¼mm. needles. If your tension square does not correspond to these measurements, see page 156 for adjustment instructions.

ABBREVIATIONS

k. = knit; p. = purl; st(s). = stitch(es); inc. = increas(ing) (see page 156); dec. = decreas(ing) (see page 157); beg. = begin(ning); rem. = remain(ing); rep. = repeat; alt. = alternate; tog. = together; sl. = slip (transfer one stitch from left needle, knitwise unless otherwise stated, to right hand needle.); cont. = continue; patt. = pattern; foll. = following; folls. = follows; mm. = millimetres; cm. = centimetres; in. = inches; st. st. = stocking st.: one row k., one row p.; g. st. = garter st.: every row k.; incs. = increases; decs. = decreases; C6B = cable 6 back: sl. next 3 sts. onto cable needle and leave at back of work, k.3, then k.3 from cable needle; m.1 = make 1 st.: pick up horizontal loop lying before next st. and work into back of it.

BACK

** Cast on 71(79:85:93:99) sts. with 2¾mm. needles.
Work in rib as folls.:

1st row (right side): k.1, * p.1, k.1, rep. from * to end.
2nd row: p.1, * k.1, p.1, rep. from * to end.
Rep. these 2 rows until work measures 5(5:5:6:6) cm. (2(2:2:2¼:2¼) in.), ending with a 1st row.
Next row: rib 4(4:2:2:6), * m.1, rib 4, m.1, rib 5(5:5:5:4), rep. from * to last 4(3:2:1:5) sts., m.1, rib to end. [86(96:104:114:122) sts.]
Change to 3¼mm. needles.
Work in patt. as folls.:
1st row (right side): k.
2nd and every alt. row: k.5(3:7:5:2), * p.6, k.8, rep. from * to last 11(9:13:11:8) sts., p.6, k.5(3:7:5:2).
3rd row: k.
5th row: k.5(3:7:5:2), * C6B, k.8, rep. from * to last 11(9:13:11:8) sts., C6B, k.5(3:7:5:2).
7th row: k.
8th row: as 2nd.
These 8 rows form patt.
Cont. in patt. until back measures 23(26:26:29:31) cm. (9(10¼:10¼:11¼:12¼) in.), ending with a wrong side row.

Shape Armholes
Keeping patt. straight, cast off 4 sts. at beg. of next 2 rows.
Dec. 1 st. at each end of next 3 rows.
Work 1 row.
Dec. 1 st. at each end of next and every alt. row until 66(74:80:88:96) sts. rem. **
Work straight in patt. until armholes measure 8(9:10:11:12) cm. (3¼(3½:4:4¼:4¾) in.), ending with a wrong side row.
Change to 2¾mm. needles.
Work in g. st. until armholes measure 10(11:13:14:15) cm. (4(4¼:5:5½:5¾) in.), ending with a wrong side row.
Next row: cast off 16(20:21:24:26), k.34(34:38:40:44) including st. on needle after casting off, cast off rem. 16(20:21:24:26) sts.
Leave 34(34:38:40:44) sts. on a spare needle.

FRONT

Work as for back from ** to **.
Cont. straight in patt. until armholes measure 6(7:8:9:10) cm. (2¼(2¾:3¼:3½:4) in.), ending with a wrong side row.

Divide for Neck
Keeping patt. straight, work as folls.:
Next row: patt. 22(26:27:30:32), work 2 tog., turn.
Leave rem. sts. on a spare needle.

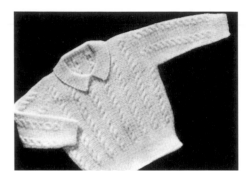

Cont. on these 23(27:28:31:33) sts. for first side and dec. 1 st. at neck edge on every row until 16(20:21:24:26) sts. rem.
Change to 2¾mm. needles.
Work in g. st. until front matches back to shoulder, ending with a wrong side row.
Cast off.
Sl. centre 18(18:22:24:28) sts. onto a length of yarn.
Rejoin yarn to rem. sts.
Next row: work 2 tog., patt. to end.
Complete to match first side.

SLEEVES

Cast on 39(41:45:49:51) sts. with 2¾mm. needles.
Work 5(5:5:6:6) cm. (2(2:2:2¼:2¼) in.) in rib as for back, ending with a 1st row.
Next row: rib 2(3:5:4:5), * m.1, rib 3, rep. from * to last 1(2:4:3:4) sts., m.1, rib to end. [52(54:58:64:66) sts.]
Change to 3¼mm. needles and work patt. as folls.:
1st row (right side): k.
2nd and every alt. row: k.2(3:5:1:2), * p.6, k.8, rep. from * to last 8(9:11:7:8) sts., p.6, k.2(3:5:1:2).
3rd row: k.
5th row: k.2(3:5:1:2), * C6B, k.8, rep. from * to last 8(9:11:7:8) sts., C6B, k.2(3:5:1:2).
7th row: k.
8th row: as 2nd.
Cont. in patt. as set, shaping sides by inc. 1 st. at each end of next and every foll. 8th(8th:10th:10th:12th) row until there are 64(68:72:78:82) sts., working inc. sts. into patt.
Work straight until sleeve seam measures 21(23:27:31:35) cm. (8¼(9:10½:12¼:13¾) in.), ending with a wrong side row.

Shape Top

Keeping patt. straight, cast off 4 sts. at beg. of next 2 rows.
Dec. 1 st. at each end of next and every alt. row until 40(40:34:40:40) sts. rem.
Work 1 row.
Dec. 1 st. at each end of every row until 20(20:22:24:24) sts. rem.
Cast off.

COLLAR

Sew up shoulder seams.
With right side facing, using set of 4 2¾mm. needles and beg. at centre of front neck work as folls.: 1st needle – k.9(9:11:12:14) sts. from centre front neck, k. up 16(16:20:20:20) sts. up right side of neck, 2nd needle – k.34(34:38:40:44) sts. from back dec. 1 st. at centre, 3rd needle – k. up 16(16:20:20:20) sts. down left side of neck, then k. rem. 9(9:11:12:14) sts. from front. [83(83:99:103:111) sts.]
Work backwards and forwards as folls.:
1st row: k.1, * p.1, k.1, rep. from * to end.
2nd row: p.1, * k.1, p.1, rep. from * to end.
Rep. these 2 rows until collar measures 5(5:6:7:7) cm. (2(2:2¼:2¾:2¾) in.), ending with a 2nd row.
Cast off loosely in rib.

MAKING UP

Sew up side and sleeve seams.
Set in sleeves.
Fold collar to right side.

Two-colour Zig-zag Cardigan

1961

Chevron-pattern cardigan with round neck, raglan sleeves and ribbed borders with turnback cuffs

★★ Suitable for knitters with some previous experience

MATERIALS

Yarn
Patons Clansman 4 ply
2(2:3:3:4) × 50g. balls Main Col. A
2(2:2:3:3) × 50g. balls Col. B

Needles
1 pair 2¾mm.
1 pair 3¼mm.

Buttons
6(6:6:7:7)

MEASUREMENTS

Chest
46(51:56:61:66) cm.
18(20:22:24:26) in.
6 months/1(1/2:2/3:4/5:6/7) approx. age

Length
32(37:40:44:47) cm.
12½(14½:15¾:17¼:18½) in.

Sleeve Seam
20(23:25:28:30) cm.
7¾(9:9¾:11:11¾) in.

TENSION

32 sts. and 32 rows = 10 cm. (4 in.) square over patt. on 3¼mm. needles. If your tension square does not correspond to these measurements, see page 156 for adjustment instructions.

ABBREVIATIONS

k. = knit; p. = purl; st(s). = stitch(es); inc. = increas(ing) (see page 156); dec. = decreas(ing) (see page 157); beg. = begin(ning); rem. = remain(ing); rep. = repeat; alt. = alternate; tog. = together; sl. = slip (transfer one stitch from left needle, knitwise unless otherwise stated, to right hand needle.); cont. = continue; patt. = pattern; foll. = following; folls. = follows; mm. = millimetres; cm. = centimetres; in. = inches; st. st. = stocking st.: one row k., one row p.; g. st. = garter st.: every row k.; incs. = increases; decs. = decreases; t.b.l. = through back of loops; m.1 = make 1 st.: pick up horizontal loop lying before next st. and work into back of it.

BACK

Cast on 61(69:77:85:93) sts. with 2¾mm. needles and A.
1st row (right side): k.1 t.b.l., * p.1, k.1 t.b.l., rep. from * to end.

2nd row: p.1 t.b.l., * k.1, p.1 t.b.l., rep. from * to end.
Rep. last 2 rows 6(6:7:7:8) times more, then 1st row again.
Next row: rib 3(7:2:6:1), m.1, * rib 3(3:4: 4:5), m.1, rep. from * to last 4(8:3:7:2) sts., rib 4(8:3:7:2). [80(88:96:104:112) sts.]
Join in B, change to 3¼mm. needles and st. st.
Work in zig-zag patt. as folls.:
1st row (right side): k. * 2A, 2B, rep. from * to end.
2nd row: p. 1B, * 2A, 2B, rep. from * to last 3 sts., 2A, 1B.
3rd row: k. * 2B, 2A, rep. from * to end.
4th row: p. 1A, * 2B, 2A, rep. from * to last 3 sts., 2B, 1A.
5th row: as 3rd.
6th row: as 2nd.
These 6 rows form patt.
Work straight in patt. until back measures 20(23:25:28:30) cm. (7¾(9:9¾: 11:11¾) in.) from beg., ending with a wrong side row.

Shape Raglans
Cast off 4 sts. at beg. of next 2 rows.
Dec. 1 st. at each end of every row until 68(72:76:80:84) sts. rem.
Patt. 1 row.
Now dec. 1 st. at each end of next and every alt. row until 32(34:36:38:40) sts. rem.
Patt. 1 row.
Cast off in patt.

LEFT FRONT

Cast on 29(33:37:41:45) sts. with 2¾mm. needles and A.
Work 15(15:17:17:19) rows in twisted rib as given for back.
Next row: rib 4(1:3:5:2) sts., m.1, * rib 2(3:3:3:4), m.1, rep. from * to last 5(2:4: 6:3) sts., rib 5(2:4:6:3) sts. [40(44:48:52:56) sts.].

Join in B.
Change to 3¼mm. needles and beg. with a 1st row.
Work straight in zig-zag patt. as given for back until front matches back at side edge, ending with a wrong side row.

Shape Raglan
Cast off 4 sts. at beg. of next row.
Work 1 row straight.
Now dec. 1 st. at raglan edge on every row until 34(36:38:40:42) sts. rem.
Now dec. 1 st. at raglan edge on next and every alt. row until 23(24:25:26:27) sts. rem.

Shape Neck
With wrong side facing, cast off 7(8:9: 10:11) sts. at beg. of next row.
Cont. dec. at raglan edge on every alt. row, and at the same time dec. 1 st. at neck edge on every row until 5 sts. rem.
Now keep neck edge straight and cont. dec. at raglan edge on alt. rows as before until 2 sts. rem.
Next row: patt. 2, turn, k.2 tog.
Fasten off.

RIGHT FRONT

Work to match left front, reversing all shapings.

SLEEVES

Cast on 37(39:43:45:49) sts. with 2¾mm. needles and A.
Work 15(15:17:17:19) rows in twisted rib as for back.
Next row: rib 3(1:3:1:3), m.1, * rib 3, m.1, rep. from * to last 4(2:4:2:4) sts., rib

4(2:4:2:4) sts. [48(52:56:60:64) sts.]
Join in B, change to 3¼mm. needles.
Beg. with a 1st row, work in zig-zag patt.
as for back.
Shape sides by inc. 1 st. at each end of
1st(7th:1st:7th:1st) row, and every foll.
6th(6th:8th:8th:10th) row until there are
64(68:72:76:80) sts., taking inc. sts. into
patt.
Work straight until sleeve seam measures
20(23:25:28:30) cm. (7¾(9:9¾:11:11¾)
in.), ending with a wrong side row.

Shape Raglans
Cast off 4 sts. at beg. of next 2 rows.
Dec. 1 st. at each end of every row until
28(32:36:40:44) sts. rem.
Now dec. on next and every alt. row until
4 sts. rem., ending with a p. row.
Cast off in patt.

FRONT BORDERS

Left Border
Cast on 9 sts. with 2¾mm. needles and
A.
1st row (right side): k.2 t.b.l., * p.1, k.1
t.b.l., rep. from * to last st., k.1 t.b.l.
2nd row: k.1, * p.1 t.b.l., k.1, rep. from * to
end.
Rep. last 2 rows until strip fits up left
front to beg. of neck shaping when
slightly stretched, ending with a wrong
side row.
Sew border in position as working, to
ensure a good fit.
Leave sts. on safety pin at top.

Right Border
Work to match left border, with the
addition of 5(5:5:6:6) buttonholes, first to
come 2 cm. (¾ in.) above beg. of border,
last to come 4 cm. (1½ in.) below beg. of
neck shaping, with rest spaced evenly
between.
Mark position of buttons on left border
with pins before working buttonholes.
1st buttonhole row: rib 3, cast off 3, rib to
end.
2nd row: work back in rib, casting on 3
sts. over those cast off.

NECK BORDER

Sew up raglan seams.
With right side facing, 2¾mm. needles
and A, rib 9 sts. from right border, pick
and up and k. 19(20:21:22:23) sts. up right
side of neck, 3 sts. from right sleeve top,
29(31:33:35:37) sts. from back, 3 sts. from
left sleeve top, 19(20:21:22:23) sts. down
left side, rib 9 sts. from left border.
[91(95:99:103:107) sts.].
Beg. with a 2nd row, work 3 rows in
twisted rib as for left border.
Make a buttonhole in next 2 rows.
Work another 3 rows in rib.
Cast off in rib.

MAKING UP

Press work lightly on wrong side, omit-
ting ribbing.
Sew up side and sleeve seams.
Press all seams.
Sew on buttons.

V-neck, Check-pattern Sweater

Loose, V-neck sweater with ribbed welts, set-in sleeves and check pattern on front, back and outside of sleeve

★★★ Suitable for experienced knitters only

MATERIALS

Yarn
Argyll Ambridge DK
12(12:12:13:13) × 50g. balls

Needles
1 pair 3¼mm.
1 pair 4mm.
1 set of 4 double-pointed 3¼mm.

MEASUREMENTS

Chest
92(97:102:107:112) cm.
36(38:40:42:44) in.

Length
64(65:66:68:69) cm.
25(25½:26:26¾:27) in.

Sleeve Seam
47(47:47:48:48) cm.
18½(18½:18½:18¾:18¾) in.

TENSION

22 sts. and 30 rows = 10 cm. (4 in.) square over patt. on 4mm. needles. If your tension square does not correspond to these measurements, see page 156 for adjustment instructions.

ABBREVIATIONS

k. = knit; p. = purl; st(s). = stitch(es); inc. = increas(ing) (see page 156); dec. = decreas(ing) (see page 157); beg. = begin(ning); rem. = remain(ing); rep. = repeat; alt. = alternate; tog. = together; sl. = slip (transfer one stitch from left needle, knitwise unless otherwise stated, to right hand needle.); cont. = continue; patt. = pattern; foll. = following; folls. = follows; mm. = millimetres; cm. = centimetres; in. = inches; st. st. = stocking st.: one row k., one row p.; g. st. = garter st.: every row k.; incs. = increases; decs. = decreases.

FRONT

Cast on 101(107:113:119:125) sts. with 3¼mm. needles.
1st row: k.2, (p.1, k.1) to last st., k.1.
2nd row: k.1, (p.1, k.1) to end.
Rep. these 2 rows for 7 cm. (2¾ in.), ending with a 2nd row and inc. 9 sts.

evenly on last row. [110(116:122:128:134) sts.]
Change to 4mm. needles and work in patt. as folls.:
1st row (right side): k.8(11:14:8:11), (p.4, k.14) to last 12(15:18:12:15) sts., p.4, k.8(11:14:8:11).
2nd row: p.8(11:14:8:11), (k.4, p.14) to last 12(15:18:12:15) sts., k.4, p.8(11:14:8:11).
3rd and 4th rows: as 1st and 2nd.
5th row: k.7(10:13:7:10), (p.1, k.4, p.1, k.12) to last 13(16:19:13:16) sts., p.1, k.4, p.1, k.7(10:13:7:10).
6th row: p.6(9:12:6:9), (k.1, p.6, k.1, p.10) to last 14(17:20:14:17) sts., k.1, p.6, k.1, p.6(9:12:6:9).
7th row: k.5(8:11:5:8), (p.1, k.8) to last 6(9:12:6:9) sts., p.1, k.5(8:11:5:8).
8th row: p.4(7:10:4:7), (k.1, p.10, k.1, p.6) to last 16(19:22:16:19) sts., k.1, p.10, k.1, p.4(7:10:4:7).
9th row: k.3(6:9:3:6), (p.1, k.12, p.1, k.4) to last 17(20:23:17:20) sts., p.1, k.12, p.1, k.3(6:9:3:6).
10th row: p.1(4:7:1:4), (k.2, p.14, k.2) to last 1(4:7:1:4) sts., p.1(4:7:1:4).
11th row: k.1(4:7:1:4), (p.2, k.14, p.2) to last 1(4:7:1:4) sts., k.1(4:7:1:4).
12th and 13th rows: as 10th and 11th.
14th row: p.3(6:9:3:6), (k.1, p.12, k.1, p.4) to last 17(20:23:17:20) sts., k.1, p.12, k.1, p.3(6:9:3:6).
15th row: k.4(7:10:4:7), (p.1, k.10, p.1, k.6) to last 16(19:22:16:19) sts., p.1, k.10, p.1, k.4(7:10:4:7).
16th row: p.5(8:11:5:8), (k.1, p.8) to last 6(9:12:6:9) sts., k.1, p.5(8:11:5:8).

17th row: k.6(9:12:6:9), (p.1, k.6, p.1, k.10) to last 14(17:20:14:17) sts., p.1, k.6, p.1, k.6(9:12:6:9).
18th row: p.7(10:13:7:10), (k.1, p.4, k.1, p.12) to last 13(16:19:13:16) sts., k.1, p.4, k.1, p.7(10:13:7:10).
These 18 rows form patt.
Cont. in patt. until work measures 41 cm. (16 in.) from beg., ending with a wrong side row.

Shape Armholes
Keeping patt. correct, cast off 6(7:8:9:10) sts. at beg. of next 2 rows.
Dec. 1 st. at each end of next 7 rows, then on the 4 foll. alt. rows. [76(80:84:88: 92) sts.]

Shape Neck
Next row (wrong side): patt. 38(40:42:44: 46), turn.
Cont. on these sts.
Dec. 1 st. at neck edge on foll. 3rd row, then on every foll. alt. row until 28(29:31: 33:35) sts. rem., then on every foll. 4th row until 23(24:25:26:27) sts. rem.
Work straight until front measures 23(24:25:27:28) cm. (9(9½:9¾:10½:11) in.) from beg. of armhole shaping, ending at armhole edge.

Shape Shoulder
Cast off 8(8:8:9:9) sts. at beg. of next and foll. alt. row.
Work 1 row.
Cast off.
With wrong side facing, rejoin yarn to rem. sts. and patt. 1 row.
Complete as first half.

BACK

Work as for front until armhole shaping is complete.
Work straight until back measures same as front to shoulder shaping, ending with a wrong side row.

Shape Shoulders
Cast off 8(8:8:9:9) sts. at beg. of next 4 rows.
Cast off 7(8:9:8:9) sts. at beg. of next 2 rows.
Sl. rem. 30(32:34:36:38) sts. onto a spare needle.

SLEEVES

Cast on 49(51:53:55:57) sts. with 3¼mm. needles.

Work in rib as on welt for 7 cm. (2¾ in.), ending with a 2nd row and inc. 7(5:9: 7:11) sts. evenly across last row. [56(56: 62:62:68) sts.]
Change to 4mm. needles and work patt. as folls.:
1st and 2nd sizes only: work 1st to 4th rows as given for 1st size on front.
3rd and 4th sizes only: work 1st to 4th rows as given for 2nd size on front.
5th size only: work 1st to 4th rows as given for 3rd size on front.
All sizes: cont. in patt. to match front, at the same time shape sleeve by inc. 1 st. at each end of next row, then on every foll. 6th(4th:4th:4th:4th) row until there are 78(62:68:76:82) sts., then on every foll. 8th(6th:6th:6th:6th) row until there are 88(92:98:102:108) sts., taking extra sts. into st. st.
Work straight until sleeve measures 47(47:47:48:48) cm. (18½(18½:18½:18¾: 18¾) in.) from beg., ending with a wrong side row.

Shape Top
Cast off 6(7:8:9:10) sts. at beg. of next 2 rows.
Dec. 1 st. at each end of every right side row until 44 sts. rem., then on every row until 34 sts. rem.
Cast off.

NECKBAND

Sew up shoulder seams.
With set of 3¼mm. needles and right side facing, k. across sts. of back, k. up 44(47:50:53:56) sts. evenly down left front neck, pick up and k. into back of horizontal thread lying between the 2 centre sts., finally k. up 43(46:49:52:55) sts. evenly up right front neck. [118(126:134: 142:150) sts.]
Keeping centre st. as a k. st. on every round, work 9 rounds in k.1, p.1 rib, dec. 1 st. at each side of centre st. on every round.
Cast off in rib.

MAKING UP

Omitting ribbing, press lightly.
Sew up side and sleeve seams.
Set in sleeves.
Press seams.

Russian Blouse 1933

High-necked Russian blouse in moss stitch with side-buttoning front, set-in sleeves and ribbed welts

★★ Suitable for knitters with some previous experience

MATERIALS

Yarn
Lister Lee Motoravia 4 ply
4 × 50g. balls

Needles
1 pair 3mm.
1 pair 3¼mm.

Buttons
6 small

MEASUREMENTS

Chest
71 cm.
28 in.
6/7 approx. age

Length
38 cm.
15 in.

Sleeve Seam
34 cm.
13¼ in.

TENSION

28 sts. and 32 rows = 10 cm. (4 in.) square over patt. on 3¼mm. needles. If your tension square does not correspond to these measurements, see page 156 for adjustment instructions.

ABBREVIATIONS

k. = knit; p. = purl; st(s). = stitch(es); inc. = increas(ing) (see page 156); dec. = decreas(ing) (see page 157); beg. = begin(ning); rem. = remain(ing); rep. = repeat; alt. = alternate; tog. = together; sl. = slip (transfer one stitch from left needle, knitwise unless otherwise stated, to right hand needle.); cont. = continue; patt. = pattern; foll. = following; folls. = follows; mm. = millimetres; cm. = centimetres; in. = inches; st. st. = stocking st.: one row k., one row p.; g. st. = garter st.: every row k.; incs. = increases; decs. = decreases.

BACK

Cast on 100 sts. with 3mm. needles.
Work 10 rows in k.1, p.1 rib.
Change to 3¼mm. needles and patt. as folls.:
1st row (right side): * p.1, k.1, rep. from * to end.
2nd row: as 1st.
3rd row: * k.1, p.1, rep. from * to end.
4th row: as 3rd.
These 4 rows form patt.
Working in patt., cont. until back measures 23 cm. (9 in.), ending with a wrong side row.

Shape Armholes
Cast off 6 sts. at beg. of next 2 rows. **
Cont. straight until armholes measure 15 cm. (5¾ in.).

Shape Shoulders
Cast off 6 sts. at beg. of foll. 8 rows.
Cast off rem. sts. for back of neck.

FRONT

Work as for back to **.

Next row: work 24 sts., cast off 6 sts., work to end.
Cont. on 58 sts. for right front side of neck opening.
Work straight until armhole measures same as back to shoulder shaping, ending at side edge.

Shape Shoulder
Cast off 6 sts. at beg. of next and foll. 3 alt. rows.
Cast off rem. sts. for neck.
Return to rem. 24 sts. and work to match first side.

SLEEVES

Cast on 56 sts. with 3mm. needles.
Work 5 cm. (2 in.) in k.1, p.1 rib.
Change to 3¼mm. needles.
Work in patt. as for back, inc. 1 st. at each end of every 6th row until there are 68 sts.
Cont. straight until sleeve measures 34 cm. (13¼ in.).

Shape Top
Cast off 2 sts. at beg. of every row until 16 sts. rem.
Cast off.

LEFT FRONT BAND

Cast on 12 sts. with 3mm. needles.
Work in k.1, p.1 rib until band fits from bottom to top of left side of front opening.
Cast off.
Sew on band.

RIGHT FRONT BAND

Work as for left band, making 4 buttonholes thus, first on 8th and 9th rows, rem. 3 buttonholes at intervals of 10 rows:
1st buttonhole row: rib 5, cast off 2, rib to end.
2nd buttonhole row: rib 5, cast on 2, rib 5.
Cont. until right band matches left band.
Cast off.
Sew on band.

COLLAR

Sew up shoulder seams.
Cast on 20 sts. with 3mm. needles.
Work 4 rows in k.1, p.1 rib.
5th row: rib 4, cast off 2, rib 8 including st. left after casting off, cast off 2, rib to end.
Next row: rib 4, cast on 2, rib 8, cast on 2, rib to end.
Work in k.1, p.1 rib until collar fits around neck and overlaps for button opening.
Cast off.

MAKING UP

Press pieces with warm iron over damp cloth, omitting ribbing.
Set in sleeves.
Sew up side and sleeve seams.
Sew collar to neck.
Sew on buttons.
Press seams lightly.

Sweater with Peter Pan Collar

Reverse stocking stitch sweater with set-in sleeves, garter stitch collar, cuffs and welts, and zip or button closing

★★ Suitable for knitters with some previous experience

MATERIALS

Yarn
Sunbeam Shantung
11(12:13:14) × 25g. balls

Needles
1 pair 2¾mm.
1 pair 3¼mm.
1 3mm. crochet hook (for button version)

Buttons
2

OR

Zip
1 10 cm. (4 in.)

MEASUREMENTS

Bust
82(87:92:97) cm.
32(34:36:38) in.

Length
54(55:58:59) cm.
21¼(21½:22¾:23¼) in.

Sleeve Seam
44(44:45:45) cm.
17¼(17¼:17¾:17¾) in.

TENSION

25 sts. and 32 rows = 10 cm. (4 in.) square over st. st. on 3¼mm. needles. If your tension square does not correspond to these measurements, see page 156 for adjustment instructions.

ABBREVIATIONS

k. = knit; p. = purl; st(s). = stitch(es); inc. = increas(ing) (see page 156); dec. = decreas(ing) (see page 157); beg. = begin(ning); rem. = remain(ing); rep. = repeat; alt. = alternate; tog. = together; sl. = slip (transfer one stitch from left needle, knitwise unless otherwise stated, to right hand needle.); cont. = continue; patt. = pattern; foll. = following; folls. = follows; mm. = millimetres; cm. = centimetres; in. = inches; st. st. = stocking st.: one row k., one row p.; g. st. = garter st.: every row k.; incs. = increases; decs. = decreases; m.1 = make 1 st.: pick up horizontal loop lying before next st. and k. into the back of it.

FRONT

** Cast on 99(105:111:117) sts. with 2¾mm. needles.

Work 11 rows in g. st.
Change to 3¼mm. needles and reverse st. st. (p.1 row, k.1 row alternately, having p. side as right side).
Work 12 rows.
Dec. 1 st. at each end of next row, and then every 6th row until 91(97:103:109) sts. rem.
Work 9 rows.
Inc. 1 st. at each end of next row, and then every 8th row until there are 105(111:117:123) sts.
Work until front measures 36(36:38:38) cm. (14(14:15:15) in.) from beg., ending with a k. row.

Shape Armholes
Cast off 4(4:5:5) sts. at beg. of next 2 rows.
Now dec. 1 st. at each end of every row until 91(93:97:99) sts. rem., and then every alt. row until 85(87:91:93) sts. rem. **
Work until armholes measure 14(15:15:16) cm. (5½(5¾:5¾:6¼) in.) measured on the straight, ending with a p. row.

Shape Neck
Next row: k.37(38:40:41) sts., cast off 11 sts., k. to end.
Cont. on last set of sts.
Dec. 1 st. at neck edge on next 6(6:6:6) rows, and then the 3(3:4:4) foll. alt. rows, ending at armhole edge.

Shape Shoulder
Dec. at neck edge on foll. alt. rows twice more, and at the same time cast off 7(6:7:7) sts. at beg. of next row, and 6(7:7:7) sts. at beg. of 2 foll. alt. rows.
Work 1 row.
Cast off rem. 7(7:7:8) sts.
Rejoin yarn to rem. sts. at neck edge and complete to match first side, working one extra row before shaping shoulder.

BACK

Work as for front from ** to **.
Work until armholes measure 10(10:11:12) cm. (4(4:4¼:4¾) in.) measured on the straight, ending with a p. row.

Divide for Back Opening
Next row: k.42(43:45:46) sts., cast off 1 st., k. to end.
Cont. on last set of sts.
Work until armhole measures same as front, ending at armhole edge.

Shape Shoulder
Cast off at beg. of next and foll. alt. rows 7(6:7:7) sts. once, 6(7:7:7) sts. twice, and 7(7:7:8) sts. once.

Work 1 row.
Cast off rem. 16(16:17:17) sts.
Rejoin yarn to rem. sts. at opening edge and complete to match first side.

SLEEVES

Cast on 53(53:55:57) sts. with 3¼mm. needles.
Work 10 rows in reverse st. st.
Cont. in reverse st. st., inc. 1 st. at each end of next row, and then every 6th row until there are 61(63:73:77) sts., and then every 8th row until there are 75(77:81:85) sts.
Work until sleeve measures 44(44:45:45) cm. (17¼(17¼:17¾:17¾) in.) from beg., ending with a k. row.

Shape Top
Cast off 4(4:5:5) sts. at beg. of next 2 rows.
Now dec. 1 st. at each end of every row until 57(59:61:63) sts. rem., then every alt. row until 33(33:33:35) sts. rem., and then every row until 19(19:19:21) sts. rem.
Cast off.

COLLAR

Cast on 43(43:45:47) sts. with 2¾mm. needles.
Work 6 rows in g. st.
Next row: k.2, m.1, k. to last 2 sts., m.1, k.2.
Working in g. st., cont. to inc. in this way at each end of every 6th row until there are 51(51:53:55) sts.
Work 5 rows.
Cast off.
Work other side of collar to match.

CUFFS

Cast on 53(53:55:57) sts. with 2¾mm. needles.

Work 6 rows in g. st.
Next row: k.2, m.1, k. to last 2 sts., m.1, k.2.
Working in g. st., cont. to inc. in this way at each end of every 6th row until there are 61(61:63:65) sts.
Work 5 rows.
Cast off.
Work another cuff to match.

MAKING UP

With wrong side facing, block each piece and press lightly with a warm iron and damp cloth.
Sew up shoulder, side and sleeve seams.
Set in sleeves.
Sew cast-on edges of collar pieces to neck edge from back opening to centre front

neck.
Sew in zip at back, OR work a row of double crochet (see page 162) along back opening edges, making 2 small button loops.
Sew on buttons.
Sew cast-on edges of cuffs to sleeve edges.
Press seams lightly.

Shoulder-buttoning Nautical Sweater 1955

Stocking stitch, striped sweater with set-in sleeves, ribbed yoke and welts, button fastening on both shoulders

★ Suitable for beginners

MATERIALS

Yarn
Sunbeam Pure New Wool 3 ply
2(3) × 25g. balls Main Col. A
2(2) × 25g. balls Col. B

Needles
1 pair 2¼mm.
1 pair double-pointed 3mm.

Buttons
6

MEASUREMENTS

Chest
46(51) cm.
18(20) in.
6 months/1(1/2) approx. age

Length
27(31) cm.
10½(12¼) in.

Sleeve Seam
17(20) cm.
6½(7¾) in.

TENSION

32 sts. and 44 rows = 10 cm. (4 in.) square over st. st. on 3mm. needles. If your tension square does not correspond to these measurements, see page 156 for

adjustment instructions.

ABBREVIATIONS

k. = knit; p. = purl; st(s). = stitch(es); inc. = increas(ing) (see page 156); dec. = decreas(ing) (see page 157); beg. = begin(ning); rem. = remain(ing); rep. = repeat; alt. = alternate; tog. = together; sl. = slip (transfer one stitch from left needle, knitwise unless otherwise stated, to right hand needle.); cont. = continue; patt. = pattern; foll. = following; folls. = follows; mm. = millimetres; cm. = centimetres; in. = inches; st. st. = stocking st.: one row k., one row p.; g. st. = garter st.: every row k.; incs. = increases; decs. = decreases; y.fwd. = yarn forward.

FRONT

Cast on 75(83) sts. with 2¼mm. needles and A.
1st row: k.1, * p.1, k.1, rep. from * to end.
2nd row: p.1, * k.1, p.1, rep. from * to end.
Rep. these 2 rows 5(6) more times, inc. 5 sts. evenly across last row. [80(88) sts.]
Change to double-pointed 3mm. needles and cont. in st. st. as folls.:
1st row: B, k. to end.
2nd row: B, p. to end.
3rd row: A, k. to end, return to beg. of row.
4th row: B, k. to end.
5th row: B, p. to end, return to beg. of row.
6th row: A, p. to end.
7th row: A, k. to end, return to beg. of row.
8th row: B, k. to end.
9th row: A, p. to end.
10th row: A, k. to end.
11th-20th rows: as 1st-10th rows, but reading k. for p. and p. for k. throughout. These 20 rows form the patt. and are rep. throughout.
Cont. in patt. until 58(70) rows have been worked in patt.

Shape Armholes
Keeping patt. correct, cast off 2 sts. at beg. of next 2 rows, then dec. one st. at each end of next and foll. 1(2) alt. rows. [72(78) sts.]
Cont. without shaping until 96(110) rows in all have been worked in patt., inc. one st. at end of last row. [73(79) sts.]
Change to 2¼mm. needles and A, and work 6 rows in rib as at beg.
Next row: rib 24(26), cast off 25(27) sts., rib to end.
Cont. on last 24(26) sts., rib 3(5) rows.
Next row: rib 2, (y.fwd., k.2 tog., rib 4) twice, y.fwd., k.2 tog., rib to end.
Rib 1 more row, then cast off in rib.
Rejoin yarn to the other 24(26) sts., and work to match, reversing buttonhole row.

BACK

Work as for front, omitting buttonholes.

SLEEVES

Cast on 41(45) sts. with 2¼mm. needles and A, work in rib as on front, inc. 11 sts. evenly across last row. [52(56) sts.]
Change to double-pointed 3mm. needles and cont. in patt. as on front, inc. 1 st. at each end of 15th and every foll. 16th(14th) row until there are 58(64) sts., then cont. without shaping until 58(70) rows in all have been worked in patt.

Shape Top
Keeping patt. correct, dec. 1 st. at each end of every row until 14(16) sts. rem.
Cast off.

MAKING UP

Overlap front over back for 2 rows at shoulders and sew at armhole edges.
Set in sleeves.
Sew up side and sleeve seams.
Sew on buttons.
Press seams.

h-neck Sweater with Giant Cable 1956

sweater with garter-striped body, ribbed sleeves, centre-front
nd slash neck with facing

le for knitters with some
perience

LS

Wool Aran
18) × 50g. balls

m.
m.
lle

MENTS

7:112) cm.
44) in.

70) cm.
27:27½) in.

48) cm.
18½:18¾) in.

4 rows = 10 cm. (4 in.) square
on 4½mm. needles. If your
are does not correspond to
urements, see page 156 for
instructions.

ATIONS

. = purl; st(s). = stitch(es);
as(ing) (see page 156); dec. =
(see page 157); beg. =
rem. = remain(ing); rep. =
= alternate; tog. = together;
ransfer one stitch from left
wise unless otherwise stated,
d needle.); cont. = continue;
rn; foll. = following; folls. =
. = millimetres; cm. = centi-
. = inches; st. st. = stocking st.:
one row p.; g. st. = garter st.:
.; incs. = increases; decs. =
C8 = cable 8: sl. next 4 sts.
needle and leave at back of
4 from cable needle.

84(88:92:96:100) sts. with
dles.
(p.2, k.2) to last st., k.1.
, (p.2, k.2) to last 3 sts., p.2,

2 rows for 7 cm. (2¾ in.),
a 2nd row and inc. 6 sts.
last row. [90(94:98:102:106)

Change to 4½mm. needles and patt. as folls.:
1st row (right side): p.
2nd and 3rd rows: k.
4th row: p.
These 4 rows form patt.
Cont. in patt. until work measures 44 cm. (17¼ in.) at centre, ending with a wrong side row.

Shape Armholes
Keeping patt. correct, cast off 5(6:7:8:9) sts. at beg. of next 2 rows.
Dec. 1 st. at each end of next 5 rows, then at each end of the 3 foll. alt. rows. [64(66: 68:70:72) sts.]
Work straight until back measures 20(21: 23:24:25) cm. (7¾(8¼:9:9½:9¾) in.) from beg. of armhole shaping, ending with a wrong side row.

Shape Shoulders
Cast off 5(5:6:6:6) sts. at beg. of next 4 rows.
Cast off 6(6:5:5:6) sts. at beg. of next 2 rows.

Shape Neck Facing
Beg. with a k. row, work 4 rows in st. st.
Cast off 2 sts. at beg. of next 6 rows.
Cast off loosely.

FRONT
Work ribbing as for back, but inc. 12 sts. evenly on last row. [96(100:104:108:112) sts.]
Change to 4½mm. needles.
Work in patt. with centre cable as folls.:

1st row (right side): p.40(42:44:46:48), k.2, p.2, C8, p.2, k.2, p.40(42:44:46:48).
2nd row: k.40(42:44:46:48), p.2, k.2, p.8, k.2, p.2, k.40(42:44:46:48).
3rd row: k.42(44:46:48:50), p.2, k.8, p.2, k. to end.
4th row: p.42(44:46:48:50), k.2, p.8, k.2, p. to end.
5th row: p.40(42:44:46:48), k.2, p.2, k.8, p.2, k.2, p.40(42:44:46:48).
6th to 8th rows: as 2nd to 4th.
9th to 12th rows: as 5th to 8th.
These 12 rows form patt.
Cont. in patt. until front measures same as back to armhole shaping, ending with a wrong side row.

Shape Armholes
Work as for back. [70(72:74:76:78) sts.]
Work straight until front measures same as back to shoulder shaping, ending with a wrong side row.
Shape shoulders as for back.

Shape Neck Facing
Beg. with a k. row, work 4 rows in st. st., dec. 3 sts. evenly over centre 12 sts. on 1st row.
Cast off 2 sts. at beg. of next 6 rows.
Cast off loosely.

SLEEVES
Cast on 40(40:44:44:48) sts. with 3¾mm. needles.
Work in rib as on welt for 7 cm. (2¾ in.).
Change to 4½mm. needles.
Cont. in rib, shaping sleeve by inc. 1 st. at each end of next row, then on every foll. 6th(4th:4th:3rd:3rd) row until there are 50(52:56:62:58) sts., then on every foll 4th row until there are 78(82:86:90:94) sts., taking extra sts. into rib.
Work straight until sleeve measures 46(47:47:47:48) cm. (18(18½:18½:18½: 18¾) in.), ending with a wrong side row.

Shape Top
Cast off 5(6:7:8:9) sts. at beg. of next 2 rows.
Work 2(4:6:8:10) rows straight.
Dec. 1 st. at each end of next and every foll. alt. row until 46 sts. rem., then on every row until 36 sts. rem.
Cast off.

MAKING UP
Press lightly, omitting welt and cuffs.
Sew up shoulder seams.
Sew up side and sleeve seams.
Set in sleeves.
Fold facings to wrong side and slip st. in position.
Press seams.

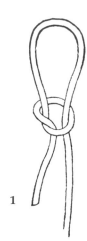

1

Casting On

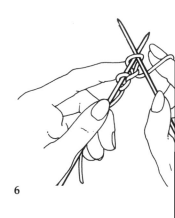

5

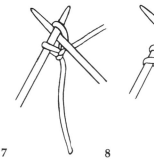

6

There are several methods of casting on stitches, each of which creates a slightly different first row of loops on the needle. The simplest method to learn is the thumb method, which is therefore a good starting point for beginners. All the methods begin with a slip loop (fig 1), which is made as follows:

1. Make an X twist of wool around your thumb.

2. Pull lower right half of this X through upper right half using needle point, and pull yarn end to tighten.

Thumb method

1. Make a slip loop as above, leaving an end of yarn about a metre (yard) long. Put loop on needle.

2. Draw up both ends of yarn to tighten the loop. Take the needle in your right hand (fig 2), holding the yarn end in your left hand, main yarn in your right hand, as shown.

3. Wind the yarn around your left hand in an X shape and put the needle through the loop (fig 3). Wind the main yarn around the needle and draw this loop through (fig 4).

4. Leave this stitch on the needle and repeat the process from step **3.** until the required number of stitches have been made. For an extra strong edge, you can double the loose end of yarn.

This method of casting on produces an elastic, hard-wearing edge.

Cable method with 2 needles

1. Make a slip loop on the left-hand needle.

2. Put the right-hand needle into the loop and wind the yarn round it (fig 5).

3. Draw the yarn through the loop on the left-hand needle with right needle and transfer loop to the left-hand needle (fig 6).

4. Put the right-hand needle between the last two stitches on the left-hand needle (fig 7), and wind the yarn around the right-hand needle as before. Draw the loop through and transfer the stitch onto the left-hand needle (fig 8).

5. Repeat step **4.** until the required number of stitches have been made.

This method of casting on produces a firm edge, and can be used where casting on is necessary within the garment as well as to begin the work. For a slightly less firm finish, put the needle into the stitch *knitwise* in step **4.** instead of between stitches.

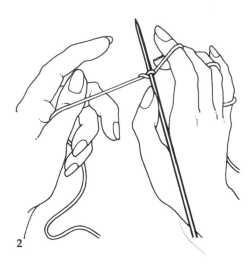

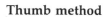

7   8

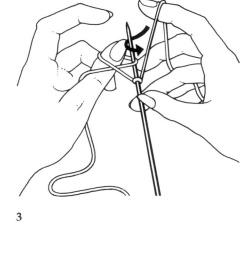

3

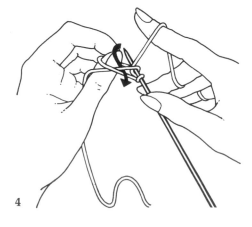

4

Cable method with 4 need

Use four needles with points for this method.

1. With two needles, cast on of stitches for one needle on

2. With the third and second on the required number of stit second needle, likewise with ing needle.

3. Ensure that the stitches are draw the last stitch on the thir close to the first stitch on the for the next row, forming a tri The right side of the work wi on the outside of the triangle. This method of casting on pro edge.

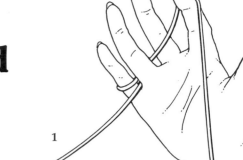

1

Knitting and Purling

Once you have created your first row of loops, or stitches, (see preceding pages) you can begin to knit. Use long, firm needles, for they are the easiest to manipulate, and the right needle can be held under your right arm to give your right hand complete freedom to knit. In order to achieve firm, even tension, it is essential to have complete control of the yarn, one simple method of achieving this is shown below.

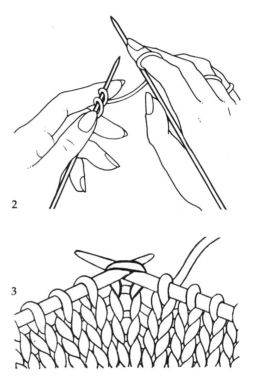

2

How to hold the yarn and prepare to knit

1. Wind the yarn around the little finger of your right hand, over your third finger, under the second and over the index finger (fig 1).
2. Rest the right-hand needle between thumb and the palm of the hand. Allow the needle to slide between thumb and hand, using only the index finger to manipulate the yarn (fig 2).

3

Knit stitch

1. With the needle containing the cast on stitches in your left hand and the wool at the back of the work, put the right-hand needle through the front of the first stitch from right to left (fig 3).
2. Wind the yarn around the right-hand needle around the two needle points with the index finger (fig 4), and turn the right needle slightly to pull the new loop of wool through the old loop and onto the right-hand needle. Slip the old stitch off the left-hand needle.
Repeat this process until all the stitches are knitted. *Abbreviation: 'k.'*. The side of the work facing you while knitting is known as the 'knit' side.

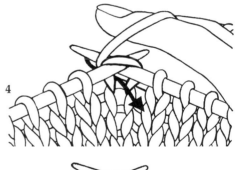

4

Purl stitch

1. With the needle containing the cast on stitches in your left hand and the wool at the front of the work, put the right-hand needle through the front of the first stitch, from right to left (fig 5).
2. Wind the yarn around the right-hand needle from above with the index finger (fig 6), and turn the right-hand needle slightly to pull the new loop of yarn through the old loop and onto the right-hand needle. Slip the old stitch off the left-hand needle.
Repeat this process until all the stitches are purled. *Abbreviation: 'p.'*. The side of

5

6

Casting on with a circular needle

1. Cast on the required number of stitches using the cable method for two needles.
2. Draw the last stitch on the needle up close to the first to prevent a loose stitch. The right side of the work is always on the outside of the circle.

Looped method with 1 needle

1. Make a slip loop on the needle, which should be held in the right hand.
2. Loop the yarn around the left thumb, and put the loop on the needle (fig 10).
3. Repeat step **2.** until the required number of stitches have been made.
This method of casting on produces a very loose cast on edge, which is suitable for lacy patterns and for hems which are to be knitted up.

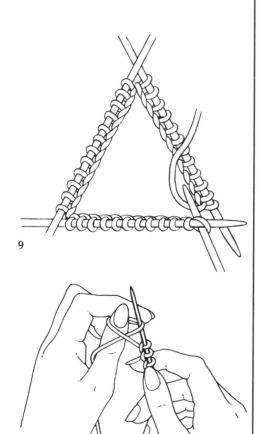

9

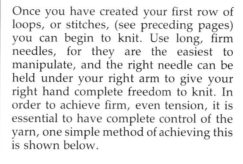

10

the work facing you while purling is called the 'purl' side.

Stitch notes

Some knitters find that slipping the first stitch in every row and knitting the last gives an extra firm and even selvedge to the work.

Garter stitch

This is one of the simplest for beginners, achieved by knitting every row. Purling every row would achieve a similar effect. *Abbreviation: 'g.st.'.*

Stocking stitch

One row purl, one row knit. *Abbreviation: 'st.st.'.* The knit side of the fabric is usually treated as the 'right' side, but some patterns are worked in 'reversed stocking stitch' (*abbreviated as rev.st.st.*), when the purl side is treated as the right side.

Ribbing

Ribbing can be worked in various widths, the most usual being one stitch knit, one stitch purl. This is worked as follows: k.1, *bring the yarn forward, p.1, bring the yarn back, k.1, rep. from * to end. On the following row all the knit sts. (which appear as purl sts. on the opposite side) will be purled, and all the purl sts. (which appear as knit sts. on the opposite side) will be knitted. For a chunkier rib, the stitch combination might be k.2, p.3, or k.2, p.2, instead of k.1, p.1, but the pattern will be worked in exactly the same way, reversing the type of stitch on the following row. Ribbing is usually referred to in patterns as 'rib'.

Moss stitch

This stitch is derived from ribbing. On the first row the stitches are alternated as for ribbing, and as for ribbing the number of stitches worked in each block vary. On the second row all the knit stitches are knitted, and all the purl stitches are purled. A 'single' moss stitch pattern, i.e. one stitch purl, one stitch plain, will work thus on an even number of stitches: k.1, p.1 to end; the second row will work thus: p.1, k.1 to end. *Abbreviation: 'm.st.'.*

Tension

'Tension' means the number of rows and stitches in a given measurement over the knitted fabric. Since every knitting pattern is based on a particular ratio of these, it is essential to check your tension before beginning to knit a new pattern. Personal tension is very variable and adjustments in needle sizes are often necessary. In particular, when the yarn suggested in the pattern is unavailable and an equivalent has to be used, great care in checking tension is necessary. There are tremendous variations in thickness between yarns of the same 'ply': the importance of checking tension cannot be overstressed.

How to check your tension

1. Work a small square, measuring at least 10 cm. (4 in.), in the pattern stitch or that mentioned in tension section.
2. Put the work on a flat surface, and, using a rigid ruler, measure 5 cm. (2 in.), (or the measurement suggested in the pattern) across stitches and rows. Carefully mark this square with pins.
3. If there are more rows or stitches in the pinned area than there should be, your tension is too tight and you should work a new sample using larger needles.
4. If there are too few stitches or rows in the pinned area, your tension is too loose and you should work a new sample using smaller needles.
Continue in this way until you have achieved the correct tension for the pattern. A variation from that suggested in the pattern by even as much as ½ stitch or row could mean that the garments will be a size smaller or larger, and the effect of the stitch too loose or tight for the design. Where a substitute yarn has been used it is sometimes impossible to obtain the correct width and depth tension. In this case the width tension should be obtained and the depth adjusted by working more or less rows as required.

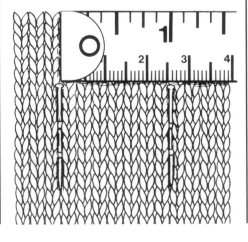

Shaping: Increasing

Knitting is shaped by the addition and subtraction of stitches. There are many different ways of doing this, some purely functional, some decorative too. Single stitches can be increased or decreased at any point in the row, groups of stitches are increased or decreased by casting on and casting off at the end of rows.

Casting on

This method is used where blocks of stitches are to be added. Cast on the required number of stitches at the beginning of a row using the cable method (see page 154), or at the end of a row by the looped method (see page 155).

Simple increasing

1. On a knit row: increase one stitch by knitting first into the front and then into the back of the same stitch. Slip stitch off left-hand needle, (fig 1).
On a purl row: increase one stitch by purling first into the front and then into the back of the same stitch. *Abbreviation: 'inc. 1 st.'.*

2. On a knit or a purl row: increase one stitch by knitting (or purling) the stitch below the next stitch on the left-hand needle, and then knitting (or purling) the next stitch on the left-hand needle, (fig 2). *Abbreviation: 'k.1 up'.*

3. On a knit or a purl row: increase one stitch by picking up the loop lying between the needles, knitwise or purlwise, using the right-hand needle. Put the loop onto the left-hand needle and knit or purl into the back of it, (fig 3). *Abbreviation: 'm. 1'.*

Decorative increasing

These methods produce a series of holes in the fabric which can be used to create lacy patterns.
1. On a knit row: increase one stitch by bringing the yarn forward between needles (as for a purl stitch), then carrying the yarn over the needle to knit the stitch in the usual way, (fig 4). *Abbreviation: 'y.fwd.'.*

2. On a purl row: increase one stitch by bringing the yarn over and round the right-hand needle, then purling the stitch in the usual way, (fig 5). *Abbreviation: 'y.r.n.'.*

3. Between a purl and a knit stitch: increase one stitch by taking the yarn from the front of the work over the needle, then knitting the next stitch in the usual way, (fig 6). *Abbreviation: 'y.o.n.'.*

Shaping: Decreasing

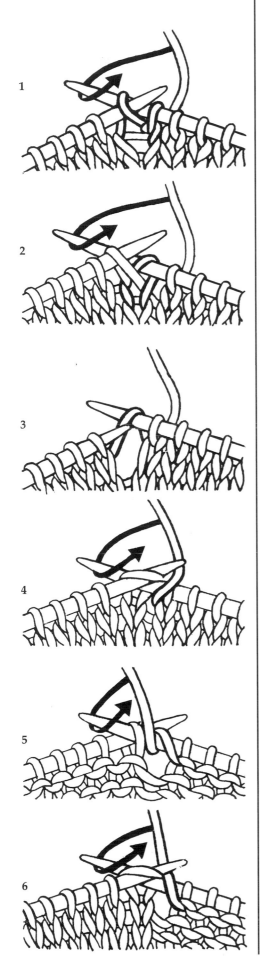

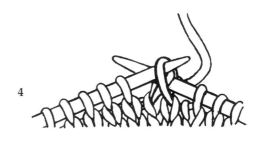

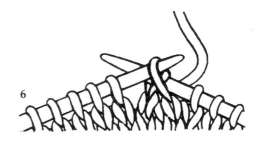

Casting off

This method is used where blocks of stitches are to be removed, for example at shoulder or neck. Casting off should be worked loosely, particularly at the neck (to allow for stretch in wear), and it is often helpful to use a size larger needle.

Simple decreasing

1a. On a knit row: decrease one stitch by putting the right-hand needle knit-wise into second and then first stitch, then knitting them together in the usual manner (fig 1). *Abbreviation: 'k.2 tog.'.*

b. On a purl row: decrease one stitch by putting the right-hand needle purl-wise through the first and then second stitches and purling them together in the usual manner (fig 2). *Abbreviation: 'p.2 tog.'*

c. On a purl row: decrease one stitch by putting the right-hand needle through the back of the first and then second stitches on the left-hand needle and purling them together in the usual manner (fig 3). *Abbreviation: 'p.2 tog. t.b.l'.*

2. On a knit row: decrease one stitch by slipping the next stitch purlwise on to the right-hand needle. Knit the next stitch, put the point of the left-hand needle purl-wise into the slipped stitch and slip it over the knitted stitch and off the needle (fig 4). *Abbreviation: 'sl. 1, k. 1, p.s.s.o.'.*

3. On a knit row: decrease two stitches by putting the right-hand needle through the next three stitches and knitting them together in the usual manner (fig 5). *Abbreviation: 'k.3 tog.'.*

4. On a knit row: decrease two stitches by slipping the next stitch purlwise. Knit the next two stitches together, then put the point of the left-hand needle purlwise into the slipped stitch and slip it over the stitches knitted together and off the needle (fig 6). *Abbreviation: 'sl. 1, k. 2 tog., p.s.s.o.'.*

Decorative decreasing

Decreased stitches lean either to left or right. Different methods of decreasing, *see above*, can thus be used to create patterns. For example, 'sl. 1, k. 1, p.s.s.o.' is used on the decreased edge of raglan sleeves. Of the methods above:
1a., 1b. and **4.** lean to the right;
1c., 2. and **3.** lean to the left.

Problems

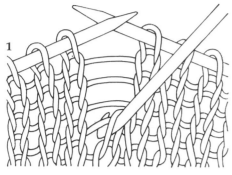

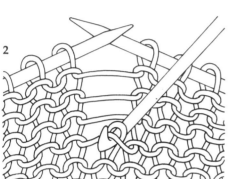

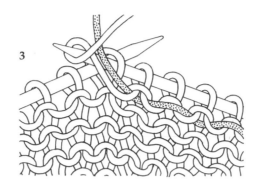

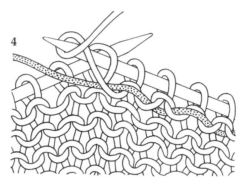

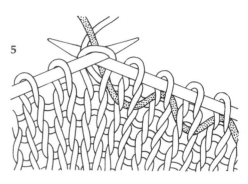

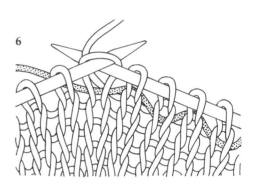

Keeping work clean and evenly knitted

Never leave your knitting in the middle of a row, or an uneven stitch will result. Don't stick your needles into the ball of wool, because this splits the yarn. When knitting very furry or pale yarns, it may be helpful to pin a polythene bag or linen cloth over the finished work to keep it clean.

Dropped stitches

Even if the stitch has dropped several rows, it is usually very simple to pick it up again using a crochet hook.

1. On a knit row (fig 1), with right side facing:
a. Insert crochet hook from the front into the dropped stitch.
b. Put hook under the thread above the stitch and pull it through the stitch.
c. Continue in this way until the dropped stitch is level with the rest of the work.

2. On a purl row (fig 2), with wrong side facing:
a. Insert the crochet hook between the bottom and second threads lying above the dropped stitch, then into the stitch from back to front.
b. Draw the thread through the stitch.
c. Put the new stitch onto a spare needle. Insert hook between the next two threads as in step a. pick up stitch from needle and draw thread through.

If you are knitting in pattern, it may be impossible to pick up dropped stitches in this manner. Unpicking will then be necessary.

Unpicking mistakes

If you make a mistake don't tear your work off the needles. Unpicking may be time-consuming, but it is simple and, when worked as below, will prevent your dropping any stitches in the process.

1. On a knit row:
a. With the knit side facing you, put the right-hand needle into the stitch below the first stitch on your left-hand needle.
b. Gently pull the first stitch off the left-hand needle and pull the yarn out of the stitch on your left-hand needle, leaving it at the back of the work.
c. Continue in this way until you have unpicked the required number of stitches.

2. On a purl row:
With the purl side of the work facing you, proceed as above, remembering that the yarn will unravel at the front of the work instead of the back.

Running out of yarn

Yarn should always be joined in at the end of a row, for best results, with a loose knot which can later be untied, and the yarn ends darned in. Splicing, an invisible method of joining yarn, is sometimes used by experienced knitters in mid-row, but it creates a weak join. If you inadvertently run out of yarn in mid-row, unpick to the beginning of the row and join there.

Snagging

If you catch your work and pull a thread, you can rectify this by easing the stitches on the same row gently with a crochet hook or a knitting needle until the loop disappears. If the snag is really bad, you can either unpick, or pull the loop through to the back of the work and ease the stitches around it.

Working with several colours:

There are two methods of dealing with the spare colours running behind the work. Over small pattern repeats, up to four or five stitches, the stranding method is used, over large pattern repeats the weaving method is used. Some patterns combine the two.

Weaving method

Carry the yarn not in use over the yarn in use for one stitch (fig 3, purl row; fig 5, knit row), and under it for the next stitch (fig 4, purl row; fig 6, knit row), on the wrong side of the work. As with the stranding method, the yarns should be carried loosely to prevent pulling of the work.

Stranding method

Carry the yarn not in use loosely along the back of the work, being careful not to pull it too tightly when picking it up to use again (fig. 7).
See page 153 for notes on working from pattern charts.

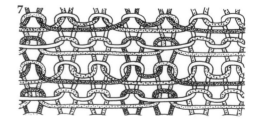

Casting Off

Casting off is used both at the end of a piece of work, to fasten off all the stitches, and also to decrease blocks of stitches within the work, such as at shoulder and underarm. Casting off should be worked loosely, often a larger size needle makes this easier. Where a block of stitches is cast off at the end of a row, the yarn must be broken off and rejoined at the beginning of the following row.

Simple casting off

On a knit row
1. Knit the first two stitches.
2. Lift the first stitch over the second with the point of the left-hand needle (fig 1).
3. Drop the first stitch off the needle leaving the second on the right-hand needle.
4. Knit one stitch.
5. Repeat steps 2. to 4. inclusive until the required number of stitches have been cast off. If block decreasing, cast off number of stitches required and knit to end of row (fig 2). If finishing off work, continue until one stitch remains. Break off yarn leaving an end of 15 cm. (5¾ in.). Draw end through remaining stitch and pull tight.

On a purl row
1. Purl the first two stitches. Keep yarn forward.
2. As above (fig 3).
3. As above.
4. Purl one stitch.
5. Repeat steps 2. to 4. inclusive until the required number of stitches have been cast off. If block decreasing, cast off the number of stitches required and purl to end of row (fig 4). If finishing off work, continue until one stitch remains. Break off yarn leaving an end of 15 cm. (5¾ in.). Draw end through remaining stitch and pull tight.

Casting off in pattern

Cast off each stitch by knitting or purling it according to the pattern being knitted. Where casting off a block, cast off in pattern and continue to work in pattern to end of row.

Casting off on 4 needles

This is done exactly as on two needles, except for the adjoining stitches at each end of needles, worked as follows each time:
1. Cast off to last stitch on needle.
2. Knit (or purl) first stitch on next needle.
3. Cast off last stitch on needle by lifting it over the first on the next needle.

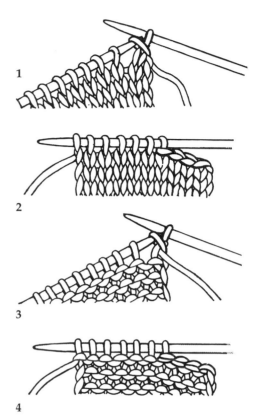

Finishing Touches

Knitting with sequins
Thread sequins onto yarn as follows:
1. Fold a 25 cm. (9¾ in.) length of sewing cotton in half, thread a needle with the cut ends.
2. Pass 20 cm. (7¾ in.) of the knitting yarn through the cotton loop, and thread the sequins onto the needle, over the cotton and onto the yarn.

When a sequin is required
1. Knit to position of sequin, slide sequin down yarn and position close to work.
2. Knit the next stitch through the back of the loop in the usual manner, pushing the sequin through the stitch to the front of the work (fig 1).

Swiss darning

Swiss darning is a type of embroidery used on knitted fabric to create a pattern which appears knitted-in. It is worked on stocking stitch, using a yarn of similar weight to that of the piece of work.

1. Thread a blunt darning needle with the yarn. Insert needle from back to front of the work at the centre of the first stitch to be embroidered over.
2. Following fig 2, insert the needle behind both strands of the stitch above.
3. Then thread the needle through the two next strands below, as marked by the arrow in fig 2. Be careful to ensure that the tension of the embroidery matches that of

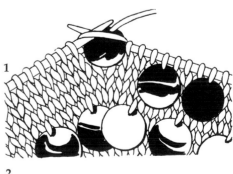

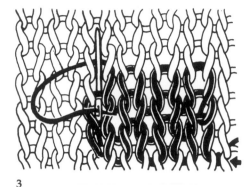

3

the original work, to prevent the fabric pulling.

4. Where the embroidery is to cover several rows, complete one row as above and insert the needle under the upper loop of the last stitch (fig 3). Turn the work upside down and continue with steps **1.** to **3.** and reverse again for following row.

Buttonholes

The patterns detail how and when buttonholes are to be made. You can alter their size by adding or taking away stitches to be cast off (on the armhole edge) on a horizontal buttonhole, or by increasing or decreasing the number of rows worked for a vertical buttonhole.

Horizontal buttonholes

1. Loosely cast off required number of stitches. The stitch remaining after casting off is counted as part of the row, NOT of the buttonhole.
2. In the next row, cast on the same number of stitches as were cast off in the previous row (figs 4 and 5).

Vertical buttonholes

1. Divide stitches to form the sides of the buttonhole.

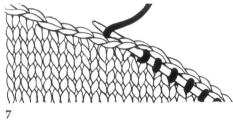

4

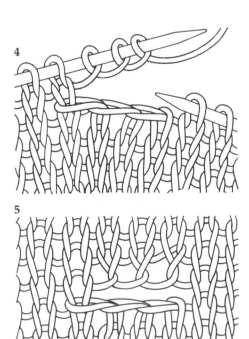

5

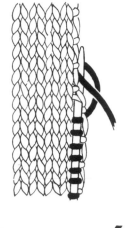

6

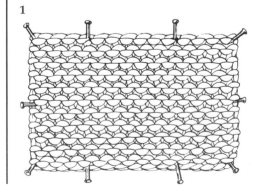

7

2. Work individually to required height, rejoin the two sides.
3. Later, work buttonhole stitch with the end of yarn left when the two sides were joined together, to strengthen the buttonhole.

Working separate front bands

When separate front bands have to be worked, as for a cardigan, it is a good idea to knit both bands simultaneously to ensure that they are exactly the same length. As you knit the buttonholes mark the button position on the other band.
When measuring the band length ensure that the band is *very* slightly stretched against the main work, otherwise the band will sag in wear.

Knitting up stitches

Always ensure that stitches are picked up evenly, thus count rows or stitches and compare with the number of stitches to be picked up before starting.

Knitting up vertically, used for knitted-on front bands

1. Compare number of stitches to be picked up with number of rows.
2. To pick up each stitch: having yarn at back of work, put needle from front to back of work, pick up a loop of yarn and bring it through to front (fig 6).

Knitting up along straight or curved edges

1. Compare number of stitches to be picked up with the number of stitches along the edge to be worked on.
2. To pick up each stitch: having yarn at back of work, put needle from front to back of work, pick up a loop of yarn and bring it through to front (fig 7).

Making Up

Careful making up is essential to the success of your work. There are pressing and making up instructions on each pattern, which you should follow. Below there are further details on how to block, press, and how to sew up seams to achieve a professional finish.

Blocking and pressing

Only press where this is specifically mentioned in the pattern.

Where the pattern instructs you to press the finished pieces of your garment, proceed as follows (fig 6):
1. Pin each piece, right side downwards, onto a well-padded surface. Do NOT stretch any part of the fabric, be careful to keep rows and stitches in straight lines.
2. Press the fabric, excluding any ribbing, under a damp cloth if specified.
3. Allow fabric to cool and remove pins.
4. Push ribbing together so that only the knit stitches show, pin out carefully and press lightly, again under a damp cloth if specified.

Sewing up seams

Use your knitting yarn to sew up seams wherever possible. If the yarn is very heavy, or very textured, substitute a similar-coloured 4 ply yarn. Your pattern will tell you the order in which to sew up the pieces you have knitted. There are several methods of sewing up seams, of which the backstitch and flat seam methods, below, are the most popular. Backstitch can be used for most seams except ribbing, where flat seaming is used. Flat seaming is also used on fabrics knitted in very fine yarns.

Flat Seam (fig 2)

1. Put the right sides of the two pieces together, matching rows if working on a straight edge.
2. Put your left forefinger between the two pieces of work. Join in yarn with several

1

stitches one over the other at the
-ing of the seam.
- the needle from front to back close
- edge of the fabric, pull yarn
-h, create a small running stitch by
- needle through the fabric again
-ack to front, one stitch further on
- the fabric.
-ntinue to end, ensuring that the
-s are not drawn too tightly, thus
- the work. Press (if pressing is
-mended for the yarn) under a damp

-titch Seam (fig 3)

- the right sides of the two pieces
-er, matching rows if working on a
-t edge.
- in yarn with several running
-s one over the other at the begin-
- the seam.
- needle into right-hand end of the
- stitches and bring out at front of
-one stitch from the edge of the
-and one stitch beyond the left-hand
- the running stitches.
- needle back into work at left-hand
- the running stitches, and bring out
- of work one stitch beyond the stitch
-d in step **3.** Continue in this way
- care not to split stitches. Use run-
-titches as in step **2.** to finish the end of
-m. Press (if pressing is recommen-
- the yarn) under a damp cloth.

-l seam notes

-ler seams: match shapings on both
- When stitching, work in a straight
-ross these shaping steps, in firm
-tch. Press seams on the wrong
-einforce with tape, in the case of
-eavy garments.

- and side seams: join with back-
-using flat seaming for ribbing (and
-hout for jumpers in very fine

-sleeves: mark the centre top of the
-and pin to shoulder seam, match
- stitches in sleeve and armhole and
-ether. Pin remaining sloping sides
-ve evenly into the armhole. Back-
-s near the edge as possible, using
-tches.

-sleeves: match raglan seams row
-, and stitch using a flat seam, with
-all stitches.

-n collars: with right side of collar
- wrong side of the work, pin centre
-r to centre of neckline, and each
- the collar to neckline edges, or

position marked in the pattern. Stitch,
taking care not to stretch the neckline, as
close to the edge as possible.

Hems: where the hem has been marked by
a line of knit stitches, or where a length of
fabric is to be turned up as hem, this
should be pressed, and slipstitched in
place.

Lapped seams: place parts to be joined
right sides together, with the underneath
fabric extending 12mm. (½ in.) beyond the
upper part. Backstitch close to the edge,
turn to the right side and backstitch again
through both layers of fabric 12mm. (½ in.)
from the original seam, using small, neat
stitches.

Front Bands: sew on using a flat seam.
Zips (fig 4): nylon zips are normally the
best type for knitwear. Reinforce the
edges of the knitting with a row of double
crochet, if necessary, and pin zip in place,
taking care not to stretch the knitting.
With right side facing, using small back-
stitches, sew in with fine thread (to match
yarn) and needle, as close to the edge of
the knitting as possible. Stitch from top to
bottom on both sides of the zip. Later,
slipstitch the zip edges on the inside.

Yarn ends

Thread each end in turn into a blunt-
ended darning needle. Darn neatly into
the back of the work, including a couple of
back stitches to hold it firmly. Trim end
close to work.
Where more than one colour has been
used, darn the ends of each into its own
colour area.

Ribbon facing

Choose ribbon in a colour to match your
yarn. You should allow at least a 6 mm.
(¼ in.) hem on either side of the button
bands, and a 12mm. (½ in.) hem at top
and bottom of both bands.
1. Press the work lightly. Cut the button
and buttonhole band facings together so
that their length is identical.
2. Fold in all the turnings and press lightly.
3. Pin to the bands on the wrong side,
checking that buttonholes are evenly
spaced: ease work to adjust this. Slipstitch around the ribbon with matching
fine cotton, using tiny stitches.
4. Mitre corners: slipstitch outer seam,
fold ribbon at corner and stitch.
5. Cut buttonholes along grain, oversew
ribbon and knitting together with sewing
cotton, then work buttonhole stitch on top
using the original yarn.

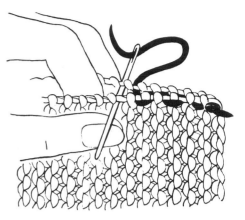

2

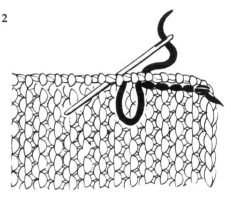

3

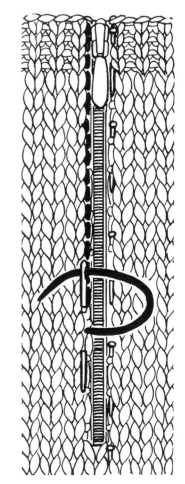

4

Crochet Finishes

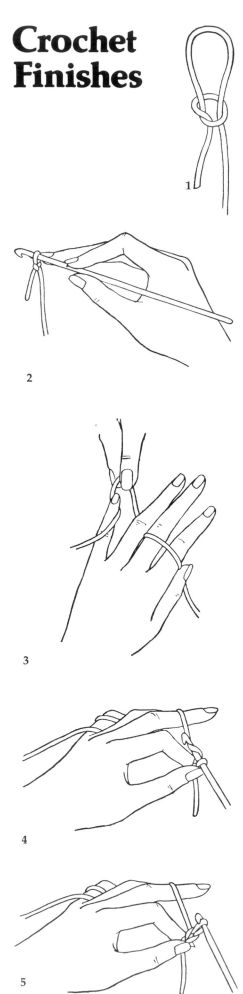

1

2

3

4

5

Crochet is sometimes used to finish hand-knitting, either as a border or to create patterns on the knitted fabric.

Like knitting, crochet is begun with a slip loop (fig 1), which is made as follows:

1. Make an X twist of yarn around your thumb.
2. Pull lower right half of this X through upper right half, using hook point, and pull yarn end to tighten.

Hold the hook like a pencil with the shank resting between your thumb and first finger, using your first and second fingers to guide the work (fig 2).

The yarn should be held in the left hand (fig 3), wound over the first and second fingers, under the third finger and then looped over the fourth finger, so that the new yarn runs first over and then round the fourth finger.

Chain stitch

Chains are used as the basis of most crochet work. The first row of any crochet garment is worked in chain stitch. Chains are worked at the end of crochet rows before turning work for the next row, their number depending on the stitch being used.

Chains are worked as follows:

1. Make a slip loop as above.
2. Hold the end of the slip loop with thumb and first finger of the left hand.
3. Put hook under yarn from left to right, then back over the yarn from right to left (fig 4).
4. Pull yarn through the loop (fig 5).

Repeat steps 2 to 4 to lengthen the chain. Chain stitch can be used on knitted fabric to create patterns, and is particularly useful where knitted-in contrast is unsatisfactory, such as in the case of narrow vertical lines.

When working over a fabric, work as for simple chain, but keep the new end of yarn behind the fabric, working with right side facing, as follows:

1. Make a slip loop, take it off the hook, put hook through fabric from front to back in position where first chain stitch is to be and put loop back on hook. Pull loop through to front of fabric, leaving the knot at back of fabric.
2. Put hook through fabric from front to back at required point, one chain's length from previous hole, put hook under and over yarn as in step 3 above.
3. Pull yarn through fabric and through loop on right side surface of fabric.

Repeat steps 2 and 3 to required length of line or design.

The abbreviation for chain stitch is ch.

Slip stitch

Slip stitch edging on knitted fabric is worked as follows:

1. Make slip loop as above.
2. Put hook from front to back between 1st and 2nd cast-off sts., loop yarn around hook as in step 3 of chain st. above and pull resulting loop to front

through fabric and loop on croche
3. Repeat step 2 to end of row.
4. If only one row is indicated pattern, break off yarn and end i this and starting end neatly. If a row is needed, make one turning and work back, inserting hook und double loop at the top of each previous row, and end off as abov The abbreviation for this is sl.s.

Treble

1. Attach yarn to edge of garment is to be finished.
2. Put hook through edge of fabri cast-off edge, from front to back yarn around hook as in step 3 of stitch above, and pull resulting l front.
3. Work 2 chain.
4. Put the yarn over the hook, ther hook from front to back through e fabric, put the yarn over the hook the new loop of yarn through the only [3 loops now on hook].
5. Put the yarn over the hook, dr new loop of yarn through the next on the hook [2 loops now on hoo
6. Yarn over hook, draw the ne through the two remaining loops hook [1 loop now on hook ready f treble].
5. Repeat steps 4 to 6 for each tr end of row.

If only one row of treble is indica the pattern, break off the yarn and in neatly, likewise neaten in the sl end.

If further rows are required, work before turning work to begin th row.

The abbreviation for treble is tr.

Double crochet

Double crochet edging on knitted is worked as follows:

1. Attach yarn to edge of garment is to be finished.
2. Put hook through edge of fabri cast-off edge, from front to bac yarn around hook as in step 3 o stitch above, and pull resulting front.
3. Now put hook through fabri front to back again, a stitch furthe cast-off edge, loop yarn around h before and pull through the fa front. There are now two stitches hook.
4. Loop yarn around hook onc and pull through both stitches.

Repeat steps 3 and 4 to end requiring finishing.

If only one row of double croche dicated by the pattern, break off t and end it in neatly, likewise ne the slip loop end.

If further rows are required, work before turning work to begin t row.

The abbreviation for double cr d.c.

Care of Knitwear

Pilling

Many yarns are prone to pilling: this means that loose balls of fibre appear on the surface of the garment. These can be removed very simply with a strip of sticky tape, or with gentle brushing.

Snagging

This, too, can usually be remedied, see description of the process on page 158.

Cleaning knitted garments

The great variety of yarns now on the market has meant that washing instructions need to be individually described for each type: thus ball bands carry cleaning and pressing instructions in the International Textile Care Labelling Code. The symbols are explained briefly opposite.

General guidelines

1. Where the garment should be hand-washed, ensure that soap flakes are thoroughly dissolved before immersing the knitwear, or use Woolite cold water wash. Never use very hot water to wash wool, follow the temperature suggested on the ball band.

2. Rinse thoroughly in tepid water.

3. NEVER wring knitwear roughly by hand, spin briefly in a machine, or squeeze gently, to remove moisture.

4. Unless otherwise stated in the pattern, knitwear should be gently pulled into shape and dried on a clean flat surface.

60°C = Hot, hotter than the hand can bear, the temperature of water from a domestic hot tap.
50°C = Hand-hot, as hot as the hand can bear.
40°C = Warm, pleasantly warm to the hand.
30°C = Cool to the touch.

Can safely be washed by hand or machine. Number above line denotes washing process for machines, figure below it denotes water temperature in °C, see above for temperature details.

Wash *only* by hand.

Must *not* be washed.

Dry cleanable in all solvents.

Dry cleanable in perchloroethylene, white spirit, Solvent 113 and Solvent 11.

Goods sensitive to dry cleaning which may be cleaned with solvents shown for **P**, but with strict limitation on the addition of water during cleaning and/or restrictions concerning mechanical action or drying temperature or both.

Dry cleanable in white spirit and Solvent 113.

Goods sensitive to dry cleaning which may be cleaned with solvents shown for **F** but with a strict limitation on the addition of water during cleaning and/or certain restrictions concerning mechanical action or drying temperature or both.

Do *not* dry clean.

Tumble drying beneficial.

Do *not* tumble dry.

Where a triangle contains the letters **CL** the article can be treated with chlorine bleach. Where the triangle is crossed out chlorine bleach may *not* be used.

Hot iron up to 210°C.

Warm iron up to 160°C.

Cool iron up to 120°C.

Do not iron.

Yarn Conversion Chart

U.K.	U.S.A.	Australia
A.N.I. Scottish Homespun	A.N.I. Scottish Homespun	Mail order
A.N.I. Shetland 2 ply	A.N.I. Shetland 2 ply	Mail order
Argyll Ambridge DK	any DK	any DK
Argyll Pure Wool Aran	Mail order	Mail order
Christian de Falbe Studio Yarns Paradise	Christian de Falbe Studio Yarns Paradise	Mail order
Christian de Falbe Studio Yarns Pure Wool	Christian de Falbe Studio Yarns Pure Wool	Mail order
Christian de Falbe Studio Yarns Watership	Christian de Falbe Studio Yarns Watership	Mail order
Emu Superwash Wool 4 ply	Emu Superwash Wool 4 ply	Emu Superwash Wool 4 ply
Hayfield Grampian 4 ply	Hayfield Grampian 4 ply	Hayfield Grampian 4 ply
Lister-Lee Motoravia 4 ply	Lister-Lee Motoravia 4 ply	any 4 ply
Lister-Lee Pure Wool Aran	Lister-Lee Pure Wool Aran	Mail order
Maxwell Cartlidge Lotus Silk 4 ply	Mail order	Mail order
Natural Dye Company Wool	Mail order	Mail order
Jaeger Alpaca	Jaeger Alpaca	Jaeger Alpaca
Jaeger Luxury Spun 4 ply	Beehive 4 ply Fingering	Patons/Jaeger Matchmaker 4 ply
Patons Clansman 4 ply	Beehive 4 ply Fingering	Patons/Jaeger Matchmaker 4 ply
Patons Cotton Top	Patons Cotton Top	Patons Cotton Top
Phildar Perle 5	Phildar Perle 5	Mail order
Phildar Wool DK	Phildar Wool DK	any DK
Picaud Coton Canelle	Picaud Coton Canelle	Picaud Coton Canelle
Pingouin Confortable Fin 4	Pingouin Confortable Fin	Pingouin Confortable Fin
Pingouin Corrida 3 4 ply	Pingouin Corrida 3 4 ply	Pingouin Corrida 3 4 ply
Pingouin Coton Perle 5	Pingouin Coton Perle 5	Pingouin Coton Perle 5
Pingouin Fil d'Ecosse Fin	Pingouin Fil d'Ecosse Fin	Pingouin Fil d'Ecosse Fin
Pingouin Pingofine	Pingouin Pingofine	Pingouin Pingofine
Pingouin Pingolaine	Pingouin Pingolaine	Pingouin Pingolaine
Pingouin Pingolaine 4 ply	Pingouin Pingolaine 4 ply	Pingouin Pingolaine 4 ply
Pingouin Pingoperle	Pingouin Pingoperle	Pingouin Pingoperle
Poppleton Lana DK	Poppleton Lana DK	Mail order
Rowan Yarns Botany Wool 3 ply	any 3 ply	Rowan Yarns Botany Wool 3 ply
Rowan Yarns Light Tweed	Mail order	Rowan Yarns Light Tweed
Sirdar Country Style 4 ply	Sirdar Country Style 4 ply	any 4 ply
Sirdar Majestic DK	Sirdar Majestic DK	any DK
Sirdar Talisman DK	Sirdar Talisman DK	any DK
Sunbeam Shantung	Sunbeam Shantung	Sunbeam Shantung
Sunbeam St. Ives 4 ply	Sunbeam St. Ives 4 ply	Sunbeam St. Ives 4 ply
Sunbeam Wool 3 ply	Sunbeam Wool 3 ply	Sunbeam Wool 3 ply
Sunbeam Wool 4 ply	Sunbeam Wool 4 ply	Sunbeam Wool 4 ply
Templeton's H & O Shetland Fleece	Mail order	Mail order
Twilley's Cotton Stalite	Mail order	Twilley's Cotton Stalite
Twilley's Pegasus Cotton	Mail order	Twilley's Pegasus Cotton
Wendy Ascot DK	Wendy Ascot DK	Wendy Shetland DK
Wendy Ascot 4 ply	Wendy Ascot 4 ply	any 4 ply
Wendy Pampas	Wendy Pampas	Wendy Pampas
Wendy Shetland 4 ply	Wendy Ascot 4 ply	any 4 ply
Yarn Store Cashmere	Mail order	Mail order
Yarn Store Natural British Wool	Mail order	Mail order
Yarnworks Cotton	Mail order	Mail order
Yarnworks Silk and Cotton Slub	Mail order	Mail order

Canada	South Africa
Mail order	Mail order
Mail order	Mail order
Argyll Ambridge DK	any DK
Argyll Pure Wool Aran	Mail order
Mail order	Mail order
Mail order	Mail order
Mail order	Mail order
Emu Superwash Wool 4 ply	Emu Superwash Wool 4 ply
Hayfield Grampian 4 ply	Hayfield Grampian 4 ply
Lister-Lee Motoravia 4 ply	any 4 ply
Lister-Lee Pure Wool Aran	Mail order
Mail order	Mail order
Mail order	Mail order
Jaeger Alpaca	Mail order
Beehive 4 ply Fingering	Patons Beehive, knits as 4 ply
Beehive 4 ply Fingering	Patons Beehive, knits as 4 ply
Patons Cotton Top	Patons Cotton Top
Phildar Perle 5	Mail order
Phildar Wool DK	any DK
Picaud Coton Canelle	Mail order
Pingouin Confortable Fin	Pingouin Confortable Fin
Pingouin Corrida 3 4 ply	Pingouin Corrida 3 4 ply
Pingouin Coton Perle 5	Pingouin Coton Perle 5
Pingouin Fil d'Ecosse Fin	Pingouin Fil d'Ecosse Fin
Pingouin Pingofine	Pingouin Pingofine
Pingouin Pingolaine	Pingouin Pingolaine
Pingouin Pingolaine 4 ply	Pingouin Pingolaine 4 ply
Pingouin Pingoperle	Pingouin Pingoperle
Poppleton Lana DK	Poppleton Lana DK
any 3 ply	any 3 ply
Mail order	Mail order
Sirdar Country Style 4 ply	any 4 ply
Sirdar Majestic DK	any DK
Sirdar Talisman DK	any DK
Sunbeam Shantung	Sunbeam Shantung
Sunbeam St. Ives 4 ply	Sunbeam St. Ives 4 ply
Sunbeam Wool 3 ply	Sunbeam Wool 3 ply
Sunbeam Wool 4 ply	Sunbeam Wool 4 ply
Mail order	Mail order
Mail order	Twilley's Cotton Stalite
Mail order	Twilley's Pegasus Cotton
Wendy Ascot DK	Wendy Shetland DK
Wendy Ascot 4 ply	any 4 ply
Wendy Pampas	Wendy Pampas
Wendy Ascot 4 ply	any 4 ply
Mail order	Mail order
Mail order	Mail order
Mail order	Mail order
Mail order	Mail order

USING THE CHART

Tension: all the patterns were knitted up and checked in the yarns listed in the first column. In many cases these are widely available, but where they are not, the nearest equivalent in both weight, character and appearance has been quoted. When using an equivalent yarn, it is *doubly* important to check your tension, in order to achieve perfect results.

Needles: unless otherwise stated in the chart, use the needle sizes quoted in the pattern.

Yarn: unless otherwise stated in the chart, yarn requirements are as given in the pattern. Individual tension variations may cause fluctuations in amount used.

Addresses: should you have difficulty in acquiring yarn, or want to order by post, the addresses to write to are listed on pages 166–168.

NEEDLE CONVERSIONS

U.K. and Australia metric	U.K. and Australia original, Canada, S. Africa	U.S.A.
2mm.	14	00
2¼mm.	13	0
2¾mm.	12	1
3mm.	11	2
3¼mm.	10	3
3¾mm.	9	4
4mm.	8	5
4½mm.	7	6
5mm.	6	7
5½mm.	5	8
6mm.	4	9
6½mm.	3	10
7mm.	2	10½
7½mm.	1	11
8mm.	0	12
9mm.	00	13
10mm.	000	15

AMERICAN TERMINOLOGY

Most knitting and crochet terms are identical in English and American usage. The exceptions to this are listed below, with the English term used in the book given first, followed by the American term.

Double crochet (d.c.) = single crochet (s.c.); stocking stitch (st. st.) = stockinette stitch (st. st.); yarn round needle (y.r.n.) = yarn over needle (y.o.n.); cast off = bind off.

Addresses

If you have any difficulty in obtaining yarns, you can write to the address given below for the head office or agent of the yarn spinner for stockist information. Where there is no agent the address of sole or main stockists are given. Where the yarn is available only by mail order, this address is given.

A.N.I.

Head Office and mail order

A.N.I.

7 St. Michael's Mansions
Ship Street
OXFORD
OX1 3DG
U.K.

U.S.A. sole stockist

Textile Museum
2320 S Street
WASHINGTON D.C.
U.S.A.

ARGYLL WOOLS

Head Office

Argyll Wools Ltd.
P.O. Box 15
Priestley Mills
PUDSEY
W. Yorks.
U.K.

Mail order

Paul Bishop
R & D Bishop
Third Avenue
Pioneer Indoor Market
ILFORD
Essex
U.K.

Canada agent

Mr P K Peacock
Estelle Designs & Sales Ltd.
1135 Queen Street East
TORONTO
Ontario
CANADA

CHRISTIAN DE FALBE YARN

U.K. and mail order

Christian de Falbe
97 Wakehurst Road
LONDON SW11
U.K.

U.S.A.

117 W 58th Street 11D
N.Y.10019
U.S.A.

EMU

U.K.

Customer Service
Emu Wools
Leeds Road
Greengates
BRADFORD
W. Yorks.
U.K.

U.S.A.

The Plymouth Yarn Company Ltd.
P.O. Box 28
500 Lafayette Street
PA 19007
BRISTOL
U.S.A.

Australia

Karingal Zic-tas Pty. Ltd.
359 Dorset Road
Bayswater
VICTORIA 3153
AUSTRALIA

Canada agent

S R Kertzer Ltd.
257 Adelaide Street West
TORONTO M5H 1Y1
Ontario
CANADA

S. Africa agent

E Brasch & Son
57 La Rochelle Road
Trojan
JOHANNESBURG
S. AFRICA

HAYFIELD

U.K.

Hayfield Textiles Ltd.
Hayfield Mills
GLUSBURN
Nr. KEIGHLEY
W. Yorks. BD20 8QP
U.K.

U.S.A. wholesaler

Shepherd Wools Inc.
917 Industry Drive
SEATTLE
Washington 98188
U.S.A.

Canada wholesaler

Craftsmen Distributors Inc.
4166 Halifax Street
BURNABY
British Columbia
CANADA

Australia wholesaler

Panda Yarns International Pty. Ltd.
17–27 Brunswick Road
EAST BRUNSWICK
Victoria 3057
AUSTRALIA

S. Africa agent

A & H Agencies
392 Commissioners Street
Fair View
JOHANNESBURG 2094
S. AFRICA

JAEGER see PATONS

LISTER

U.K.

George Lee & Sons Ltd.
Whiteoak Mills
P.O. Box 37
WAKEFIELD
W. Yorks.
U.K.

U.S.A. agent details and mail order

Fransha Wools
P.O. Box 99
Parkside Mills
BRADFORD
Yorks.
U.K.

Canada major stockist

Mrs Hurtig
Anita Hurtig Imports Ltd.
P.O. Box 6124
Postal Station A
CALGARY
Alberta T2H 2L4
CANADA

THE NATURAL DYE COMPANY

Mail order only

The Natural Dye Company
Stanbridge
WIMBORNE
Dorset
BH2 14JD
U.K.

MAXWELL CARTLIDGE

Head Office, U.K. and S. Africa mail order

Maxwell Cartlidge Ltd.
P.O. Box 33
COLCHESTER
ESSEX
U.K.

U.S.A. and Canada mail order

Victoria Street Designs
430 So. Lake
PASADENA
91101 CALIFORNIA
U.S.A.

Australia mail order

Ida Rix
c/o Port Sorrel P.O.
LATROBE
Tasmania
AUSTRALIA 7307

PATONS and JAEGER

U.K.

Jaeger Handknitting or
Patons & Baldwins Ltd.
Alloa
CLACKMANNANSHIRE
SCOTLAND
U.K.

Mail orders

Woolfayre Ltd.
120 High Street
NORTHALLERTON
W. Yorks.
U.K.

U.S.A.

Susan Bates Inc.
212 Middlesex Avenue
Route 9a
CHESTER
Connecticut 06412
U.S.A.

Australia agent

Coats & Patons Aust. Ltd.
321–355 Fern Tree Gully Road
P.O. Box 110
MOUNT WAVERLY
Victoria 3149
AUSTRALIA

Canada agent

Patons & Baldwins (Canada) Ltd.
1001 Roselawn Avenue
TORONTO
CANADA

S. Africa

Mr Bob Theis
Marketing Manager
Patons & Baldwins (S. Africa) Pty. Ltd.
P.O. Box 33
RANDFONTEIN 1760
S. AFRICA

PHILDAR

Canada

Phildar LTEE
6200 Est.
Blvd. H. Bourassa
MONTREAL Nord HIG 5X3
CANADA

U.S.A.

Phildar Inc.
6438 Dawson Boulevard
85 North
NORCROSS
Georgia 30093
U.S.A.

Mail order Information

Phildar
4 Gambrel Road
Westgate Industrial Estate
NORTHAMPTON
NN5 5NS
U.K.

PICAUD

U.K. and mail orders

Brown's Woolshop
79 Regent's Park Road
LONDON NW1 8UY
U.K.

Priory Yarns
48 Station Road
OSSETT
W. Yorks.
U.K.

U.S.A. agent

Merino Wool Co. Inc.
230 Fifth Avenue
Suite 2000
N.Y. 10001
U.S.A.

Canada agent

Innovations C.F. Ltd.
11460 Hamon
MONTREAL
Quebec H3M 3A3
CANADA

Australia agent

Olivier Aust. (Pty.) Ltd.
53 Liverpool Street
SYDNEY 2001
AUSTRALIA

PINGOUIN

U.K.

French Wools Ltd.
7–11 Lexington Street
LONDON W1R 4BU
U.K.

Head Office and mail orders

M R Mesdagh
Laines du Pingouin
59061 ROUBAIX
Cedex 1
BP 9110
FRANCE

U.S.A. agent

V Hoover
Pingouin–Promafil Corp. (U.S.A.)
P.O. Box 100
Highway 45
JAMESTOWN
S. Carolina 29453
U.S.A.

Australia stockist

C Sullivan Pty. Ltd.
47–57 Collins Street
ALEXANDRIA N.S.W. 2015
AUSTRALIA

Canada agent

Mr G Meurant
Promafil (Canada) Ltd.
1500 Rue Jules Poitras
379 ST LAURENT
Quebec H4N 1X7
CANADA

S. Africa agent

Mr Peter Grobler
Saprotex
Pingouin Wools
Yarns and Wools Pty. Ltd.
P.O. Box 12
52 Jacobs 4026
NATAL
S. AFRICA

POPPLETON

U.K. and mail order

Richard Poppleton & Sons Ltd.
Albert Mills
Horbury
WAKEFIELD
W. Yorks.
U.K.

S. Africa

Woolcraft Agencies
P.O. Box 17657
2038 Hillbrow
JOHANNESBURG
S. AFRICA

ROWAN

U.K. and mail order

Rowan Yarns
Green Lane Mill
Washpit
HOLMFIRTH
HUDDERSFIELD HD7 1RW
W. Yorks.
U.K.

U.S.A. and Canada mail order only

The Westminster Trading Corporation
P.O. Box 116
MILLFORD
NEW HAMPSHIRE 03055
U.S.A.

Australia agent

Beedies Gallery
479 Chapel Street
SOUTH YARRA
3141 Victoria
AUSTRALIA

Addresses

Continued

SIRDAR

U.K.

Sirdar P.L.C.
Flanshaw Lane
Alverthorpe
WAKEFIELD WF2 9ND
W. Yorks.
U.K.

Australia agent

Coats & Patons Aust. Ltd.
321–355 Fern Tree Gully Road
P.O. Box 110
MOUNT WAVERLEY
Victoria 3149
AUSTRALIA

S. Africa agent

Mr Bob Theis
Marketing Manager
Patons & Baldwins (S. Africa) Pty. Ltd.
P.O. Box 33
RANDFONTEIN 1760
S. AFRICA

U.S.A. agent

Kendex Corp.
31332 Via Colinas
107 Westlake Village
CALIFORNIA 91362
U.S.A.

Canada agent/distributor

Diamond Yarn (Canada) Corporation
153 Bridgeland Avenue
Unit 11
TORONTO M6A 2Y6
CANADA

SUNBEAM

U.K.

Sunbeam Wools
Crawshaw Mills
PUDSEY LS28 7BS
W. Yorks.
U.K.

Mail order

Woolfayre
120 High Street
NORTHALLERTON
N. Yorks.
U.K.

U.S.A. agent

Grandor Industries Ltd.
P.O. Box 5831
4031 Knobhill Drive
SHERMAN OAKS
CALIFORNIA 91403
U.S.A.

Phillips Imports
P.O. Box 146
PORT ST JOE
FLORIDA 32456
U.S.A.

Australia agent

39 Tennyson Street
EAST MALVERN
Victoria 3145
AUSTRALIA

Canada agent

Estelle Designs and Sales Ltd.
1135 Queen Street East
TORONTO
Ontario
CANADA M4M 1K9

S. Africa agent

Brasch Hobby
57 La Rochelle Road
Trojan
JOHANNESBURG
S. AFRICA

TEMPLETON'S

U.K. and mail order

James Templeton and Son Ltd.
Mill Street
AYR KA7 1TL
SCOTLAND
U.K.

TWILLEY'S

U.K. and mail order

H G Twilley Ltd.
Roman Mill
Casterton Road
STAMFORD
LINCS. PE9 1BG
U.K.

Australia stockist

Panda Yarns
17/21 Brunswick Road
EAST BRUNSWICK
3057 Victoria
AUSTRALIA

S. Africa stockists

F W Nyman and Co. (Pty.) Ltd.
P.O. Box 292
DURBAN 4000
S. AFRICA

Mr Ben Van As
Chester Mortonson (Pty.) Ltd.
P.O. Box 1179
JOHANNESBURG 2000
S. AFRICA

WENDY

U.K.

Wendy International
P.O. Box 3
GUISELEY
W. Yorks.
U.K.

U.S.A. and Canada agent

White Buffalo Mills Ltd.
545 Assinidoine Avenue
BRANDON
Manitoba
CANADA

Australia agent

Craft Warehouse
30 Guess Avenue
ARNCLIFFE
N.S.W. 2205
AUSTRALIA

S. Africa agent

Woolcraft Agencies
P.O. Box 17657
2038 Hillbrow
JOHANNESBURG
S. AFRICA

YARN STORE

Shop and mail order

The Yarn Store
8 Ganton Street
LONDON W1V 1LJ
U.K.

YARNWORKS

U.K. and mail order

Yarnworks Ltd.
27 Harcourt Street
LONDON W1H 1DT
U.K.

The endpapers are photographed from The Natural Dye Company Cardigan pictured on pages 8 and 29